COMING TO POWER

COMING TO POWER

WRITINGS AND GRAPHICS ON LESBIAN S/M

S/M: A form of eroticism based on a consensual exchange of power

Boston • Alyson Publications, Inc.

First published, 1981, by the authors. Revised and updated editions published in 1982 and 1987 by Alyson Publications, Inc. 40 Plympton Street Boston, Mass., 02118.

Distributed in the U.K. by GMP Publishers, PO Box 247, London, N15 6RW, England.

Third U.S. edition: October, 1987

ISBN 0-932870-28-7

Table of Contents

Introduction:
What We Fear We Try to Keep Contained

This is an outrageous book. It has many purposes and will have many effects on those who read it, on those who only hear about it, and on others who will never know that it exists.

S/M fantasies and S/M sex between feminist lesbians have been one of the most avoided topics of discussion in the movement. We've allowed it to remain a scary skeleton hidden in the corner of our otherwise carefully cleaned-up closets. Few of us have been able to admit to anyone our interest in S/M or have been able to talk about the content of our fantasies. Some of us could not even admit those fantasies to ourselves. Social and political costs run very high. In the public arena of the lesbian, feminist, and gay press, positive feelings about S/M experiences have been met for the most part with swift negative reaction and authoritative reprimands. In this context, trashing has been re-named "feminist criticism," honest dialogue has been submerged by wave after wave of ideological censure calling itself "debate," and those of us who continue to resist this treatment are accused of being contaminated by the patriarchy. *What we fear we try to keep contained.* The intense political battle over S/M is increasingly polarizing members of the lesbian-feminist community. Is S/M good or evil? Is it "feminist"? Anti-feminist? Or should we even be bothering to discuss it at all?

This turbulence is symbolic of a much deeper, more invisible and less-than-direct ideological power struggle. S/M lesbians have been accused repeatedly of being a threat to lesbian-feminism as it is currently defined. In certain ways this may be true. But what is the fear which lies behind the virulent attacks and the apparent building of an anti-S/M mini-movement? Why the concerted attempts to invalidate, to politically neutralize us?

We are here and we are not silent. This, in itself, becomes a challenge to much of the propaganda put out over the years which has denied any connection between lesbian-feminism and S/M. More than a few lesbian-feminists have formulated theories which are dependent on targeting S/M. We are told S/M is responsible for practically every ill and inequity, large and small, that the world has ever known, including rape, racism, classism, spouse abuse, difficult interpersonal relationships, fascism, a liking of vaginal penetration, political repression in Third World countries, and so on. In 1981, "sadomasochism" has become a buzz word. It is tacked onto just about anything hated or feared. Thus, we hear that there have been sadomasochistic eras in history, or that some people have sadomasochistic mentalities which warp them beyond hope.

Anti-S/M attitudes are embedded in many areas of lesbian-feminist ideology. As S/M lesbians, we say that our experience contradicts many of those closely held theories, and that this examination of our experience is a feminst inquiry. Because we have some fundamental disagreements with existing theories, anti-S/M lesbian-feminist theorists correctly perceive us as a threat, but we are only a threat insofar as we are a threat to their status. The wall of resistance is strong. Lesbian-feminist politics have lost flexibility. Our own presence cannot be resolved by the currently accepted politics, therefore some of us are being caught in the odd situation where we must, politically, disown ourselves. Those of us who have been working actively in the movement for many years are being labeled anti-feminist, mentally ill, or worse. Lines are drawn and we find ourselves, quite unexpectedly, on the "other" side. We are being cast out, denied. We become heretics.

It doesn't have to be this way—but the alternative is a much longer, more difficult road. We must reexamine our politics of sex and power. The challenge of talking personally and explicitly about all the ways we are sexual, and about how our sexuality differs, is not so much destructive as it is corrective, and necessary. The logical place to begin is to talk about our sexuality *as it is.* We must talk about what we do as much as who we do it with. We will find many differences among and between us, but it is better to do this work than to continually hide from our fears and insecurities. We must put the rhetorical weaponry aside and willingly engage each other, without simply jumping ahead into a new sexual conformity. We must have precisely the same dialogues about the texture of our sexuality as we have been having about classism, racism, cultural identity, physical appearance and ability. How do all these differences converge, to make us who we are? We must all ask and answer these questions.

This is the second book SAMOIS has published. The first, a 45 page booklet, *What Color is Your Hankerchief? A Lesbian S/M Sexuality Reader* (now out of print), was hurriedly produced in 1979 in response to the high demand for positive S/M information. It contained a number of reprints of previously published articles, along with a few short essays written for the book, safety information, a glossary, and a bibliography. At this writing, it has sold over 2000 copies in four printings. The positive response to the booklet has been greatly affirming to us. In the many letters we've received, we've heard funny stories and fearful ones as other lesbians tell us their own coming out stories. Our correspondence has been worldwide. British, German, and Polish lesbians have written; a Maori lesbian wrote wanting to find other S/M lesbians of color with whom to communicate; we have received much information from the Conversation Group, Women and S/M, a women-only support group within the Dutch organization Vereniging Studiegroep Sado-masochisme (V.S.S.M.), who are doing consciousness raising in The Netherlands and Europe.

What we learned from our first publishing project is that lesbians do want more information about S/M, from political analysis to fantasy material. Obviously, we needed to do another book.

The process of putting together *Coming to Power* has been long and difficult, tedious and frustrating as well as joyous. Originally there were as many as 15 of us in the Ministry of Truth (SAMOIS' publications and public information committee), reading manuscripts and working on this volume. Our structure was very loose. In the first round of decision making, we made selections by a "yes," "no," or "maybe" majority vote. At no time in the entire process did we try to reach consensus. It was a rare instance when we all agreed. We were well into trying to decide what was to be included, before we began to talk about why we each wanted to *do* the book. During this time, the size of MOT decreased to a relatively stable, on-going group of five to eight women. Some of us had writing and/or publishing experience, others did not. We soon found we had greatly varying ideas about the focus of the book, what the book should include, and who we thought its audience would be; we also discovered that we had a staggering number of different political, sexual and vested interests in putting the book out. There were highly-charged disagreements about content, the politics of editing each other's work, how we defined quality of writing and artwork, how to represent a diversity of experience and opinion, and how we viewed the fiction we chose to include.

Overall, the content presents many different voices, attitudes, and definitions of S/M. Some pieces are consciously irreverent; others cover activities outside the realm of traditional S/M. *Coming to Power* is *not* all-inclusive of lesbian S/M, nor could it be.

Although the book will probably be interpreted by some as "what SAMOIS thinks," it does not represent the collective opinion of the organization or the politics of individual members. No one person in MOT likes or is happy with everything in this book, including sections of this introduction. At best, we have agreed to disagree.

The most difficult part of our process was making decisions about which fiction would be included. As individuals we lobbied for our favorite stories and against others with which we had personal or political difficulties. We struggled for several months over the issue of *fantasy*. How do we define it? What is our attitude towards it? What is its use, its purpose? Is it all right if a fantasy doesn't include overt consent? In what ways, if any, are we feeling unnecessarily defensive about a particular piece, due to the current political climate?

For many of us, these are ongoing discussions that have been only partially answered in creating this book. Because there were several stories that made many of us uncomfortable, we debated whether we should add disclaimers with the fiction pieces, a statement akin to: "Remember, this is only a fantasy." Some of us felt this was a reaction to the anti-porn movement or a way to avoid criticism. We knew that even the most pristine story about S/M would upset *someone*. And what would the authors think if we warned readers, in effect, not to take their stories seriously?

We talked about whether the fiction portrayed S/M lesbians as strong, self-defining women. Was a caring interaction shown between the characters? Was safety portrayed? How was consensuality (overt or implied) shown? Several of us, after having spent years constantly slugging it out in political catfights, threw up our hands in frustration saying, "Oh shit, *we know* it's a fantasy. What's the big deal?!" We talked about the stories with a mixture of humor, concern, lewdness and wonder, asking, "But could you *really* do this?" We pretty much agreed with an old inside saying, "Fantasies are hungrier than bodies," meaning that our fantasies can often be more extreme than anything we'd ever want to experience in reality. Most of us were also in agreement with the idea that fantasy is, by definition, consensual: if you don't like what you're fantasizing, you have total power to change the scene.

A related issue was whether each piece of fiction reached beneath the stereotype of S/M to portray the experience. Should this be a criterion for accepting the story? And who could speak for the "valid" experience? Some of us concluded that, as masturbation material, a "hot" story need only be a succession of images to be "good." A more complex story might better portray the broader relationship between the characters beyond the S/M scenario, but as a piece of erotica, it might not be as much of a turn-on. Obviously, these talks involved examining what was "erotic," i.e., by our loose definition, what was sexually stimulating. We found that what was intensely arousing for one person, left others feeling indifferent or even angry. The same holds true

11

for the graphics we have chosen. If we had tried to publish only the things all of us collectively "liked," there probably wouldn't be any book. In the end we decided not to attach disclaimers in favor of trying to explain to you some of our process and tell you some of the many questions we asked ourselves.

Here, then, are different kinds of fiction written with a broad range of experience. Some of it is strictly fantasy-focused, some uses conventional S/M imagery, and some is more experimental.

For as much territory as this book covers, it has many limitations. In some areas we know what is missing, in others we can only speculate. Not represented here are experiences clearly identifiable as being written by disabled women or women of color. We know that some of this material is currently being prepared for publication elsewhere. We urge others to record their own stories. We hope lesbian and feminist journals will become more open to the many exploratory discussions and visual artwork which haven't appeared here.

There are many reasons why we did not receive more material than we did, or broader examinations. Our outreach could have been better, more extensive. We did several mailings—to newspapers, bookstores, various organizations, and to people already on our mailing list. We handed out flyers at events, and members who were traveling further distributed our request for materials. Some of the usual avenues of communication we found closed to us. Several feminist and lesbian publications would not print our call for material. This prevented many lesbians from knowing about the book or how to get in touch with us.

Of those whom we did reach with our publicity, some, we know, didn't feel comfortable as "writers," and so did not offer submissions; for others, the risk of coming out publicly or being associated with S/M lesbians was simply a risk too great to take. (Fully one-half of the material in this book has been published under pseudonyms.) Still other women, we can imagine, had more pressing priorities in their lives at the time we were soliciting material, and so were not able to prepare work for the book. And yet—out of 120 submissions—we offer you in this volume nearly three dozen.

Coming to Power is a statement, a confrontation, and a

challenge. It calls for a re-evaluation of existing lesbian-feminist ethics, saying, "You must own your 'illegitimate' children." We offer you this document and hope that you will use it well, for personal exploration and as a tool for dialogue.

Katherine Davis, for the Ministry of Truth
September 1, 1981

Reasons

BARBARA ROSE

BUT WHY DO YOU DO IT?

Because it is erotic! Because I like sex to be as erotic as possible. When I am in bed with a woman whom I like and trust, and am turned on with, I want to soar, to feel my body and hers shuddering with delight, with ecstasy. I don't want to think about the dishes still sitting in the sink since the day before yesterday. When I make love, I want only to feel, to think about my body, her body, our pleasure—nothing more. I want to feel her fingers in my cunt, thrusting, pushing; my sounds of pleasure, the build of excitement. I want her to take me, totally, away from my life, away from my rational world. Only in bed do I remember my toes, my thighs, my sensitive hands. She can take my breath away with a look, a word, an unexpected touch. Her mouth sucking my fingers sends moans to my lips—I become my fingers, my fingers are my cunt, her mouth my own. She stops sucking, and I breathe, savoring the sensations in my body, wanting more, knowing she will give me what I want, knowing that she will push me only as far as I allow her to.

BUT, WAIT! THIS ISN'T S/M SEX!

Ah, but it is. It is giving, trusting, opening my mind and my body to possibilities, to fantasies I never before dreamed possible. I can be her slave, her servant, her teacher, her mother—I can be anything, anyone. I am my own lover. She is part of me, and I am part of her. She will not hurt me because it is my desire which directs us, my desire which she shares. I flinch as she smiles and slaps my face. I lose my breath, feeling only my cunt and my belly. She kisses me deeply; I cannot, do not even care to, discern the difference between this pain, this pleasure. I am my body, nothing more.

WHERE DO YOU DRAW THE LINE?
The distinctions fade in my mind, my body. Sucking her fingers, her tongue in my mouth. I am kneeling. She ties my hands behind me. I forget where I am, who I am. My nipples harden without her touch. I wait in anticipation of her next move, aware only of my body, her presence, confident that she will take me again to the next erotic level, wherever that is. I know I can stop this anytime I choose with a single, pre-arranged word. This moment, all I feel is the erotic energy flowing between us, the tension of not knowing how or where or even if she will touch me. I am trembling, my entire cunt on fire. I smell leather, breathe deeply, and feel her boot against my clit. "Don't," I whisper. "I don't want to come, not yet." She pulls her boot away, and I see my juices on its toe. I look up to her stern face, see the pleasure in her eyes. Silently, I begin to lick, to taste myself mixed with leather. I am drunk on the sensations I am experiencing. There is no today or yesterday or tomorrow. There is only now, my body ready to explode with pleasure. I don't understand.

I DON'T UNDERSTAND.
This is what I have wanted, fantasized. My nipples are still taut, my wrists restrained. The tension in my body is exquisite. Once again I am taken away from myself—no, I have given myself the pleasure I desire, the pleasure I deserve. She bends down and takes my chin in her hand. Again, I cringe, not knowing what to expect, at the same time knowing that her actions will serve only to push me farther into ecstasy. She kisses me deeply.

On the Beam

She could feel the wall now. It had emerged slowly, sailing in from her old fears. Loomed up graceful and familiar and more and more real. Here, riding the crystal cutting edge of passion as it sliced through her tensions, she watched the brilliant unfolding that was herself. She was becoming more and more complex, and she watched as each new expansion from her center left her jewel self more faceted, more blindingly reflective than before. "I can feel my beauty," she said. Then this wall, this point at which her unfolding stopped. What caused her need for protection was long forgotten, smoothed over by habit. What remained was a fortress around her most vulnerable core. The picture that came to her was granite, or maybe slate. Always cool and grey, sometimes rough, sometimes smooth. Impassive but not scarey. After all, this boundary had been with her for years. She ran a mental finger across its surface.

In a split second she time travelled back to make one of those connections that takes much longer to talk about than to experience. She was wrestling with her lover. She was keenly aware of feeling both her own strength and her desire to be forced to the floor. She enjoyed pushing as hard as she could against her strong womon lover, this good friend who shared the hard work of trust, this mutual risk taker who could accept closeness as easily as she understood the need for aloneness, and who could push back against her with an easy, knowing smile.

Slipping on sweat and panting and always winning and not wanting to, until finally her lover pinned her and sent pure inner energy, ki energy, through her. And this energy felt just like a rock. Struggle was useless, although she continued to push and arch until she was spent. She could not move such living, ungiving grey.

And here was that wall again. That same feeling of being blocked by womon stone. Except this time she saw and felt her inner wall as her own power turned back on herself. She was stunned. She had not expected to feel this part of herself. A buzz of excitement rippled through her body. Something new was happening.

She felt a searing leap of pleasure as a whip crack snapped her back to the fantastic scene in front of her. A quick focus on her lover's hands reaching inside, tearing her edges apart in a sudden wild rip that left no time for decisions. The slap of leather on flesh and she felt herself leap straight up and forward, chains notwithstanding, only to slam into that inner stone. A moment's flash— "That I could trust so completely to let another womon slash away layer after layer!" She was amazed at herself, and thrilled.

Then another crack of the whip, a fast full rush of body love and joy, and again her whole self slammed into that wall of grey. Soft sweaty belly crushed against solid earth of her own creation. "I want through this," she whispered silently.

Her muscles strained to free her arms held spread-eagle overhead by chains at the wrists. Her hips and legs danced in sensuous helplessness as the leather around her ankles kept her spread open slightly wider than was comfortable. Suspended there, she was aware of nothing touching her but chains, leather, and her own heat and sweat. She was not stretched too taut. She had room to fight, and she did.

At first it all felt good. She let herself stretch and snap with each sharp pleasure from her lover. She thrashed and tugged and arched and whimpered, all the while acutely aware of the sensitive physical balance her bondage had her in. The chains around her wrists were too cruel for her simply to drop all her weight and hang. But the thick soft leather around her ankles fooled her into thinking she could move. Her open stance made her very aware of her availability. She would writhe, take up all her slack, not be able to stand up at the same instant she realized she could not collapse. A very narrow edge. Her cries were frequent and getting louder.

Suddenly the blows stopped, and with her body singing her hair was grabbed tight and her head forced slowly all the way back. Past comfort. Wrists calling. She found herself staring deep into the eyes of her lover, who was saying, "You're getting too loud, Sweety. And you know how that ruins my concentration. I'd hate to miss." Before she was gagged, her lover slid the whip handle through her wetness and kissed her long and deep.

Gagged then, and panting, and roaring just a little, she watched as her lover fetched some candles. Her body pulsed with wanting as she was slowly circled. The beam overhead and the rings attached to the floor left her accessible from any point. She could feel her lover's eyes on her skin. "I'm going to blindfold you, but first I want you to watch the wax fall," her lover said. And then her lover bit her ear and sighed into it. She arched belly out and her head snapped back into her lover's waiting hand. The pressure of the grip was almost enough to twist her to her toes. She could not move. Cathectic cries streamed from her. And as the heated wax dropped she saw the soft deep fury in her lover's eyes.

The leather blindfold fit snugly. There was no outside vision. She could see only herself. Her lover bit her ear again and stayed there awhile sucking and sighing; climbing wetly right inside her head.

Another arch as she felt her nipple grabbed hard, then a slight change of feeling that stayed. The other nipple the same. And her body was swept up and away and back as the clamps pinned her to the air. She was so aware of her vulnerability, so bitingly aware. No shadows here, no explaining away. Glaring light on this living sculpture of her desires. Face to face.

The blows started again, more intensely now as her lover swung a cat. All the tails hitting ass and thigh. "Rocketing straight up and in and through all at once," she flashed. She felt driven from behind and pulled hard at from the front. Her tits stretched way out. She could feel only herself and the moment. She was flying inside. She was completely in the room.

And that granite was there, too, inside her for her to dash herself against. As her passion grew her awareness of her old limits grew, and she began to be afraid to try and move them. After all, they felt like stone. She wanted to close up, withdraw. "Stop, stop, stop, stop!" she cried in her fear and her lust. She remembered the agreed upon signal and this was not it. She felt her fear turn to anger and she screamed in rage at her lover. She was a thunderstorm hanging from the ceiling, all turmoil and electricity and sudden deep screams.

Faster and faster the cat hit, building to a rapid steady rhythm. Her lover's breathing nearly matched her own. Her whole body in flames—her insides battered from the rough granite of her own wall. Her wetness spreading down her legs.

This was her wall that she built a long time ago and it was time for her to tear it down. All her lover was doing was what she had said she had wanted done to her. She knew she was feeling her own ki energy holding herself back from her own pleasure. So she grabbed tight onto the trust between herself and this good womon lover of hers, sucked in a lungful of air, and let herself fly kicking and screaming breast first into her granite. She felt it give way. Again and again she let the blows from her lover send her crashing into the rock. Each hit made her stronger. Tensions she didn't know she had let go as her wall yielded and crumbled. Skin boundaries melted into air. Pure sensation now.

Sucking in her passion, screaming her right to own her body, she rode this ocean until she was lighter than the water. Then the graceful, easy drift of a feather on still air. Her lover had her body freed in plenty of time to sway with her and croon her to an easy full landing. "Oh, that I could trust myself this much," she smiled. Then she floated secure and safe in her lover's arms. Both womyn tender and connected.

Still smiling long after, she felt very softly smug. She knew that the next time the struggle wouldn't be there. The next time it would be pure pleasure.

How Many More?

CRYSTAL BAILEY

The house was quiet, darkened by the coming night. One window was streaked by sunset and we laid wrapped in our arms on the couch. I had a swift, sudden desire to see us from the outside, to know what our big bodies looked like, tangled together. We both were feeling sleepy, eyes drooping and closing all by themselves; I was pleasantly drifting. Chris and I had been talking about sexuality with me in particular trying to explain what I thought I wanted; or a someone that I wanted:

"I like to play games, I love to come on strong," I told Chris. "I want to find someone who gets into the games as much as I do. I'm learning more and more about gentleness within the structure of roughness—I like learning how far I can push someone before their body resists. It's so important to find out where someone feels safe, then I can ask them to step away from it until they get scared; we pull back again where it's safe and then I push them to step out a bit further."

Chris' blue eyes never left my face. I couldn't tell what she was thinking. Idly I rubbed her shoulder with my hand.

"And I love it when my partner gets off on my strength, when I know she knows I can control her physically if I had to or if I desired that." My words were mostly a probing, a groping for visions and ideas of the sort that are somewhat elusive.

Chris fidgeted in my arms; I thought she might be nervous. "I'm interested in it, it's arousing, but . . ." she looked for words of her own.

She and I had fooled around with S/M before, some very mild

explorations. I was aware of her interest but she always seemed aloof, as if approaching it from a distance was as close as she wanted to be. I rarely talked of my S/M fantasies to her because I never knew how she would react. Her body seemed particularly tense, her breath was coming in little gusts, an unevenness that suggested that she was harboring bothersome thoughts. "What's up?" I asked quietly, peering into her face.

"I'm really interested in that part of you," Chris said.

I wasn't feeling much like talking anymore and didn't comment, pushing my face into her sleeve instead.

"Mandy," she whispered from the tense stillness of her body.

"Hmmm."

"Would you take me to the sleeping cabin and spank me?" Her voice was somewhat tight, carrying a bit of strain as if the question had been a hard one.

I came eyes-open awake, slightly startled, and searched her face in the clustered darkness.

"Would you *really* spank me?"

I propped myself out of her embrace into my elbows. I was suddenly thrown a game to play and I felt a little unsure, a reaction I wasn't going to share with her. "Yes," I said evenly.

"As we walk to the sleeping cabin will you tell me what I have to do when we get there?"

"I will tell you exactly what you are to do and I expect you to do it; otherwise I will be displeased and will have to punish you further. Understand?"

She nodded her head, eyes closed. I closed my hand around her wrist and squeezed until she opened them and looked at me. Her gaze had ribbons of titillation all through it.

"Will you really spank me? Will it hurt?"

I looked down at her, my friend—we knew each other well. She wanted me to spank her, I wanted to give her what she wanted. "Yes, it's going to hurt. I'm going to hurt you, Chris."

She gasped slightly, her breath was excited and very uneven. "Will you pinch my nipples. . . maybe before you spank me?" She seemed to taste each word for their full effect. They affected me too, my hands yearned to rid her of her clothes.

"When you are lying across my lap, just before I expose your ass, I'll unsnap all of your pretty red buttons and then I'm going to reach inside your shirt front. I'll let you know I'm pinching your nipples, Chris." I thought briefly of her rounded white ass being marked and reddened by my hand, of how wet her cunt must be getting; mine was certainly oozing. "Get up," I ordered her, rolling off the couch myself, reaching for my boots.

"Can I pee first?"

"All right, but hurry."

She disappeared into the other room. I collected blankets and a sheet. The sleeping cabin had mouse tenants who ate such things. When Chris returned I silently watched while she put on her shoes and then I gave her the sheet to carry. I took the blankets. We left the house and walked briefly through the night along a path that was crowded with grasses eager to lay their wet—soundlessly—onto our legs. I hardly noticed. Partially hooded by clouds, the stars watched our walk.

"When we get to the cabin," I said, "I want you to put the sheet on the bed. I will light the candle and then, when you are done, I'm going to punish you."

"Have I been bad?" Her voice was low and hesitant.

"Yes, and I think you should be punished."

She stopped and turned to me. "In the morning if my ass isn't red enough, will I have to have another spanking?"

I was silently amazed at how boldly her desires were showing. "Yes, you will," I said.

The cabin door stuck slightly. I applied a bit of shove with my palm and stepped inside. A mild mustiness perfumed us. I groped for matches, scratched one into flame and lit a candle and the room with a softness. Chris went immediately to the bed and began to dress its bareness with the sheet. I watched her, standing by her side.

"You'll have to do it again, Chris, there's a hole in the sheet. It should be at the bottom of the bed." I indicated the hole with a movement of my foot.

Silently she undid what she had already done and started over. A small drift of uneasiness feathered into my chest, thoughts tumbled: how to weave her fantasies into my own? Did I like the boss/slave part of the game? Did I really know how to push her and yet stay where there was a semblance of security for both of us? I pushed my thoughts aside, determined to give her what she wanted and receive what I wanted in return. Silently, eyes averted, she removed her boots. Then her eyes trembled into mine and I felt bold.

"Turn around, Chris," I said in stern tones.

Slowly she did so, tremoring from. . . anticipation? . . . possibly a little fear? I hoped so, I wanted her to be somewhat afraid of me.

"Pull your pants down and ready yourself for your spanking."

Her slender fingers undid her buttons, slid down her zipper.

"Slowly," I said, "I want to see your ass exposed very slowly."

She nodded, trembling even more, and head bowed, she showed me her ass; her pants slid unnoticed to a heap at her ankles. "You'll hit me softly at first so I'll get used to it before you hit me harder, won't you?"

I wanted to lunge at her, throw her onto the bed, rip open her shirt, fall mouth upon her breast; I wanted to fire the depths of her cunt with forceful fingers. I wanted her to cry out, to reach as if to stop me. I wanted us to be furious and fast, her to be tied and spread, to make her feel the strength of my arms holding her down. I sat on the bed. "Come here, Chris. I want you to lay yourself over my lap. I want your ass up high, just right for me to spank it."

Her chest showed the quickness of her breath. She stretched herself onto my lap and her rounded white ass, not very plump, was ready, lusciously waiting. I struck my first blow, a somewhat light one, the first warning of what was to come.

"Oh!" Chris blushed and pressed her face into the pillow.

I slapped again, harder, a volley of slaps, coming down on the lower cheeks, then higher up where the cheeks spread out some and then even lower down where the cheeks sloped into her legs. Her skin reddened and I liked it. I soothed her skin with caressing circles of my hand; my right hand reached underneath her and closed on one of her nipples, pinching it with increasing pressure until I sensed that her moans meant the pain was becoming too much. "You like that?" I asked her. "You want me to spank you more?"

"I don't know," she whispered into the pillow. "When you're through spanking me, will you play with my clitoris?"

24

"If I'm satisfied with how you take the spanking I'll play with your clitoris."

"Will you fuck me gently?"

My answer was the palm of my hand against her ass until she was crying out no, no, no, and twisting her body away from my blows. Her resistance excited me. I gripped her roughly and bore down on her ass three more times before I let up—partially so that I could catch my breath and to give each of us time to center before we started up again. My next few blows made her clutch her pillow, twisting beneath my grasp, telling me it hurt, it hurt. I pushed her a short ways past her resistance and then once again let up, soothing her burning flesh with light touches.

"How many more are you going to give me?" she asked haltingly.

I thought about it, trying to decide how many more she could take; how many more did I want to give her? "Six," I said. "I'm going to give you six more and each of them will hurt."

"I'm hurting now," she said.

I urged her ass higher; "Come on," I said roughly, "get it up there." The first slap snapped against her skin, the second, the third—oh, oh, she cried—another, and the last two were delivered with as much strength as I could muster. Feeling almost feverish, I rolled her onto her back. I was eager to fuck her, to take this woman I had so soundly spanked. Softly I sent my hands touching her into moaning. Her punishment over, she was ready and longing for the wetness of her cunt to be dipped into. I straddled her with my legs, mouth to her nipple, took the other with one hand, my belly and cunt lowered onto her belly and cunt; she arched up to meet me, spreading her legs. Her wetness kissed my leg. Slowly I traced my fingers along her face. She opened her eyes and I saw in them a look I'd never seen there before. Her eyes lingered, their color dark, in pain and pleasure. I teased the inside of her thighs, swiftly gliding over her cunt with just enough pressure to cause her to pant, gasp.

"Fuck me please, Mandy." Her hands reached to pull me down on her.

I sank all my weight onto her, pinning her to the bed. "Beg me, Chris," I said, forcefully. "Beg me."

"Please fuck me."

"Beg me harder."

"Please. Please. Fuck me."

Her voice never broke into a weakness that I might despise, she didn't lose my respect, she didn't cower, but she begged; she wanted it and I could tell. I sent myself inside of her. Deep. I took her, rode her with my body, sucked on her breasts, sucked their fullness into my mouth, pressed my face into the soft. Rocking, thrusting, in and out, in and out, I pleasured in our cries, our grunts and moans; everything was sensation and motion. I didn't hold back, I roughed her, took her, found her clitoris and rubbed its firmness as I fucked her wet swollen cunt. I wanted to bite her and did, bringing from her a spatter of sharp cries. Images of her ass reddening beneath my hand, images of me slapping, slapping, making her take more than she thought she could, danced inside of me until, clutching and wrapping her in my arms, we rode the crash of our spendings together.

We were very quiet for quite awhile. I lay relaxed, our bodies lightly touching, thinking of what we had just shared. Apparently she was too.

"What're you thinking Mandy?" She slid her arm under my head so that I could snuggle on her shoulder.

"Oh, not much." I tried to organize the thoughts that drifted and straggled through my mind.

"Was it ok for you?" she asked. Such a soft voice.

"Yes. Yes, Chris, it was ok for me. I liked it, I like figuring out how to mingle my needs for fulfillment with yours. A couple of times I got a little scared of the game, or maybe it was the power I was a little scared of—anyway, those were only moments." I looked up at her. She was focused on the ceiling, her forehead squinched into lines. She seemed somewhat distant, probably sorting out inner tangles. "Did you enjoy it?" I asked.

"Yes, I liked it." She seemed confused, as if she didn't really understand why she did or as if she didn't really know how she had come to explore it. I sensed that the experience had pulled open some rather deep doors for her.

"Mandy?"

"Hmm?"

"Do you think you might spank me again? Do you think I need

it again?" Her body pulsed and trembled, already falling once again into a readiness, into a sweeping tumble of naked want.

I snaked out of her embrace and looked at her quietly for a few moments. My hand crept to her belly and I wanted to splay her across my lap again, yes, I wanted to spank her yielding flesh with my hand. "Yes, Chris, I think I had better spank you again."

If I Ask You to Tie Me Up, Will You Still Want to Love Me?

JUICY LUCY

I am white middle class early 30's thin a femme all my life, separatist psychic witch astrologer ethicist. I made that last one up. It means that I approach my life as a series of ethical choices requiring thought & heart & honesty & courage. I take myself & my life very seriously & relate best to lesbians who also approach their lives seriously & ethically. I observe & analyze & learn from lesbians in our relationships to each other & the world, & believe very strongly that we can find our way out of self-destructive self-hating patterns. In other words, that we can remember our selves & grow in strength to self-love & joyful self-expression. Does all this make you feel you know something about me? Perhaps you'd like to get to know me? I also enjoy sexual S/M immensely & recognize it as a healing tool for me. Now how do you feel about me? About getting to know me? Look at how these words affect you. Does your mind start to close down when you read "S/M"?

Among lesbian feminists a closed mind is the usual reaction to sexual S/M. Many feminists are quite vocal in their condemnation of S/M, parading ignorance bigotry & condescension as analysis. One would think those opposed to S/M would inform themselves of some basics about this issue before discussing it.

But that's a problem with S/M. Ignorance & assumptions are widespread while information & personal testimony are either not easily available or ignored. So the myths keep getting circulated & the insults keep coming & I have had it. I am tired of other dykes' fear & cruelty & willful stupidity being turned against me & being held at fault for their desire to victimize someone. I am tired of the horror in 'friends' eyes when they find out I practice S/M. (Glory in S/M is more like it. I haven't had to practice for a long time now. I found I was quite good at it without the need for much rehearsal.) I am tired of being accused by hysterical dykes who beat up their lovers of being a rapist/brutalizer/male-identified oppressor of battered womyn. *I* was a battered womyn for years & claim the right to release & transform the pain & fear of those experiences any way I damn well please.

So. I decided that rather than just react, once again, to the insults of the uninformed I would try to do some informing. Understand that I ask no one's approval & that I am not implying that every dyke get into S/M. I think that the hysteria level will drop considerably when more lesbians know what it's about, which ultimately will make my life easier. I am out about this in the lesbian community because I know of no other way to get lesbians to hear about & discuss it. Being out when there is still so much ignorance & fear has put me in some very disgusting positions & I'd like the fog to lift.

First some definitions & discussion of vocabulary. I make a distinction between emotional S/M & sexual S/M, & I'll discuss emotional S/M later on. By sexual S/M I mean a consensual exchange of power involving physical pleasure & eroticism that involves 2 or more lesbians. (I know hets & fags do their own kinds of S/M & I couldn't care less. If you're interested in that you'll have to talk to someone else about it.)

Sadist & masochist are terms I have a schizophrenic reaction to. When & how I use these terms changes depending on the context & on who I'm with. In a sexual context sadist & masochist are roles that define erotic poles of power & have meanings of passion trust & intensity that flow from a fully consensual situation. In a non-sexual context sadist & masochist are roles in power-over situations involving pain & cruelty where the consensual agreement to these roles is unacknowledged or absent. Perhaps because of my schizophrenic reaction to these words I find I am learning to be very clear & specific about my meanings, expecially when talking to non-S/M dykes. S/M dykes know what I mean. I also use the terms top & bottom to describe the two basic power positions in S/M.

The exchange is: sadist/top/dominant/sender flowing into masochist/bottom/passive/receiver. However, it is an oversimplification to talk about the erotic exchange as though it only flowed one way. Each side has many levels of apparent & actual power. In sexual S/M the exchange is mutual, with both sides giving & receiving erotic intensity. For example, the trust/openness of the bottom is a constant turn-on to the top, even though it's the bottom who's being had. The power & erotic exchange always flows full circle. If it doesn't then it's not satisfying & the satisfaction of all concerned is a prime goal in S/M. This is one of the differences I find between S/M sex & vanilla sex, because so often in the latter each dyke is concerned primarily with her own satisfaction & the lover's needs are met as part of a payment or trade-off. In S/M sex each seeks to open as much as possible, to push past the limits, to turn each other on so intensely that there is no possibility but full satisfaction, not just physically but emotionally & psychically as well.

Many non-S/M lesbians are quite offended by the language of S/M. Well, if you haven't taken the risks you don't get to make the rules. A sweet friend has begun using the phrase Power & Trust as a substitute for the phrase S/M, & I like that & use it some. However, S/M dykes who haven't heard that phrase might not know what I meant & non-S/M dykes might assume I meant some "nice" watered down version of what I actually do sexually. That would be like some lesbian coming off as bi-sexual so pricks wouldn't be threatened. Whenever I'm in new surroundings I very specifically use the phrase S/M so whoever I'm talking to knows I *mean* S/M.

Here is a list of things S/M is not: abusive, rape, beatings, violence, cruelty, power-over, force, coercion, non-consensual, unimportant, a choice made lightly, growth blocking, boring.

Now a list of things S/M is: passionate, erotic, growthful, consensual, sometimes fearful, exorcism, reclamation, joyful, intense, boundary-breaking, trust building, loving, unbelievably great sex, often hilariously funny, creative, spiritual, integrating, a development of inner power as strength.

31

These are my lists. Every S/M lesbian I know would agree with the first & could probably add several more nots. Not all would agree with the second; for example spiritual & exorcism. This article comes from my own experiences, so while I can generalize about S/M please understand that there is a wide variety of experience & other S/M dykes relate to S/M differently from me.

My own growth into S/M started about 5 years ago when I developed a deeper understanding of the basic power roles in patriarchy. I was straight till my mid-20's, & when I came out was determined to leave behind power-over relationships & the power imbalance of het life. After some time as a lesbian I began to see that we all have power-over & power imbalances drilled deep into us. I began to see a pattern of emotional pain between lesbians that no one seemed to be talking about. It was as if we didn't get enough pain from the outside world so turned to our friends & lovers for more. I saw myself & other dykes constantly setting ourselves up in situations that couldn't possibly meet our expectations & then being so hurt when the inevitable came true. I saw us pushing & pushing & pushing at each other until the obvious explosion happened & we were shattered. I saw the roles reverse when the weaker one got her revenge & became for a time the strong one. I started calling this pattern emotional S/M, because I felt it had so much to do with roles frozen in a pattern of abuse & pain. These roles, of sadist & masochist, are the roles of heterosexuality & patriarchy. Power is in its nature a flowing of energy, an exchange. Sometimes we give & sometimes receive but the energy, the power, always flows. Patriarchy & heterosexuality attempt to freeze power, to make one side always dominant & one side always passive. Naturally what comes from this is violent & at its core death-centered & life-denying. The most obvious example is the power relationship between het women & men. It is the origin of the masochist & sadist positions. Lesbians don't seem to be stuck in one side of these power roles; I've often seen the roles reverse during a relationship. Butch & femme roles relate to these emotional S/M roles but do not make an exact correlation because some femmes are sadists & some butches are masochists.

Our roles aren't usually consciously chosen, but they often

determine the dynamics between us. No matter how good or loving our intentions we often live out a pain scenario because these hidden roles, which function like needs, are unacknowledged. The lesbian whose lovers always leave her, the one who constantly has too much responsibility & looks haggard, the one who's always depressed & never quite sure why—these are some of the masochists I have known & loved. This is not a joke. The one who falls in love with a new lesbian to end an old relationship, the one with a burden whose friends are always made to feel vaguely guilty, the one who's so cool emotionally her lovers always look hysterical by comparison—these are some of the sadists in my life. There are other examples. I know any of you could look around & recognize these or other variations on the same theme. Do you see yourself?

By saying "sadist" & "masochist" I do not mean that I or any of these other dykes consciously decided to cause pain. Pain is simply the inevitable result of unacknowledged power roles. I have never known lesbians to say to each other something like "Let's start a relationship & hurt each other a lot, OK? You be needy & demanding & fearful & manipulative, & I'll be cool & tough & withdraw farther from you while meanwhile becoming completely dependent on you. Then you fall in love with someone else in secret & leave me with no warning. We'll both be broken for months by grief & guilt. Sound like a good time?" Its never this consensual, though the roles are often this clear. These pain dynamics show up in friendships & political work as often as in lover relationships. When a lesbian's role is really obvious I have known other dykes to comment on it but these roles are often more subtle than that. I have not yet met a lesbian who did not have these roles in her, & the extent to which they affect her ability to relate to & be happy with other lesbians & herself depends on her awareness of the roles & her willingness to own her own participation in these dynamics.

Once I started seeing this pattern I began trying to eliminate it from my life. I have more than enough pain & seeing my own sadism & masochism was very awful. I began to look for lesbians who could understand my perceptions & who were equally committed to getting rid of this shit, & to limit or close off contact with those who couldn't & wouldn't. Several years went by, & while I was clearer & stronger & had more supportive & balanced relationships I still kept finding unequal power & elements of emotional S/M in my life. But the spirit provides, & she brought me a confrontation with sexual S/M & my own self.

I developed an enormous crush on an acquaintance. One day she had a leather studded collar around her neck, & when I asked her why she told me it was because she was into S/M. (I really appreciate & admire her courage. This was in an all womyn environment & she took a huge risk to do some CR around this. She caught a lot of crap, needless to say.) It took me a while to get my jaw off the ground. I had been really naive. It had never occurred to me that lesbians were into S/M, I thought that was just something for fags & hets. I realized that I was attracted to both her & her lover & had been for some time so *something* must be going on. I had a lot of respect & trust for these dykes & just knowing they were into S/M didn't make them any different. It had the potential of making me be different to them, but that was my shit, not theirs. I was terribly frightened, because I thought S/M was beatings & violence & I'd had so much of that as a straight womon what did it mean about me that I wanted to be sexual with someone who did these things? Soon I calmed down enough to realize that I didn't really know what S/M was & that these lesbians were kind & strong & I couldn't imagine them liking to hurt each other. I got hold of some literature from SAMOIS (a lesbian feminist S/M support group: Box 11798, San Francisco, CA 94101) & got so freaked by my recognition of & agreement with most everything I read that I got a pinched nerve from my neck down my left arm to the tip of my middle finger. Then I *really* knew something was going on.

My lover of 3 years & I discussed all this & agreed to explore this some. We started by tying each other up with soft scarves & that sort of thing, & I was scared all over again because I really liked it. I got beyond being afraid of myself pretty quickly & got the pleasure of it. I found that the terror & powerlessness of the rapes & beatings was being defused. After all, this was my scenario, not some prick's. As bottom, I got to say exactly what I wanted, & nothing I didn't want would happen. I finally had a way to let the masochistic side of me, which was there anyway whether I wanted it or not, exist instead of always trying to deny & push away & be afraid of a part of myself. I could face my own hidden side, look in my own face of fear, & reclaim myself. And this wasn't intellectual, wasn't words & theories, this was hot times with my honey love. I am most always orgasmic, but this was a step into something else again.

As time went on I learned more about myself emotionally & physically, & found that my limits are farther out than I would have thought. Some of what would feel painful in a non-S/M context or non-sexual context becomes very arousing during S/M. For example, nipple clips. I wouldn't wear them walking down the street—they'd hurt. However, once I reach a certain point of arousal they are *really* nice. The same is true of my whip. It's very soft leather, 8 thongs about 18″ long with a wood & leather handle, & at the beginning of sex I only like it lightly. As things progress, lightly isn't enough. Be very clear about this—this is not a beating I'm talking about. I've been beaten a lot & I know the difference between pleasure & pain. This is an intensification of sensation, a heightened stimulation of certain areas & it *feels good to me*. I have other toys; leather wrist & ankle restraints, handcuffs, a g-string, some chain. Never underestimate the feel of cold metal on a hot body. I am getting more into the eroticism & creativity of scenes—the "theatre" aspect of S/M—& want to get an appropriate collection of lacy whatevers. As time goes on & I release barriers I allow myself more experiences & build my collection of toys. You don't need toys to do S/M, just the desire to explore yourself. But I want to be very clear & honest about what S/M is to me. That's why I'm talking about what I use. In terms of what I do, imagine most anything & I probably do it or have considered it. I don't want the nitty-gritty of S/M for me to be some dark & hidden thing, & I want lesbians to understand that anything you want is alright as long as you don't coerce or abuse anyone to get it.

S/M is very cathartic & healing for me. A lot of nonspecific anxiety is gone from my life, especially anxiety around sex. One benefit I'd not looked for came in my fantasies. All my life I'd tried not to have fantasies 'cause they were almost always about rape & mutilation & death. Sometimes I'd feel like I couldn't push them out of my mind, like I'd been permanently invaded. Well those fantasies are almost all gone. Instead I have a constant supply of wonderful sensual erotic fantasies about lesbians, myself, this earth, anything I want. That just happened by itself, & I love it. I find a strengthening & confidence in myself that I really like, & the emotional S/M I'd still participated in happens less & less. I find that pattern sometimes but can recognize it sooner & get out of abusive & potentially abusive situations easier.

Being bottom comes so smoothly to me it's like diving into warm water. & at first that was the only role I'd let myself explore. We are trained young & deep to be passive, receptive, accepting, & so it was easier for me to reclaim the strength in that side of the power flow. Sometimes as bottom when it's being really good I feel myself open psychically so much I could take in the whole universe & I can feel spirit enter me like a lover.

Being top came harder to me. Power & cruelty have so often gone hand in hand in my life & I feared that in myself, feared my own power & taking it so openly. But as I've pushed past this barrier I've found myself claiming power with more honesty & courage than ever before in my life. The fine high feeling of pushing a womon who will trust herself to my will past barriers in herself into orgasm after orgasm is indescribable.

It's important to me that I can explore both sides of eroticism, the giving & the receiving. I am & have been both a sadist & a masochist, in all the meanings of those words, & I want to know & work with all of who I am.

S/M can bring one very close to the edge. Sometimes when making love the horror & memory of past experiences floods me with no warning & I need to know that the one I'm with will be very loving to me 'till the storm passes. This is why I know that good tops are the most compassionate & sensitive beings on earth.

Trust is an absolute essential. To build valid trust requires some ability to risk & some common sense. Since S/M is consensual there's always some talking, before & after, so that you both (or all) know what's going on. It's a lot easier to trust a dyke when you've told her what you don't want so you know she won't accidentally cross your boundaries. It's important to agree on a safe word, something you could say that would automatically stop the action. I find it much easier to really let go when we've agreed on a safe word, & I think because of the intensity it's safer. Besides, sometimes we say "no" & "stop" & we don't mean that at all, we're just into it. I like to use the word "mercy" myself. I've found that I use the safe word much more often because my emotional boundaries are being crossed rather than because my physical boundaries are being crossed. Again, everyone's experience is unique to her.

I've found that S/M has really helped me get rid of a lot of passive-aggressive shit & communications problems. You really learn how to be clear about what you want & that it's all right to want *anything* you want. I think a lot of the misunderstandings & not hearing each other & not being brave enough to be honest get burned away in S/M. It's in the nature of the situation that you become more honest & courageous.

The main issues are to talk it through openly & make sure you agree, trust each other (& if you don't trust her, either find someone else or examine your own blocks, whichever is relevant), agree on a safe word, & get all the pleasure & joy there is between you in that situation. S/M is basically about good times. It's a part of who I am to analyze & have to understand everything. I think the vast majority of S/M dykes are not so analytical—they just know a good thing when they find it. Ultimately I wouldn't have been interested in S/M, whatever its healing value, if it hadn't been such a good time.

I'd like to talk a little about some of the common reactions & "criticisms" I get about S/M. At the beginning of this article I mentioned some of the responses I've gotten. First I want to say that even before S/M was an issue for me I'd noticed that few lesbians are comfortable talking about sex. In discussing S/M this discomfort shows in several ways, one obvious one being that since S/M is specifically sexual lesbians don't seem to feel any responsibility to listen to & understand experiences that are different from their own. Dykes from different countries, races, classes, ages, etc. understand the importance of listening to each other's lives. It doesn't always mean we get anywhere, but there's an understood value of listening to & taking seriously what a lesbian of different experiences says about her life. Because S/M is sexual this value disappears, I think partly because S/M invariably enhances sex. Consequently, S/M is denied as a political choice or 'real' life experience.

Our sexual energy is literally our life force at its rawest—no shields, no disguises, no polite mistaking it for something else. This is especially true with S/M. Sexuality is energy as tangible as that which turns the earth. It is both power & a pathway to power. I see most lesbians being terrified of their own power; witness how quickly lesbians try to tear down any dyke in their midst who acts powerfully & begins to rise above the group. That common lesbian phenomenon of striving for the lowest common denominator is a direct result of fear of self/fear of one's power. S/M is about sex, about power, & about our right to work with our sacred life's energy as intensely creatively & courageously as we wish. Nothing is hidden in S/M. It's all right out front, & if you're afraid of yourself S/M will terrify you. S/M is a sexual pathway to a more & more powerful self, & I think this is the reason so many lesbians react with knee-jerk responses of condemnation bigotry prudishness & moral holier than thou crap. For those lesbians who are afraid of sex & afraid of power, S/M, which is about sexual power & specifically about lesbians becoming *more* powerful through their sexuality, is frightening. Consequently, the common resistance I find to discussing sex at all is magnified when trying to discuss S/M with non-S/M lesbians.

One common reaction is the fear that once a lesbian gets into S/M she'll never want or be able to be sexual like she used to be. It's the victorian thing of being "ruined." Well, my experience is that S/M has given me so much confidence & knowledge of my sexuality that there's always a quality of S/M in my lovemaking. If my lover is not into S/M she most likely doesn't notice the S/M quality like I do. (I'm referring here to casual & short-term affairs. Naturally, my long time lovers & heart friends are all aware of & into S/M with me to one degree or another.) With S/M everything gets charged, so that even subtle movements of the hands & body have an S/M connotation to me now. That doesn't mean that every dyke I'm with is going to have an S/M "experience." Far from it. It means that I don't shut off my own sources, &

that the extent of how much the one I'm with experiences S/M sex is up to her & to what we agree on together. Also, I wouldn't usually get into serious S/M sex with strangers right away because I need time to build a basis of trust. So obviously I haven't forgotten how to make love in a less intense way than S/M. Once again, everybody's different. I just want to show that this fear is simply that, a fear, not a realistic look. It's also true that given a choice between S/M sex with a lesbian I care for & trust, & sex with a lesbian I care for & trust who's not into S/M, I'd take the S/M experience every time. Don't be misled. I've never had a choice like this—it just sounds like a nice fantasy. Wouldn't we all like to be hustled by several different lesbians at the same time?

The most serious area of difficulty for most lesbians is the confusion between lesbian S/M & prick violence & pornography. Bondage is very in as a porn image, whips & chains are appearing more & more, & men's violence against womyn seems to be spiralling up again. The distinction here is that lesbian S/M is consensual, bringing pleasure & strength. Porn & violence bring pain mutilation fear & death. It's the difference between being powerful & loved & being a hated victim. Part of the problem is that the issues of violence & power are very charged for womyn, & it seems to be hard for some to remember that while two things may look similar from the outside that doesn't mean they're the same thing. Some womyn in Women Against Violence Against Womyn & related groups have lost this perspective & been very bigoted & hostile to S/M dykes & a lot of shit has been exchanged. Many S/M dykes have little or no patience any more, so polarization has happened fairly quickly in some places. What's important to me is that lesbians remember that all ways a lesbian strengthens herself & brings pleasure into her life without coercing or oppressing anyone else are tools against our victimization & oppression.

In my own life, I've had friends scream insults at me, tell me I'm to be pitied, like a man, oppressive to womyn, disgusting, not welcome in their home, untrustworthy, etc. I've had old lovers & friends/acquaintances of many years simply stop answering my letters. Some lesbians tell me all the reasons why it's "wrong" & then come onto me. Others simply get very polite & ignore the whole thing like I'd never made myself open to them, never brought up the subject. I wish lesbians were braver & that we didn't scapegoat each other so easily.

Though I'm often afraid, I've learned I can't afford to ever let that block my life. This world is full of ugliness & pain & grief & horror. I do what I can to lessen the awfulness for myself & others, & to build the self-respect & self-love of lesbians starting with myself, always. I celebrate the female principle, the creatrix spirit, & love the life I make for myself. I believe that we are all able to be self-creating in joy. S/M is a very big part of these things for me. So what I've come to now is if you want to talk about it that's fine, if you come with respect. If not, then keep it to yourself. I'm not interested.

But it's worth it to me to be out. I've made some wonderful friendships, had the pleasure of seeing lesbians reach past fear to trust & so find new strength in themselves, & had the satisfaction of clarity & integrity in a world that wants us to live in shame. I want that trust strength clarity & integrity recognized by the lesbian community, not just for myself but for any S/M lesbian. I want non-S/M lesbians reading this article to examine their own lives & think very carefully before they ever again put down lesbian S/M. And I want S/M lesbians who read this to know that there is no place for shame & self-hate in us about something so loving & kind. Heal & be healed. Spirit surround you.

Proper Orgy Behavior

J.

ORGY #1

Thoughts I keep to myself:

Oh, jeez, *look* at those women over there. One is whipping the other. Uh oh and I promised myself I'd be cool and non-judgemental...but...but...how can they *do* that? Why would she want to be *whipped*?

Oh, it's just too weird. Why did I come to this orgy anyway? Me, monogamous me, who's never even done a three-way with friends.

Oh, she's really going at it now. I think I'll take my glasses off so I can't see.

ORGY #2

Thoughts I *still* keep to myself:

Well, here I am again...and there are those two women again. All that *leather* she's wearing. I wonder if she gets hot in it? She's just standing there, slowly whipping her friend; it seems so impersonal.

I wonder what it feels like? Why is it such a turn on?

Oh, it's just too weird!

ORGY #3

Thoughts I say out loud to friends:

Listen, I know this might sound unusual coming from me, but...well...I'd like to see what it feels like to be whipped!

My friends are delighted, and we find a swingboard for me to lie down on. I tell them that I am feeling very vulnerable and do

41

not want any sexual play this time, only whipping. "Only whipping," I gulp. I then tell them that my safe word for stopping the action is "red," and "pink" is for lightening up.

One by one, they take turns. They ask my permission first, and are loving and gentle in their manner. In the semi-darkness of the room, I am aware of other women quietly watching us. I close my eyes so as not to be distracted from my body's feelings. I take a deep breath and try to relax, but I am anxious. Will it hurt? Can I take it? What AM I doing? I wait nervously, then...Smack! The first hit. Ahh, I expel air and automatically pull away from what hurt me, but the crop comes down again quickly: Smack! Smack! "Ayyy, that hurts," I protest. I am surprised at how much it stings. They laugh and I relax. So, it really does hurt. I feel I know now what it is I'm playing with and settle back into myself to experience my reactions.

Smack! Smack! No time for thinking...smack! Smack! Smack! "Oohh, aaahhh," I moan. Then I feel hands gently rubbing my sore bottom. Oh but I feel like crying, the tenderness is almost too much. The rubbing stops and I tense, knowing there will be another swat. Smack! I tense and then relax into it as the pain rushes up my body and is over. "That wasn't so awful," I think. Smack! Smack! Tense, rush of pain, calm...I realize I have a rhythm going now, I feel I'm on one side of a barrier, then the swat comes and the pain, and I surrender to it and am through it, through to a wonderful floating calm. As we do it again and again I lose sense of time and people. It feels like just me and the pain and the calm.

"I want you to count the next strokes I do, from six to one," my friend whispers in my ear. It's jarring, hearing her voice, and I'm angry that she broke into this intense private space I'm sharing with the crop. But I murmur, "O.K."

Smack! I try to come out of this non-thinking space enough to remember what I'm supposed to do but I can't get my mind to focus and I giggle. "The numbers won't stay in line," I report. "Does it matter?" And I try: "1...5...4...7..." She smacks me again, laughs, and then says sternly, "*Yes*, it matters: try harder." I do because her hits have gotten stronger. I pull my mind together, take a deep breath, and race through the numbers so none have time to fall out of place and get lost in the floating darkness inside of me.

After I succeed, she whispers how well I did, and that she knows how hard it is to count or do anything linear in the space I'm in.

So this place I'm in must be alpha-intense, floaty, non-linear— one of my favorite places this whipping has brought me to: alpha. Yes, I know there are other ways of getting here, but I'm enjoying this one. I'm liking the sensations, and rhythm, the pain. *How amazing, I am even enjoying the pain.*

Another friend takes over now and uses a whip, softly, caressingly at first, then harder. Smack! Smack! Ahh, I relax. A harder smack. "Ayyy," I yell, then relax as the pain is over. A rhythm is going again, then quiet. My friend leans over me and softly asks, "Are you O.K.?" I nod, yes. "Do you want a little more?" And she chuckles. I smile and nod yes and so she continues. Smack! Smack! Ahh, barriers up then I'm through and flying, over and over we go. "More?" she asks again. I smile yes. I know she knows this place I'm in, so deep inside myself, just me and my feelings, no thoughts, no judgements. Feeling so centered and safe and strong; feeling my own center, my own power. My friend pushes a little more to see how much I can take and I push myself to match her, but when I say "pink" she softens her blows. I am so deep inside and flying so high it's awhile before I realize that she has stopped.

She says, "I think that's enough for your first time." "Oh," I say disappointedly. I want to go on. The smacks, the rushes, the calm all feel a part of me now. "I was just getting started," I say. "No, enough for now. You think you can take more but you really can't." And then she reassures me, "You can *always* do it again." Yes, I smile, feeling very peaceful and self-satisfied.

My friend starts to gently rub my back and bottom. How strange to feel her hands on me, me who loves being touched, who thought a whip and crop so impersonal. . . but just now they had felt so intimate and demanding and most of all, so *very* personal.

A Bedtime Story

ANONYMOUS

The billboard of dreams
—TODAY'S ATTRACTIONS—
flashes neon in my mind . . .
and I smile my curious
semi-smile at my own curious
dreams . . . impossible,
or so they seem . . .

(to R from H)

We have a strict Mistress-Slave relationship which has been ongoing for several months now and we've acted out various scenarios,
with you always the slave. We haven't really discussed where we
want our energy to go at this point, but I'm hoping to switch roles
sometime soon. But right now we're taking it nice and easy and
that's just fine. I'm very comfortable with the intimacy we are
experiencing.

One night after I'm fast asleep, I wake up to your sucking on
my breast. It's a very pleasurable sensation: I undulate and reach
to hold you but find that you have me bound, wrists and ankles, to
our four-poster bed. "Mutiny!" I cry, and you silence me immediately with a quick slap. I'm shocked and pleased. It's about 4:30
am but you flood the room with light—you look wonderful! You're
wearing my studded G-string and a sexy black camisole I've never
seen before. Without a word, you open our toy bag and pull out
the tit clamps. I resist as much as I can while you put them on

me... and you slap me again for my insolence. I feel so excited I could come right now! But you move away and begin playing with yourself at the foot of the bed, in plain sight. "Sit on my face!" I excitingly command. Abruptly you stop masturbating and position yourself so that you're straddling me. You have a stern look on your face and you say, *"Beg* me." My eyes are wide open now. You pull your top over your head and toss it to the floor. Kneeling over me with a breast near my mouth, you say "Suck me now." You press your breast into my compliant mouth and I suck you all right! You begin pulling away from me but my mouth is still anchored to your firm breast... then you jerk away and leave me panting... you begin massaging your own breasts, playing with the nipples which are like two hard rocks by now... you're still straddling me, and you start rocking your pelvis back and forth, while with one hand you continue to play with your own nipples and you slowly finger your flower of a clitoris with the other... I'm trying to arch my back so I can touch you with my hot, wet vulva, the friction of your soft thighs on my hips is driving me crazy! Your moaning is growing louder, your eyes are shut, and your head is slightly flung back. "Sit on my face!" I cry. "Please!" Abruptly you stop moving, that stern look on your face again, "Beg me."

I can hardly believe my ears, but I earnestly plead with you to let me devour you until you come... so you finally lower yourself onto my awaiting tongue and soon we are lost together, moving in sync... it seems you could swallow me just now... and then...

and then...

and then...

it's the Fourth of July all over again... and again... and again...

Act II, Scene I

A. J. SAGAN

"No." More a moan than a word.

The heavy strands of black braided leather bit into my ass and shoulder blades once more. And again. And again.

And my cries continued, breathless, reverberating in my throat, barely making it into the air. My body, bound and helpless, jerked at the blows, writhing without my will.

"No. Ohh." A moan trailing off into a shuddering sob.

I waited for the next cut of the whip—but it didn't come. And it still didn't come.

"Don't stop yet," I said in a low tone somewhere between a plea and a reproach.

"Just a short break" she said softly, running a hand soothingly over my burning skin. "For you *and* for *me.*"

"Okay."

My wrists were bound by black leather cuffs which were in turn attached to chains leading up to a couple of eyebolts placed about two feet apart in the door frame. My feet were free and just resting on the floor, so that, although I was chained with my arms up, I was not actually hanging or suspended.

She stepped around to my front still holding the nine-stranded black whip in one hand. She ran the other hand over my breasts fondly and began playing with my nipples, pulling and rolling and plucking at them and finally squeezing so hard that I winced and groaned. This made her grin widely, then laugh a little. She put the whip over my head and pulled my face to hers with a smooth demanding motion. We kissed. Very easily, barely touching lips.

47

My knees buckled and my lips began to fall apart. Gradually she pushed her tongue into my mouth gently, yet hard and insistent touching all surfaces. A rapture like fear stole through me, gripping bodily. My crotch tingled with our body currents. The muscles of my cunt and my ass were clenching and releasing, slow and hard.

Still kissing me, she returned to squeezing my left nipple, which seemed more sensitive than the right. That sent another current to my crotch. She had me—and I hoped that she would keep me there. Slowly she withdrew her mouth from mine, leaving me still wanting her. Letting go of the whip around my neck but still holding on hard to the nipple, she reached over to a little table and picked up a small cylinder—the poppers inhaler. She took off the top and held the inhaler to my nose. I breathed in slow and deep. She recapped it and put it back on the table picking up something else.

The poppers began to come on. I felt a rush of heat. Muscles letting go. The air seemed thick. Closing my eyes, I fell deep, deep inside an inner well of intensity, surrender, and desire. I opened my eyes and saw in the dim light a gleam of metal in her hands. Two sturdy metal clamps tipped with rubber pads—one for each nipple. I moaned anticipating their hard pinch and that piercing thrill of erotic pain.

She attached them quickly and smoothly. As each one clamped down, a deep part of me shrank away convulsively. I felt on the verge of tears once more. My voice quivered within me, my breath rasped. She began licking and lightly biting my ears while pulling on the clamps. She whispered in my ears: "Poor, poor nipples hurt so much, don't they? But they have to. Yes, for a while yet. Maybe the whip can help you to forget about how much your poor nipples hurt." She had me inhale the poppers again and then positioned herself behind me once more with whip in hand.

The heavy black whip hissed through the air landing over and over on my thighs, shoulders, and ass. What marks there would be when we were done! At each stroke I twisted, moaned, strained, wanted to come. Harder, I thought, it should be harder. "Hit me harder," I begged. And harder it was. Once she stopped for just a moment, rotated the clamps ninety degrees from their previous position, an excruciating change, and hung weight from the clamps

which pulled them tighter if that were possible. She gave me poppers again and then continued the whipping.

Soon I was almost ready to say "Mercy" which would, as we had
agreed, end things, if only for awhile. She anticipated me. "Are
you sure you want to ask for mercy already? You've got a lot more
coming to you! And, believe me, I know what I'm doing." I was
still and silent, masking the inner struggle of my feelings. What *do*
I really want?

"What is it, then?" She played the whip lightly over my breasts.
Her body pressed against mine. A hand pulled rhythmically on
my pubic hair. Deep inside me I had the sensation of falling.

"I want to go on."

"Good. I've barely started something really good. You won't
want to stop it. I'll stop when it's time. I know what you can take.
And I know you need it, too."

She resumed whipping me from behind. Now harder than before.
And faster. I was bursting with feeling. If only I could come like
this, I thought. If only. If only.

I began crying, real crying, sobbing, losing my breath and gasping for it. Shaking. Tears streaming down my face. But still I
didn't want to ask for mercy. I hoped that it would end soon but I
had let go, leaving it to her to end it. I had, after all, given myself
to her. I was hers and she wasn't done with me yet.

Suddenly the whipping stopped. I felt as if I were awakening in
a strange place with no recollection of how I had gotten there. A
sudden stab of pain in each nipple, followed by relief, brought me
back as she removed the clamps. She undid the wristcuffs from
the chains and half carried me to the bed.

"We need a break," she said to me urgently. I murmured wordless agreement. Holding her holding me I felt renewed energy
surging through us. I knew that we weren't finished yet tonight.

Curtain

Hot and Heavy:
Chris Interviews Sharon and Bear

Chris: Why don't you tell me some background . . . about how sex was for you before you got into S/M.

Sharon: Well, there was always this stuff of holding back. I'd always do things that were too hard or rough for whoever I was with. So I'd always hold myself back.

Chris: Physically?

Sharon: Yeah. And I'd make love more to them than they would to me. And I know when they did it to me it was always sort of boring because they were doing it I guess the way they wanted it done to them, and I wanted it done to me different.

Bear: You made love to them the way . . .

Sharon: The way *I* would like to be made love to, and they made love to me the way *they* would like to be made love to, I guess, which wasn't satisfying to *me*. Only I learned how to make love to them how they liked it, how to get them off and stuff, so they'd always have a satisfying experience, but I'd always be frustrated at the end.

The first woman lover I had was really soft, really passive. We had sex a lot only because I wanted it a lot. Her saying everyone was responsible for their own orgasms! We'd make love and then I'd have to get myself off . . . that was the pits. It *still* happens . . . But then I was lovers with one woman a couple of years ago when I did have orgasms with, because she was really into doing it to me, she really liked it, she really liked giving me pleasure. When I first came with her it felt like a miracle. I love sex a lot, I get wetter than anybody, dripping, sopping wet, but there's something in there . . . if somebody's just doing it to me out of guilt or because they

50

think they owe it to me, I don't get off, I don't get off on it. I just *can't*. Bear is the first person I've met who likes it as much and as often as I do—and maybe even more (laughs). When she comes on to me it's a real pleasure, you know, it's like "Oh my God!" It really can be equal. This is the most equal I've ever felt with anyone.

Bear: For the longest time I felt like a sex fiend, I wanted to make love so much, all the time! It's really nice having a lover that it's OK, you know?

Sharon: You're making me real passive, though. . .not passive, but I can lay back and take it forever.

Bear: Really! (laughs)

Sharon: The second or third time we made love I thought "Oh my God, she's doing too much to me!" Cause no one had ever come on like that to me before. I'm not used to taking it. It's hard for me to be passive. I'd like to give it a try, though (laughs).

Chris: (to Bear) How was it for you, with other lovers before Sharon?

Bear: Well, most of my lovers have been aggressive to me, have come on to me—not in bed, but came on to me to get me interested. But once we were in bed it was left totally up to me to be aggressive. It was really unsatisfying as far as them making love to me. I was always in that position of—what's the joke?—68. You know, "You owe me one, you *owe* me one!" Finally, not with Sharon but with my last lover, she was aggressive with me. She was also a big woman. For the first month or something I just laid back and ate it up, let her make love to me. As far as I was concerned I was getting even or something, which wasn't a good idea, really.

Chris: She didn't know you were. . .

Bear: She didn't know what the fuck was going on. Still, I would be aggressive, but I could never be as aggressive and as strong as I wanted to be.

Chris: What do you mean by aggressive—making the first moves or actually being physically aggressive?

Bear: Being physically aggressive. I would make love to them, and they would not make love to me. I would spend hours making love to these women—hours! Then they would roll over and make love to me for five minutes, and that would be it. When I did want to wrestle with them in bed a little bit, do more than just lay there and diddle with each other, "Ow, it's too hard! Ow, you're scrinching me! Ow, my breasts! Ohh, don't tickle." It was just so fucking frustrating. Now that I'm with Sharon, it's really quite exciting and different. I don't want to be with smaller women, if that's what it's about. With smaller women, I feel like it's a conditioned response by now, that I have to touch them so soft. I just feel like I'm in a girdle all over, you know what I mean? (Laughter) And it itches! I don't want to be like that anymore. I feel like I've been ripped off too long. I've had women come on to me for months at a time, and I really didn't want to be lovers with them, because I was bigger than they were. You know, "I *love* your body, I *love* your body," and the first time I got in bed with the woman it's "Oh you're hurting me," and "Oh be careful."

Sharon: For me, I like "rough sex," that feeling of struggle. The excitement of struggle turns me on. Struggle turns me on more than talking with somebody, actually. And wrestling—wrestling's great! Bear was the first person that could beat me wrestling.

Bear: I played a dirty trick on you, Sharon.

Chris: (to Bear) Oh yeah? What did you do?

Bear: Well, she kept saying, "I want to wrestle, I want to wrestle, I want to wrestle." I had mentioned somewhere along the line that I'd done martial arts, but I don't think she took that in. So finally she was smarting off and saying, "Ahh, I want to wrestle." So I said "OK, let's go somewhere. We'll wrestle." So we went down to the Marina and I beat her—two or three times. Since then we've gotten into wrestling, and that's real fun for me because I have a hard time getting anyone to wrestle with me.

Sharon: I *love* to wrestle with Bear. Even though she beats me it's getting harder for her to beat me. I've never learned the techniques, but I'm strong and I've wrestled a lot, and I've fought; I learned how to fight when I was five years old.

Bear: I've always been strong too. I've got a picture of me in a class, when I was about 6 or something, and I'm a head taller than anybody, and my chest is wider; I'm the biggest kid in the goddamn picture. (laughter)

Chris: Have you ever felt that people have been intimidated by your size?

Bear: Oh yes. I have met people, and I don't know where it comes from but they told me later that they thought I was like 6 feet tall and 600 pounds, you know, and were afraid to be around me—literally scared of me. And I'm not *that* big, but I am strong, and I always have been stronger and bigger, I guess, than the kids I went to school with. Ever since I can remember people have been scared of me. It's hurtful, it really is hurtful, and it makes you hold back a lot.

Chris: Are you talking about in everyday things?

Bear: In sex a lot, mostly, and in everyday life, too. But when people back away from you and you don't even know them, it's hard to get beyond that. I've *always* thought of myself as big and strong, and I always *liked* that about myself. But somewhere along the line you begin to wonder a little bit, "What the fuck is going on"? Because *you* feel good about yourself, but other people are intimidated, scared.

Chris: I know that just from my height, *people are intimidated by me, and a* lot *of people are stronger than I am! But just because I'm 5 or 6 inches taller than them. . . I'm really quite a sweetheart.*

Sharon: Me too! (Laughter) When somebody told me that people were intimidated by my size—this was in SAMOIS when someone first told me that—first it hurt my feelings, and then I got mad. When I feel like people are intimidated by my size or afraid of me—that's when I feel like being pushy, like, "Well, *fuck* you," and pushing them aside, when I wouldn't ever think of doing anything like using my size to. . . I *don't* use my size to intimidate people —people just get intimidated *by* it. But when I feel like people are feeling that way, it makes me want to really intimidate them.

Bear: "I'll give you something to be afraid of. . ."

Sharon: Right. Like when somebody says, "You make me nervous," I say, "Well, you should be." I'm just not going to play it anymore. There was a time when I was intimidated because other people were intimidated, you know what I mean? I'd feel weird, I wouldn't be able to feel strong and feel good around them. I've gotten stuff about my size for so long that I don't want to play it anymore. I don't feel like approving myself to anybody. I don't feel like telling them, "Look, I'm a regular person. I'm strong, and I'm gentle too." (Pause)

Bear, talk about how you got interested in S/M.

Bear: Well, about two years ago, I went to SAMOIS' first educational meeting, with a couple of friends. Soon after that I started being lovers with this woman and I thought I'll be brave and I'll tell her I'm interested in S/M. She gave me a real hard time about it. She didn't want to hear it. So I said OK, forget it, and I went on with our relationship, continued on with vanilla sex, with diddling around. About three months later she started complaining that I was doing things to her without telling her about it. And I never did *anything* to this woman that I hadn't done to a lot of *other* women! I was *not* playing any games with her. It was driving me crazy because I was *not* doing anything. It ended up really badly. I was real scared to get into it, because this was her reaction, and I cared about her. I was scared to get into it for myself. That's why I was hesitant to go to any of the orientations while I was still seeing her—and even later when I was by myself. I was just plain scared. I think mind-fucking is so much worse than S/M, and everybody else plays that. Nothing's clear; they just do these mind games—makes you feel crazy.

Chris: Well, that's what people are trying to call S/M, and that's what we're trying to say isn't S/M—mind games, power trips.

Sharon: That's not to say that there aren't some people into S/M that are like that, but it's not true that S/M is like that.

Chris: Right.

Sharon: There are people that do vanilla sex that are fuckers, that are shitheads, that are mean—power-mongers that power-trip you and get you in the place that they want you. I was lovers with this woman for a year and a half that told me all the time that she was ambivalent about being lovers with me.

Chris: Jeez!

Sharon: We finally just stopped being sexual, because it just wasn't good anymore. It never *was* as good as it could be. She was my first fat lover; our bodies felt real good together and all that. I watched myself go through these stages of. . . I mean, it's learning; I guess it's growing up; I guess it's learning not to let everybody's shit affect you, cause that stuff can. Maybe it's being into S/M and being more clear about power trips, too. I hold my own now, and I don't get on anybody's power trip; I don't let them do that anymore.

(Pause)

Bear and I had met for the first time a few years ago, so I knew her a little. Last year, it was the day after Halloween—I went over to Ollie's. Here she is walking in the door. We hung out awhile together, then we got bored with Ollie's. We came over to my house and smoked a joint. Then we went to the Jubilee. I forgot what happened, but somewhere during the evening she said, "Oh, you like it rough?" or something like that. Well, I ended up going home with her that night, it was real quick—we knew it was hot! (laughter) Don't waste no more time!! That night I did a little testing her out; I did a few things and then afterwards I asked her how she liked it, and she liked it. Then I decided, "Well, maybe we'd better—you know, all this communications stuff in SAMOIS, well, maybe we should talk about sex." I asked her to come over the Tuesday after that, and we're sitting in the front room talking, and I was thinking in my head, "God, how am I going to bring up S/M?" and just as I got the words together, just about to say something, she asks, "What do you think about S&M?" I said "*I* was just going to ask the same thing." It was great! I was searching in SAMOIS for this big tough woman and there she was at Ollie's! (Laughter)

Chris: Do you want to talk any about class and sex?

Sharon: No...(Pause) Well, one thing is that I'm *very* comfortable in Bear's house. My last lover owned her own home...you had to take your shoes off to go into the fucking house. It was a cold house, not warm and homey, it *felt* cold. A "don't get anything dirty" house. With Bear, we're so similar, even our kid pictures look alike. It looks like we could have been in the same family. We both smoke cigarettes, we both drink beer, we both smoke pot, we both are working class, we both are younger sisters in the same line-up of three kids in the family, the same ages between the siblings. I don't know if there's anything else to have in common! She has a car; I don't...

Chris: Does she have pets?

Sharon: She has a bitch cat...

Bear: Hey!

Sharon: ...and a dog. No, I *like* her animals. Yeah, we've both got animals.

Bear: When I go home to feed the animals, or let the dog out,

55

she understands.

Sharon: We both go, when somebody says a big word, "What the fuck does *that* mean?" We always know what each other's talking about.

Bear: It's true. I've never had to ask you what you mean.

Sharon: That's a drag, to be talking to somebody and have them say something I don't understand. It's nice not having that, with Bear. It's another kind of power trip that people have if they talk so I can't understand them: they've got one up on me. If they have to explain to me what they're talking about... I'm sort of antagonistic about it—is that the word? Sometimes it's not worth it to ask what it means; I don't care. But if someone does it a lot I make a point of saying something—"and what does *that* mean?" (Laughs). I say it in a way so I'm not being put down. I don't feel bad about not knowing what something means anymore. Somebody said to me once, "Look it up." I about smacked her. This woman's a feminist, but that's no consciousness, that's no *class* consciousness. Don't talk to me unless you can talk so I can understand. Because I'm not stupid. These people who went to college and know all the big words—they're real naive about life stuff, lots of stuff I know a lot about. Sometimes they seem real stupid to me—the only difference is that *they* use big words. They use big words to cover up their stupidity. I don't know...*I* don't use big words, and some people don't know what I'm talking about. But Bear does. And then there's some people I can talk to and it doesn't matter what words we use, we can talk to each other. It can make it difficult for relationships.

Class and sex...hmmm...class and *strength* has something to do with it, for Bear and me. That we're both big and strong had something to do with being working class. And physicalness, being more physical.

Bear: The only *big* women that I've been lovers with have been working class. I think I'm attracted more to working class women, partly because of the verbal thing, being able to communicate. I had middle class friends when I was growing up too, same as Sharon. I didn't know what was going on with class, of course, then, but it made me feel shitty: I didn't have the clothes, my family didn't have an extra car to run me around, I grew up in a small town so that meant I walked, or didn't go places. It's this undercurrent of not having it, not being able to talk the way they do, that makes you feel bad, makes you feel uncomfortable.

Sharon: It doesn't make me feel bad, it makes me pissed off.

Bear: *Now* it makes me pissed off.

Sharon: Well...everything has something to do with sex (laughs). I mean if you're not able to be yourself with somebody in other ways in the relationship, then the sex isn't going to be as good either. Anger, niceness, stuff like that. Like if people can't take anger, if they can't just hear it and let it go, *do* it and let it go...I mean I had so many fucking mediations with people it made me sick, mediations because you can't get mad. Yell at each other, battle it out, and go on. Or laugh...I laugh more ...there's a difference in the way working class women laugh. It's more a guffaw than a "he-he-he." There's a certain working class type of humor, little sayings and stuff that come from your parents, that sort of tips you off that they're working class. It's sort of raw—real and raw—where I don't feel the realness and rawness coming from people from intellectual backgrounds. And anger...I notice that when I'm relating to Bear, sometimes she'll just roar, or we'll roar at each other, and it'll be gone, and with somebody else it might have gone for a long time.

*   *   *

Sharon: I don't know if it's possible to have a lover smaller than me who could be exciting. Maybe. I get turned on with lots of people but I don't necessarily get *satisfied*...

Once I had a lover bigger than me. She had a nice touch, she touched me good but she was fragile in a lot of ways. She had a hard time rolling around. I liked her body and I liked how she felt but we couldn't do anything rough. So I was holding back again.

Chris: What's the difference between getting turned on and being satisfied?

Sharon: Being turned on is just the beginning. Being satisfied is...I don't have to come to feel satisfied...when there's a real connection there, when we're really doing it *together*.

Chris: Something you said before about holding back, and wanting to go to the other person's limits, or to your limits...is there any-

thing in trying to go to your limits that scares you?

Sharon. . .I *have* gone to my limits a few times. It's only when I felt safe, and trusted the person. Going to my limits means I go through this door. There's two kinds of making love. One is when I'm thinking all the time and I'm doing what they like but I'm not really in this other world like I like to be. If you can cross through that line of consciousness then that's going to my limits. I never got to that place with other people, you know, that I had to be careful with; I always had to be conscious. With Bear I can let go and I'm not aware of anything else in the room. I'm connected to her almost psychically. I know exactly what's going on, it's not a thinking anymore, it's a knowing, doing. It's not like I'm not aware anymore, I'm very much aware, *more* aware of what's happening, I'm just not thinking. It's not a thought process. It's like another dimension. (Laughter) It's like going to the outer limits and *out* of them (more laughter). *That's* satisfying to me. Not *everytime* is like that. There's light, sort of fooling around, and there's really "into it" sex.

Fist fucking gets to that point, for me. It's another world, doing that. And I like fucking a lot—a lot of women aren't into that.

Chris: What do you mean by that?

Sharon: Penetration! In and out, in and out.

Chris: That's supposed to be male, and bad, these days.

Sharon: Oh. Is it?

Chris: Yeah, Like aggressive sex. To have good mutual, equal, caring sex, it's gotta be soft and tender.

Sharon: No!

Bear: Boring. I was so bored with that.

Chris: Me too but I could never figure it out before.

Sharon: People who are bored with sex, if they only tried something like S/M! (Laughter) I mean S/M *isn't* boring sex! It's creative. I feel like it's just opening up so many doors for me. Sex is more fun and better than ever. I've always liked sex, I've never *not* liked it, it's just that sometimes I got bored with it. There was something more that I wanted that wasn't there. With S/M, I still feel like there's some things I wouldn't do. I don't want to play with someone unless I know where they're coming from, why they want to do it. I played with someone who tops from anger—

that's no fun. I felt like a piece of shit. And that felt like sadistic stuff to me, what they did.

Chris: In the "bad" sense of the word.

Sharon: Yeah. That's not what I'm into. And if I'm being top, I'm not into a woman being all passive. I like the feeling of struggle. What turns me on is hard contact. At the end you can be all gooshy and mushy and soft, but there's something that opens the doors with that for me. If somebody is being real passive by just lying there and getting off on what I'm doing, it doesn't turn me on. I like the feeling of somebody really *wanting* me. If they just want me because I'm good to them and they get off on what I do, it's not good enough anymore. I went through that stuff. For a while I liked it that people liked what I did to them, but then when I didn't get off...Or if somebody lies there waiting for me to do something to them, it makes me feel like, "I'm not going to anymore. You're going to have to act like you want it." I went "oh yeah" for so long. I don't know if this has something to do with my size or what, but for a long time...well, I guess I still am surprised when people are attracted to me or like me before I go after them. For a long time I had to make the moves. If I wanted somebody or wanted something, I had to go after it, because it never came to me without me doing it. So I'd make the first moves making love, starting a relationship, doing everything...I have different ex-lovers who when they show up every once in a while, I realize how far I've come since I saw them the last time. I don't play the shit I did with them before, that I had to do to have lovers. I guess I used to think I had to do that. If we were going to be sexual, I would have to make the moves. If I never made the moves, then I think we would never be sexual. That's the way it felt. So I just decided I wasn't going to do it. This woman I'm thinking of, she wasn't doing nothing for me, and what she *did* to me was real namby-pamby, stuff that bored me; it's just...boring. In comparison to Bear I just don't know if I can take anything less. (Uproarious laughter)

Bear: I take that as a compliment.

Sharon: You should!

Taking The Sting out of S/M

KITT

The word dyke. My past conjures up images, like a well-learned lesson. Tough, athletic, male-emulating, not attractive enough or lucky enough to get a man, perverted, sick. No one gave me the definition with the instruction "recite it from the top." It was filtered through episodes of "Father Knows Best" and the culture of "See Dick run! Sally is a pretty girl."

Sado-masochism. Another word from my past, resplendent with images of: pain, torture, an urge to hurt, a delight in abuse, out-of-control animalistic desires carried to an undesirable extreme, perverted, sick.

Like an unfinished sculpture, the clay of many words is taken into the hands of women, feminists, lesbians for remolding. A multitude of Pandoras is opening up the confining boxes of words and images, letting them out to permeate every crevice of life, to no longer suffocate in compartments created by men, created to keep us in our place. We are reclaiming and remodeling words used to describe us, words used against us, words used to belittle our bodies and sexuality: woman, mother, bitch, whore, frigid, aggressive, cunt, pussy. And in the process, we are reclaiming our lives. We are exploring the richness and many textures of the fabric "woman." We are discovering diversity: both the diversity within ourselves and the diversity amongst women and within our subcultures.

And then there is the three-letter word "SEX" which still causes every head to turn in interest, excitement, shock, or discomfort. The responses range from pleased to prurient to puritanical. So

women have begun reclaiming our sexuality. We have come together, talked about sex, given support around sex, and had sex.
We have stopped flipping the channels to get away from our personal x-rated and censored fantasies, and some of us have come
out as lesbians. We have developed our fantasies into full-length
features, and some of us have come out around S/M.

Yes, some of us have come out around S/M. It started with
fear, excitement, perhaps elation, and then a quest to find others
with whom we could share concerns or discuss issues. The process
reads like a feminist roadmap in consciousness-raising, but this
time, it steered straight into a collision with a large part of the
"lesbian-feminist community." In reality, members of the women's
community seem to support two diametrically opposed philoso-
phies. The first is one of allowing women to grow and expand
their individual parameters. Many women have come with an
open mind to learn about S/M, though they may or may not choose
to practice it. Yet, others, while paying lip-service to the philosophy of embracing women's diversity, desire one unified image
of women-coming-together. They desire an Amazon Army in
which everyone conforms to the group mind's standard of "political correctness." Lesbians who practice S/M, deviating from
this confining image, are regarded as sexual outlaws. Thus, this
community offers a choice: acceptance for conformity, or ostracism
for sexual freedom. And who is accusing whom of restricting
women by holding them in bondage? It was not so long ago that
the Women's Movement, wishing to keep the movement cohesive,
attempted to suppress open lesbianism. All in the name of the
struggle for women's freedom.

The strong, negative reaction to S/M is due in part to the fact
that we have hand-me-down words, still clothed in many layers
of patriarchal connotations. (Both the words sadist and masochist
are derivatives of the male authors' names who wrote about these
sexual practices: Count Donatien de Sade, 1740–1814, and Leopold
von Sacher-Masoch, 1835–1895). Many members of the women's
community, as outsiders, see only the hurting in the S/M experience, never the touching of the fine line between pleasure and
pain to heighten pleasure. They see the acting out of power, never
the demonstration of consensuality. They see the pain or humilia-

tion, never the sharing, concern, love. Yet, all of these aspects are part of the S/M experience; they just are not part of the stereotypes by which the experience is judged.

In spite of this expressed disdain and disgust toward S/M, the disdainful and disgusted ones invariably bring up the topic in conversations. Anti S/M women seem to talk about S/M as much as women who enjoy S/M experiences. Behind the shock and horror, there seems to lie an element of fascination, of titillation, and perhaps even of self-identification. On the occasions when I have questioned women who at first have reacted negatively to S/M, they have admitted to fantasies of holding down or being held down by a partner, forcing or being forced sexually. Whose x-rated and censored fantasies are they really reacting to?

The practice of S/M needs a closer examination. Just as every lesbian I talk to defines herself in her own unique and highly personal terms, every woman whom I have met, who fantasizes about or plays with S/M, experiences it individually. There is a full spectrum in the diversity of S/M practices, such as tying with silk scarves, slapping, bondage, or whipping. All of it involves playing with the issues of power and control. And I mean playing in the full sense of the word. S/M scenes bring back memories of childhood games of playing house or playing school: pretending so hard that things become real, forcing the students/children or being forced, sometimes punishing or getting punished, and calling it off or moving on to another game when it gets boring or too intense. There is a lot of power in pushing those limits to see how much the other person or you can take (while retaining the power to cut it off at any given moment). And who is really in control? Everyone who is playing, regardless of whether S/M is played out alone while masturbating or whether it involves two or more partners. Each woman retains the total control to delight herself or others in this intensified and heightened sexual experience, or to use safe words to change or end the scene. Sex becomes a musical instrument with its strings tightened, raising the key to a sharper and clearer sound. Sharper: the tingling is no longer centered on genital orgasm, but can involve sensation and release throughout the body. Clearer: an intense interchange of communication, trust, openness, and caring is part of every S/M consensual experience.

It has taken a long time of rolling the word lesbian around in our mouths before it has become comfortable. It has taken a long time to wear down the stereotypes and rebuild the words. In the meantime, those who were "out" had to deal with stereotypes about themselves, and those who were not "out" held the closet door tightly closed to keep distance from these negative images. The S/M experience is beginning this same process. As long as stigmas are attached to S/M, both the S/M experience and those involved with S/M will be held at a distance because of fear, and will be surrounded in myth and stereotypes. Stereotypes that we have to confront: sado-masochism, domination, bondage, aggressive, dyke, woman...

Silk and Leather Dream

ANONYMOUS

She wears silk and leather. Soft silk sliding under my hand and through my fingers. Her breasts, rounded, full. She grabs my wrist guiding me down into the heat of the leather between her legs.

Slowly she takes the long red silk scarf from her pocket and lovingly wraps it around my wrists, drawing my arms up and over my head to the headboard of the bed. I lie there, spreadeagle, arms out of my control, as her breasts, covered in the cool, self-contained silk, rub over my body. She lowers herself over me, crushing my body into the bed. I am unable to move, unable to push her off, as the breath is squeezed from my body. The leather against me, pushing between my legs, hard, hot, impossible to avoid, even as the silk tells me how cool and distanced she could be at any time.

Raising her knee, she grinds into my clit until I feel the bone underneath pushing taut against my skin. On and on until the leather glistens with my juice. Another piece of silk appears and she rubs it over my breasts in ever larger circles until my sides and thighs and every part of me is drawn, electric. Her nails scrape my sides, scratching, tingling, outlining every rib. Her hand descends, and my legs spread wider than should be possible, as first one finger, than another and another join and pierce, pushing hard and fast, forcing bone against clit. Another finger enters my asshole—rubbing, massaging, ignoring the tightness of muscles fighting the invasion. The silk keeps rubbing. Breasts, ribs, ass— never stopping until I come, and keep coming—the smell of leather filling the air, the creaking of her leather coming in time to my own cries of joy.

KATE 1·2·81

Handkerchief Codes: Interlude I

Left side	Color	Right Side
Fist Fucker	Red	Fist Fuckee
Anal Sex, Top	Dark Blue	Anal Sex, Bottom
Oral Sex, Top	Light Blue	Oral Sex, Bottom
Light S/M, Top	Robins Egg Blue	Light S/M, Bottom
Food Fetish, Top	Mustard	Food Fetish, Bottom
Anything Goes, Top	Orange	Anything Goes, Bottom
Gives Golden Showers	Yellow	Wants Golden Showers
Hustler, Selling	Green	Hustler, Buying
Uniforms/Military, Top	Olive Drab	Uniforms/Military, Bottom
Likes Novices, Chickenhawk	White	Novice (or Virgin)
Victorian Scenes, Top	White Lace	Victorian Scenes, Bottom
Does Bondage	Gray	Wants to be put in Bondage
Shit Scenes, Top	Brown	Shit Scenes, Bottom
Heavy S/M & Whipping, Top	Black	Heavy S/M & Whipping, Bottom
Piercer	Purple	Piercee
Likes Menstruating Women	Maroon	Is Menstruating
Group Sex, Top	Lavender	Group Sex, Bottom
Breast Fondler	Pink	Breast Fondlee

R E D (Fist-fucking)

On her knees in the ill-lit room, she focuses her straining eyes on the hand she holds. She is ignored, except for an occasional booted prod reminding her of her status. She carefully clips each nail, being sure to avoid undue pressure on the fingers. Gently filing the clipped nails smooth, she kisses each long finger as she is finished with its manicure. She shivers a little, struggling to keep her expectations down. She knows that it is enough for her to be allowed to touch these hands, and knows not to be so insubordinate as to expect any attention from them. She kisses the palm of each hand; then hears a rough voice momentarily directed at her, "Lick!" Joyously, humbly, she licks and sucks at the blunt fingertips, takes two and three fingers at a time deep into her mouth with a fervor that shows her eagerness to warm and please her mistress. Again, the voice, "Enough," One of the hands makes an abrupt gesture. In response, the slave pours lotion into her hands, then cups them around the square hand of the woman seated above her. She rubs the lotion in with gentle strokes, concentrating with an effort on this work. It is hard not to feel her cunt, pulsing and beginning to drip. She continues rubbing and caressing the hands until they are fairly saturated with oil, but does not stop for fear of her mistress' disapproval. Finally, when she fears her quivering thighs will no longer support her, she feels a hand on her chest, pushing her suddenly backward onto the floor. She hardly dares to breathe, hearing the words, "Well, you've done an adequate job on my hands. I suppose you want something now, you greedy girl." Still silent, she looks up from her position on the floor, imploring with her eyes for mercy and relief. She feels her cunt throbbing so hotly that at first she thinks she must have imagined two fingers thrusting inside her. Arching her pelvis off the floor to meet the welcome pressure, she feels the two fingers changed to four. Gasping with pleasure, she begs aloud, "More, oh please mistress, more of your hand in me!" She hears a chuckle, and suddenly her body is only her cunt, stretching and swallowing this curling, pushing fist. The hand is pushing down to take more, more inside her. She feels nothing but this rocking, this fucking, this warm and total possession of herself.

GRAY (Bondage)

My lover is tied in our favorite place in the big bedroom window. But for the first time, the curtain is wide open. Almost six feet of her look out and down over the side door as our friends and acquaintances arrive for a meeting. She follows my orders to call attention to herself by voicing a greeting to each one. If her voice is a bit timid I tighten the cords to stretch her more across the window.

She is dripping and grateful—upright and spreadeagled. She teases herself by brushing her nipples on the cold expanse of glass

67

but knows it's unsafe to rub against it to come. I am proud of her form and her courage.

I leave her in the window while I attend the meeting. At the break a few friends come upstairs with me. We torture my lover's body with attention and later, while she still stands and aches for release, fall upon each other. Only when we are alone again do I lovingly tie her to the bed and fuck her to the ecstasy she has so beautifully earned.

W H I T E A N D W H I T E L A C E (Novice and Victorian)

Finally, she is old enough for The Womanhood Ritual in which she is taught the joys and responsibilities of wearing ladies clothing. Dressed in a simple lilac camisole, she is down on her knees and raising my petticoats one by one. When she reaches my nakedness I hand her my white silk stockings and instruct her to gradually smooth them up over my leg. The top requires extra smoothing across the thigh and each time she moves, her hand pushes against my cunt so that I start dripping with luscious anticipation.

She crawls across the room with her still girlish bottom exposed and brings me my crimson garters. I snap their elastic against her cheek to show her their strength. As she puts each one on me, I require her hand to form a fist that I come down hard against just by lowering my hips. When I tire of this game, I order her to stand.

She rises, exposing breasts larger than they ought to be on one so young. Clearly it is time to control this youthful exuberance. She has pleaded for the discipline of a corset day and night for the past two years. I give the signal for The Ritual to begin.

Her best friend and her older sister enter together and curtsy to me. They are told to lace her up, far tighter than they themselves have ever been laced, for Bianca is a special pet of mine. The little one's cheeks turn red and her eyes are filled with wonder as she experiences the beginnings of physical love. We help her into her very first pair of five inch satin heels and she spends the rest of the day learning how to serve me in a womanly way.

Being Weird is not Enough:
How to Stay Healthy and Play Safe

CYNTHIA ASTUTO AND PAT CALIFIA

NEGOTIATION

Careful and complete negotiation can make the difference between a scene that is safe and hot, and one that you will shudder to remember. It is also an excellent way for the top to begin to take control. The bottom should be asked about her vanilla sex history; any medical problems (asthma, back problems, poor circulation, diabetes, hemophilia, etc.) which may affect her flexibility, pain tolerance or limits; prior experience with S/M; a list of things she absolutely will not do, might do, and wants to do; fantasies; if she has used a safe word (a word that is not likely to be used accidentally during sex which means "I'm having trouble, let's get out of role and talk about the scene") in the past (since this will be easier for her to remember than a new one); and her reason for wanting to play with the person who is asking her all these rude, personal questions.

A top should also supply the bottom with any relevant information about her physical and emotional limits and what she expects to get out of the scene. A top has as much right as a bottom to say no, use a safeword, or make demands to ensure the scene will be satisfying for her.

Usually, two women who are turned on to each other can find enough in common to devise a scene that they will both find erotic. However, if a bottom's central fantasy is something which the top does not feel skilled enough to perform (or does not enjoy doing), or if the bottom feels she cannot meet the top's demands for a particular type of attitude or service, it may be better to forego playing.

If a scene is going to include more than two people, or take place in a public setting like a group sex party, the negotiation gets a little more complex. Here are some things that it might be a good idea to discuss. Should the scene be kept confidential? What happens when the scene is over? Is a third party supposed to split up and play with other women at the party? Does a third party understand any limits the couple has set between them? For example, they may have any kind of sex with each other but only safe sex with others, or they may reserve certain kinds of S/M play only for each other. How do participants feel about inviting others to join their scene or allowing others to watch? If voyeurizing or bringing others into the scene is not okay, one of the tops should take responsibility for deflecting unwanted requests to join in, or dispersing the audience. Do the women involved want a special safeword for feeling jealous or insecure?

Some S/M people do not include genital sex in all of their scenes. It may not occur to novices that this is something which also must be mentioned and negotiated. *Never assume anything.* Always ask.

EMOTIONAL SAFETY

It is much easier to quantify rules for physical safety than it is to define the parameters of acts which may have unpleasant emotional or psychological fallout. Even if you are careful to check out one another's limits and desires, something upsetting can happen in a scene. It is more constructive to talk this over after playing than it is to blame one another, unless there was a conscious attempt to keep a secret, ignore a clearly stated limit, or hurt someone's feelings. Give each other reassurance and comfort, then file the scene for future reference.

Check in with each other after a scene to process any reactions you might have, even if they are all positive. Tops can be as insecure about the impact of a scene as bottoms.

In general, it's a good idea to leave them wanting more. Fantasies are hungrier than bodies. A bottom (or a novice top) who

70

knows she could have done more is more likely to ask for a repeat engagement than someone who is freaked out about how heavy she got. This doesn't mean it's not okay to experiment with new techniques or play at a more intense level; it does mean that S/M should not be treated as if it were a race or a contest.

Emotional safety is especially important during all head games and verbal games (especially humiliation), gender play such as cross-dressing (which includes putting a butch in femme drag as well as women wearing men's clothes and strap-on dildoes), and submission. When you play with subjects that people have bad or ambivalent feelings about, there is potential for a really hot scene leading to catharsis of those negative feelings. However, there is also a greater potential to leave someone feeling devastated and wounded. It is important that the players have genuine respect and affection for one another, and that they handle volatile issues with sensitivity. Although the side-effects of S/M play may feel therapeutic for some of us, it is not wise to substitute S/M for therapy.

Another area of emotional safety that should be addressed has to do with roles and a perception in some parts of our community that there are more bottoms than tops, and that bottoms are not quite as important or valued as tops. This creates a feeling of sexual scarcity that may lead a bottom to make unwise choices about who she plays with and to fixate upon any top who seems even marginally available – whether or not she is compatible with her. This attitude is known as "bottom's disease," and it is very unattractive. Going home with another bottom or going home to be your own top is always better than going home with a top who is unsafe, does not enjoy doing the things you like, or is not really attracted to you. A top is not a public utility and should not be treated as if she were obligated to provide entertainment (or lifetime commitment) to any bottom who feels needy.

Not all role-connected abuses are committed by bottoms. A top who feels that she is worth more than any bottom may develop a syndrome known as "top's disease." She may feel entitled to privileges that no one has a right to demand from other people, she may become rigid and pompous, she may feel that the bottom is always in her debt, and she might develop a phobia about bottoming.

Seasoned sadomasochists know that experienced bottoms have a status and a mystique which is equal to that of a well-respected top. (And as much leadership potential.) During their "deviant careers," most people eventually experience both the bottom and the top roles. Although being a switchable is certainly not the only way to be a healthy sadomasochist, we could all make S/M a safer and more enjoyable experience for each other if we would validate any role choice our peers make.

PENETRATION

Perhaps because it can so easily symbolize possession and control, this is one type of vanilla sex which is often employed in S/M scenes. The basic safety rule here is, "If it don't fit, don't force it." The second safety rule is, "Too much lube is almost enough." Penetration should not be painful. If it is, back up, slow down, and take something out.

There are two types of penetration: that done with parts of the body, and that done with objects. When hands are used for penetration, nails should be clipped short and filed smooth. One advantage of using your hand is that you can tell if the opening (vaginal, anal, or oral) is tense or relaxing, or whether the lining is feeling smooth and wet or abraded. A woman who has never had children may be unable to comfortably accomodate a fist, although if she really likes penetration and practices a lot with a partner who makes it feel good, it may be possible for her to increase her capacity. There are also relatively few women who do anal fisting, but it is not unheard of, and there is no reason not to do it if there is enough room for your hand and you follow all safety precautions.

Water-soluble lubricants cause fewer problems with vaginal infections than oil-based products. However, for fisting, many women prefer a thick grease like Crisco which will protect the mucous membranes. Douching the next day with warm water to which you have added a couple tablespoons of white vinegar will reduce the chances of vaginal infections.

Objects which are sharp, breakable, or contain wires (like poseable or moveable dildoes) should never be inserted. And something that has been in the anus should never be put in the vagina without washing it thoroughly. Nor should an object go from one of her orifices into one of yours without being cleaned.

The vagina is self-contained, so you can't lose objects in it, but a dildo without a flanged base can be accidentally shoved past the anal sphincter. Some anal toys are balls of various sizes strung together. Sometimes one of the balls can come loose as they are being pulled out of the ass. If this happens, don't panic and *don't take an enema.* Go sit on the toilet and push down. Chances are the missing toy will pop out enough to be retrievable. Only if the object does not come out by itself in three or four hours should you go to an emergency room.

If you see any blood after penetration, apply ice to the area. If you have more than light spotting, or if the bleeding does not stop within a few minutes, go see a doctor immediately. This is especially important if you might have torn the lining of the rectum. Take your temperature! A fever is another warning sign that cannot be ignored. If fecal matter contaminates the abdominal cavity, you can get peritonitis and die.

See the section on "Health Issues" below for further information.

BONDAGE

Although tying somebody up with silk scarves sounds much lighter than using leather bondage cuffs, you are more likely to pinch nerves in the wrists and ankles with scarves (or plain rope). Nerve damage can occur (especially along the thumb) long before a limb feels numb – and can result in a permanent loss of feeling or even impede motion. Learn how to tie a few basic knots. Do not use junk knots that will get tighter if the bottom struggles. Get a pair of soft, wide, leather bondage cuffs. They provide essential protection.

Bondage which is too tight can cut off circulation. Check hands and feet frequently. If they feel cold or look blue, remove or loosen the bondage posthaste. A pair of bandage scissors can be used to cut ropes in emergencies. Keep a spare set of keys for handcuffs or other locking bondage devices. And check to make sure you have the key before you lock anything!

If someone is in standing bondage, they are more likely to pass out than if they are tied spread-eagle on your bed, especially if they have not eaten, are very turned on, and have been allowed to ingest alcohol or poppers. A clip called a panic snap, available at leather shops, mountain climbing stores, and livestock suppliers, should be made the centerpiece of any standing bondage. A panic snap can be released even if weight is hanging from it, so you do not have to lift someone who is unconscious up and over the edge of the clip, as you would with a normal, double-ended snap. If someone does pass out or become dizzy, have them lie down and elevate their feet. Keep them warm and lying down for at least half an hour.

Suffocation is another potential danger in bondage. A bottom who is tied up should not be left alone face-down on a soft surface. Bondage which can tighten around the neck is unsafe. During masturbation, some people tie themselves up in such a way that their breathing is impeded. This can be *very* dangerous. It only takes a few seconds of pressure on the carotid artery in the throat to cause unconsciousness. If you pass out while you have yourself in strangling bondage, you can remain unconscious long enough to choke to death if no one is there to untie you.

Suspension should be performed only with special equipment. Someone's full weight should never hang from their wrists, ankles, or other joints. Safe suspension requires a device like a parachute harness which will distribute weight over the torso, or a pair of boots nailed to a board (if the suspension is going to be upside down), and a strong pulley or other hoist. Suspension should be done only if you are strong enough (or have enough help) to catch the person and lower them safely if the mechanism fails. It is usually unsafe to leave someone upside down for more than twenty minutes.

CORPORAL PUNISHMENT

Whether you are using an object or your bare hand to strike someone, there are certain areas of the body that should never

74

take a blow: the head, throat, and neck (excepting the cheeks, which can be slapped, preferably while you are holding the head still – and a slap should never be hard enough to forcefully jerk the neck or jaw); the stomach; the spine and kidneys; the backs of the knees or any other joint; the lower calf; the shins. Confine corporal punishment to the shoulders, the ass, the thighs, upper arms – areas that are well-padded.

Centrifugal force works to ensure that the maximum force of any blow will be at the tip of the instrument. Cats and other tailed whips have a tendency to wrap around the ass and hit the hip-bone. If you are not sure of your aim, put a pillow on the other side of your bottom to protect her side.

Even though the entire ass is safe to hit, the higher up and further toward the side you go, the thinner the padding and the more a blow will hurt. It is not a bad idea to cover her tailbone with your hand or a rolled-up towel if you are not sure you can avoid hitting it.

Stiff, short implements (paddles, riding crops, doubled-up belts) are easier to control than longer, more flexible implements (cat-of-nine tails, canes, blacksnakes).

Some people want a whipping that involves more noise and threat than actual pain. The more turned on someone is, the more pain they will be able to tolerate. The slower a whipping is paced, the less likely the bottom is to panic and turn off to what is happening. There are also different kinds of pain, and a bottom may prefer a deep, thudding sensation to a stinging sensation, or vice versa.

EROTIC TORTURE

We have grouped miscellaneous ways of causing pleasurable (but intense) sensations under this heading. There are probably dozens of other ways to stimulate the body. The best way to learn how to use a new technique safely is to consult a responsible top or bottom who likes it and is experienced.

Clips and Clamps – Anything that will compress flesh falls under this category. The same clamps that will cost you $20 in a leather shop will cost you $2 in a hardware store, stationery store, etc. Eroticize your local Five & Dime! Women with cystic breasts should avoid heavy breast play. You can test a new clamp on the skin between your thumb and first finger to get an idea of how painful it is. Unless a clamp is so tight that it should not be used at all (i.e., it crushes tissue), there is no fixed time limit for leaving it in one place. Remember that as a clip cuts off blood flow, feeling fades, and removing it is one way to get feeling to return quickly – and unpleasantly! The longer a clip is left on, the more it will hurt when it comes off.

Hot Wax – Use a candle that melts at a low temperature. Avoid beeswax candles. Keep them away from flammable objects (like the top's hair and poppers). The higher you hold the candle, the cooler the wax will be when it hits the skin. Trailing an ice cube after a stream of falling hot wax can be delicious.

Mentholated Ointments – Unless the bottom is allergic to them, Tiger Balm, Vicks VapoRub, and other ointments can be used in small quantities on sensitive areas to produce heat and squirming. Test a small patch of skin before using a new substance. Since most of these things are oil-based and hard to remove, keep Witch Hazel around to take them off quickly.

Abrasion – Emery boards, dog grooming brushes, scalp massagers, and anything else with a rough texture can be used to abrade the skin. Avoid using things that might leave grit embedded in the skin. See "Blood Sports" and "Health Issues" below.

Electricity – There are two basic types of electrical toys. One uses static electricity, the other uses a stepped-down version of house current. Ultraviolet wands or high frequency generators look like vibrators and shed purple sparks. They use static electricity and are safe to use on any part of the body (except the eyes). Other electrical toys should not be used to pass current through the chest cavity or heart. A simple way to guarantee this is to never use them above the waist. A further safety precaution is to only use electrical toys which operate on battery current. If they plug into the wall, there is a transformer inside them which steps down the house current. A malfunction of the transformer could result in someone getting a very nasty shock. Contrary to the stereotype, a properly constructed electrical device can be as titillating as a vibrator – or agonizing. Most have rheostats which will allow you to control the intensity.

This term can refer either to playing with piss, or playing with enemas.

Piss can contain viruses. Your own piss is safe to drink, although you should probably ingest extra water afterward to flush toxins from your system. Piss falling on unbroken skin is also safe. Piss that gets in someone's eyes or in a cut can transmit disease, if it does not come from a healthy person.

Shit contains many types of disease-causing organisms. The guidelines for piss regarding disease transmission apply.

The safest enema is plain, tepid tap water, administered from an enema bag held at about waist height. The faster water is allowed to flow into the bowel, the more cramping and pain there will be. Cold water will also cause cramping. Very few people experience a painful enema as erotic. But a slow, properly administered enema can be relaxing and give a feeling of warmth and fullness that is quite arousing. S/M porn often contains unsafe recipes for enemas. Nothing caustic should be put in an enema, and undiluted alcohol should never be used because the alcohol enters the bloodstream almost immediately through the walls of the intestine and can cause poisoning. A few tablespoons of wine in an enema is probably safe, but may cause drowsiness.

BLOOD SPORTS

Any time you break the skin, there is the risk of disease transmission and infection. This can be minimized by cleaning the area and your hands, and by using sterile implements. A blooded implement should never be re-used on another person unless it is sterilized. This includes razors used for shaving, since they may cause nicks which go unnoticed. Straight-edge razors are very sexy, but difficult to learn how to use. Practice on an inflated balloon sprayed with shaving cream. If you can shave the balloon without breaking it, you can graduate to skin. You can obtain straight-edge razors with disposable blades from beauty supply houses.

Select the area where you are going to cut carefully. Avoid joints, nerves, or blood vessels. Safe areas include the front of the thigh, the shoulder, and the upper arm. Have the subject wash the area with Betadine or green surgical soap. Then clean it again with alcohol prep pads. Do not cut impulsively – any mark made on skin may be permanent. Keep the blade perpendicular to the skin. Use a sharp implement, since it will make a clean cut that will heal much better than the ragged edges of a cut made with a dull blade. You can get disposable, pre-sterilized scalpels from medical supply companies. However, remember that these are the sharpest objects you will ever hold in your hand, and treat them with utter respect. Let the bottom tell you when to begin cutting, and either have them in very secure bondage or know them well enough to know they will not jump and cut themselves or you. Begin with light pressure, and allow at least 30 seconds before cutting again, since it may take that long for the wound to bleed. It takes practice to know how deeply you have cut. Remember that a little blood goes a long way. If you are making an elaborate cutting, you may need to clean the blade periodically with alcohol prep pads. After you have finished, clean the wound with alcohol.

If your hand should slip, first aid for bleeding is direct pressure on the wound. If you can grab something absorbent, use it – if not, simply put your hand on the bleeding and press down. Continue pressure until bleeding stops. Do not try to apply a tourniquet – see a doctor if bleeding continues.

Piercing can be done using pre-sterilized, disposable hypodermic needles or sewing needles that have been autoclaved. Thirty minutes in a pressure-cooker will not sterilize something, but it is better than just using alcohol. Permanent piercings should be done by someone who is trained by an expert, and jewelry should be autoclaved before it is inserted. Temporary piercings can be made in loose folds of skin, provided you do not go through nerves, glands, or major blood vessels. Small weights can be hung from temporary piercings.

HEALTH ISSUES

A complete overview of lesbian health is beyond the scope of this article. Supplement this information with more detailed texts on the subject.

It is a myth that sexually transmitted diseases are not a problem for lesbians. The fact that we are a relatively small, closed community with a fairly low rate of sexual activity with multiple partners results in statistics which tend to show we are a healthy bunch. However, the traditional definition of STDs does not include some things, like vaginal infection, which lesbians can pass to one another during sex, and very little research has been done on lesbians and sexual health.

Because AIDS is a fatal disease that can be transmitted during sex, more attention has been focused lately on ways to be sexual while preventing the spread of disease. The safe sex guidelines below should be used by anyone who is active with multiple partners, especially if they have a history of having sex with gay or bisexual men or intravenous drug users.

Most of the documented cases of lesbians with AIDS occur among women who have injected recreational drugs. This is probably the easiest way to transmit this disease. If you shoot drugs, do not share your needles, works, or cooker. Taking time to clean this equipment may decrease the risk of spreading disease if you do have to share it. You can soak everything in a solution of 1 part bleach to 9 parts water for 20 minutes. Draw the solution up into the needle. Rinse everything, especially the needle, before re-using it – you don't want to inject bleach!

Latex is a barrier to the AIDS virus. If you have sex with a male partner, insist on using condoms from start to finish. Supplement the condom with a spermicide which contains at least 5% nonoxynol-9. This spermicide has been shown to kill the AIDS virus in test tubes. Condoms can also be used on dildoes to make it easier to keep them clean, and should definitely be used if they are going to be shared.

Latex or vinyl gloves not only are a barrier to the AIDS virus and other organisms that cause STDs, they can cut down on the amount of friction present during fucking and make it more comfortable and safer. Lubricants that are oil-based should not be used with latex products since they weaken the rubber. Use water-soluble lubricants like KY or Foreplay. Some lubricants, like Foreplay, contain nonoxynol-9. However, Foreplay (and spermicides) may cause vaginal irritation in some women.

Use lubricant from a squeeze bottle, not a container you put your hand into. This keeps the lubricant uncontaminated. If you are using a big container of lube, put small portions of it in paper cups and throw any lube that's left in the paper cup away.

Dental dams are thin squares of latex that dentists use to create a surgical field. They can be used during cunnilingus or rimming (eating someone's ass) to prevent transmission of disease. Put some water-soluble lube on the side that will be next to your partner's body. It will make your tongue feel nicer through the dam. Discard it after use, and get a new dam if you want to continue to have sex.

Toys can be cleaned using the bleach solution, 70% rubbing alcohol, hydrogen peroxide, or boiling water. Leather which has gotten blood on it is very difficult to clean. Some people feel that putting a leather toy aside for three weeks allows adequate time for drying to kill any virus. This has not been confirmed by research. To be absolutely safe, an implement that has drawn blood which cannot be cleaned should be used on only one person.

***

These guidelines are not the final word. Some of the statements above are a matter of personal opinion. We have devoted more space to the types of S/M play that carry the greatest potential dangers. Therefore, this article does not necessarily reflect the most common S/M practices in our community.

Report of a Conference on Feminism, Sexuality and Power: The Elect Clash with the Perverse

MARGARET HUNT

The debate over lesbian sadomasochism and the related controversy over how feminists should respond to pornography has been going on now for almost five years, and it shows no sign of being on the wane. From October 25 to October 30, 1986, more than a hundred feminist activists met at Mount Holyoke College for a symposium entitled "Feminism, Sexuality and Power" intended, in the words of the conference brochure, to explore "the variety of ideas about the ways that sexual practices are affected by history, culture and politics" and to provide an opportunity to "challenge and broaden the way we think about sexuality."

Originally, it seems, the conference organizers had had in mind a quite broad-based approach to the problem of sexuality and power. They planned a program which included a substantial amount of material on the ways class and race interacted with gender in the organization of sexuality, and they took special care to represent a variety of erotic lifestyles and to avoid the prevalent Western bias of much scholarship on sexuality. What they got was a pitched battle over the question of lesbian S/M, an issue which so dominated the conference as to make all other matters fade into the polished neo-gothic Mount Holyoke woodwork.

Why should this apparently sectarian issue monopolize feminists' attention to such a degree that, at this conference at least, it became virtually impossible to talk about anything else? The reason is that the S/M debate is a focus for a number of more basic conflicts that go to the heart of what the women's movement means. The "Feminism, Sexuality and Power" conference was a disappointment in terms of illuminating the subtler connections between eroticism and power, or of suggesting creative ways to end the real human tragedies caused by the collision of sexuality with the disproportionate power to coerce enjoyed by the state, men, heterosexuals, whites, employers, and adults. But it was useful too, because it clarified the larger implications of the anti-S/M position in ways that haven't been done before.

The anti-S/M group is largely coterminous with that wing of the movement which favors, in principle, some kind of censorship of pornography. This amalgam of persons and groups was variously referred to at the conference as "radical feminists" (their favored term for themselves), "the anti-pornography people," "the anti-sex group," and "moral purity feminists." For the purposes of this discussion I am going to call them "radical feminists," though as one who has long considered herself a radical feminist I want to come right out and say that I am profoundly disturbed by many of the positions these new "radical feminists" are now taking as their own.

As I suspect is true of a lot of women, including feminists, my reaction to porn varies. Some of the "soft-core" stuff I find titillating, but I often find myself alienated from what tends to be its heterosexist bias – one of the reasons I'm strongly in favor of lesbian sex magazines. On the other hand movies, books, etc. which make a cult out of killing and coercion not only offend me but fill me with outright fear and loathing. I'd put porn that focuses on killing and coercion in the same league, though I'd have to say that in terms of impact, films like *Rambo* reach a lot more people, including children, than the very small percentage of porn that is comparably violent. Were I in favor of censorship (which, for a variety of reasons, I'm not), it would be much more along the lines of regulating images of senseless, anonymous, repeated killing, without regard to whether they purportedly take place in the context of sex or a Cambodian jungle.

As a woman who has been involved for the last decade in one way or another in the battered women's movement, it is true that I am especially sensitive about representations, pornographic or not, which portray women as victims of violence or which suggest that as a group we invite violence or coercion. I

82

have participated in boycotts of record companies, complained loudly about violent portrayals of sex, and once, about ten years ago, I even helped heave a concrete block through the plate glass window of a store whose management had refused to remove displays featuring bruised and bloody female mannequins. But I didn't do any of these things because I thought the sole or major source of male oppression was sex acts, pure and simple, *or* their representations. Even ten years ago, when I was much more of a separatist than I am now, it was obvious that the story was a lot more complicated than that, and that to attribute oppression so single-mindedly to a particular style of sexuality was not only diversionary but potentially very divisive for the movement as a whole.

Like many other feminists my basic attitude toward lesbian S/M over much of the last decade has been unenthusiastic. I never condoned kicking people who did those things (whatever they were – I wasn't sure) out of the movement, probably because I was reluctant, as a fairly "out" lesbian, to engage in labeling other people as perverts. But I was troubled by the dominance/submission dichotomy in S/M and unsure about whether or not it could be reconciled with feminist egalitarianism. I was definitely open to the suggestion that indulging in bondage, whipping, etc. indicated some kind of character flaw that would make it difficult to function well in a feminist setting.

But gradually I began to get more and more uncomfortable with the anti-S/M position. My objections were both personal and theoretical. The personal ones revolved around the frequently-heard claim that women who engaged in S/M were condoning violence against other women. First of all the women who did "those things," some of whom I had known for years before they "came out" as sadomasochists, seemed like everyday feminists in other respects. Some were involved in the shelter movement, including people I have worked with for years and whose work I respect immensely. Some worked in rape-crisis centers, some had been active for years in programs relating to low-income women, some were among the earliest feminists to push for women's studies. Like any feminist cohort they included women who were incest-survivors, women coping with the problems of single motherhood, and women trying to cope with sex or race discrimination in the workplace. It seemed crazy to accuse them of condoning violence against other women. It also seemed profoundly wrong to imply either that they had never been victimized sexually or otherwise by men, or that their experience of that victimization was automatically less authentic because of the sorts of fantasies they indulged in consensually in the bedroom.

The second area of discomfort was theoretical, and it had to do with my own research into the history of sexuality. The belief that particular sex acts "cause" other kinds of acts, that they have a special power to shape social mores is a very recent one, not shared by most of the peoples of the world, nor even by most Westerners before the late nineteenth century. In the West this mode of thought emerged as the result of a complex confluence of trends, among them the rise of the science of sexology, the appearance of distinctive sexual subcultures (specifically male homosexual subcultures), and the need to legitimate a range of new repressive measures aimed at working-class populations (and especially working-class youth) in major European and American cities. We tend to associate this mode of thought primarily with the persecution of gays. A good example is the belief, common in the armed forces, that homosexual acts sap a soldier's ability to fight; another is the argument that lesbianism leads naturally to suicide. Feminists can all too easily slip into this method of reasoning as well.

One of the major questions raised by the S/M controversy is how true this habit of thought really is. Because of course S/M raises these issues in the starkest possible way. If someone gets off on playing the dominant role in a sex act is it not reasonable to harbor a suspicion that such predilections might infect their other human relationships? Reasoning like this is familiar, comfortable, even, but it does not square with reality. There are connections between what people do in the bedroom and what they do in the rest of their lives, but these are far more complex and paradoxical, even contradictory, than this line of reasoning suggests. Personally I believe that the explication of these connections is an important project for feminism, but both feminists and lesbians need to be wary of assuming simplistic or over-literal correspondences between consensual sex acts and personality types, politics, or social mores. These are approaches which have proved deeply problematic for us in the past.

Subtlety of thought with respect to the connections between sex acts and the rest of reality was not much in evidence from the radical feminist side at the "Feminism, Sexuality and Power" conference. For these people it was axiomatic that heterosexuality itself bore a large part of the blame for women's oppression in society (the same kind of reasoning I've just been describing writ large). This is something more than the old "Feminism is the theory, lesbianism is the practice" kinds of slogans some of us used to throw around in the mid-seventies. The new radical feminist cosmology not only equates all or almost all heterosexuality, even between two consenting adults, with rape (the assumption being that women are being coerced into it even when they think they are doing it of their own free will) but tends to see heterosexuality (i.e., rape) pervading the whole of reality. All the world's a stage, according to this view, on which is being enacted a kind of gigantic cosmic rape scene. There is a never-ending dialectic between heterosexuality and all other oppressive acts in society: the bedroom defines, legitimates and perpetuates "Hetero-patriarchy" (as one panelist, Julia Penelope, called it) in a horrifying cycle of sick fantasy, rape, violence, and victimization.

The main problem with this view is the exaggerated emphasis that it places on sex acts in explaining women's oppression. For these people economics, culture (apart from representatons of sex), socialization, reproductive issues, have all faded into the background. Race and class barely exist for them at all as analytic categories. Political action around these issues is seen as being at best diversionary and at worst merely collaborating with "Hetero-patriarchy." They believe that feminists should be focusing their energies primarily on eliminating or purifying sex acts, and, by extension, sexual fantasies, as in this system erotic fantasies are as potentially damaging, and play as central a role in the construction of the cosmic rape scene as do the sex acts themselves.

For the radical feminists at Mount Holyoke the task was three-pronged: 1) purifying the movement of people who do S/M; 2) instituting some kind of censorship of pornography, a project which included getting rid not only of *Hustler* and others of its ilk but also best-selling lesbian-feminist publications such as *Bad Attitude* and *On Our Backs* which allegedly fill women's minds with the desire to perpetrate violent criminal acts on their sisters (i.e., they sometimes print S/M porn), and 3) convincing currently heterosexual women to stop participating in their own oppression by continuing to have sex and/or orgasms with men.

The attack on S/M was led off by Janice Raymond, feminist author and director of the Women's Studies program at the University of Massachusetts at Amherst. The gist of her remarks was that lesbian S/M recapitulates and reinforces the oppressive structures of the society. And not just any oppressive structures but the very worst. At one point, she compared people with tolerant attitudes toward pornography and S/M to those who deny the Holocaust ever happened. This was very distressing not only to some of the people in the audience who did S/M (including several who were Jewish), but to a prominent feminist historian of the Holocaust who was attending the conference. Raymond's co-panelist, Julia Penelope, focused on what was to become a recurrent theme of the conference, the accusation that the S/M community, and indeed the whole "Pro-sex" a.k.a. "Libertarian" faction was insensitive to the victimization of women and girls as represented in the sexual harassment of children, rape, battering, and the like. Penelope was particularly incensed by the fact that Gayle Rubin, the previous night's keynote speaker and a prominent spokeswoman for lesbian S/M, was known to be in favor of loosening legal constraints on non-coercive intergenerational sex. In Penelope's view this translated into support for (or at least criminal insensitivity toward) the exploitation of children.

Not a simple issue to be sure, as anyone who has followed the recent feminist thinking on incest as well as the man/boy-love debates knows. Personally I oppose the abolition of constraints on intergenerational sex because I don't believe the rape laws work well enough to be an adequate replacement for them. On the other hand I am uncomfortable with the way existing laws are predicated on the belief that "normal" children are incapable of sexual feeling or subjectivity. I am aware that over the years this legal principle has been used to label thousands of children (particularly heterosexually active adolescent girls, but also homosexual adolescents of both sexes) as "deviant" and to justify institutionalizing them. As I've said, it's a vexed issue.

For Julia Penelope, however, the issue is crystal clear, because she believes that in the case of children who engage in sexual acts with adults it is ultimately impossible to demonstrate whether or not coercion took place. The distinction between coercion and consent which is central to the juridical meaning of rape is meaningless in a situation where one of the two actors possesses all the power and the other possesses none, where one actor is totally dependent upon the other for her day-to-day survival, sense of self, and sense of being loved. I found Penelope's analysis of incest quite compelling but her larger point, that lesbian S/M was merely the sexual abuse of children in disguise, struck me as about as convincing as the argument that long-time feminist activists who engaged in S/M had the same mind-set as Nazis. Leaps of logic like these only make sense if one really believes that adult women who choose to be the bottom in an S/M exchange are equivalent to children, while their tops are equivalent to pathological murderers.

The pivotal issue here is consent, and whether "real" consent is ever possible in patriarchal society. For those who engage in S/M the issue of consent is absolutely central. It is the presence of consent which legitimates acts that in a different, nonconsensual context would be oppressive, degrading, or criminal. S/M is something which is freely chosen by people fully in command of their faculties. Conversely, for people who want to argue that lesbian S/M is essentially identical with or in some way promotes criminal acts of violence against women, it is important to refute the idea that true consent, real free choice can ever really exist in the world. According to this line of reasoning both sadists and masochists are guilty of false consciousness. They think they are free agents in the world when actually they are caught in the same patriarchal, power-mad trip as everyone else. If the world is ever to be purged of this, lesbians who do S/M will have to be purged too.

Later on in the conference this same line of reasoning recurred with respect to heterosexuality. According to Sheila Jeffreys, English feminist-activist and author of *The Spinster and her Enemies: Feminism and Sexuality 1880-1930* (Pandora, 1985), heterosexual women *think* they are freely choosing to sleep with men, and some of them are even so deluded as to reach orgasms with men. But in actual fact they are completely without choice, victims in a totalitarian world organized by men. It follows from this, Jeffreys went on, that when a woman reaches an orgasm with a man she is only collaborating with the patriarchal system, in her phrase "eroticizing her own oppression." The solution to this is a propaganda campaign aimed at convincing heterosexual women that orgasms are bad unless they are with other women. And not just any women, but women who have agreed to totally purify themselves in thought and deed of patriarchally-inspired roles (e.g., butch/femme) or any breath of dominance-submission (e.g., S/M). Jeffreys then went on to say that birth-control was merely a tool of patriarchy, designed to paper over the excesses of male hetero-domination and give women the illusion of having some choice.

Hearing this I suddenly found myself offering up a little prayer of forgiveness for (almost) every uncharitable thought I ever had about straight women. Jeffreys is proposing to treat them as despicably as our heterosexist society has treated lesbians and gay men. My next thought was, what happened to the "old" radical feminist emphasis on free sexual expression? Reproductive choices? What happened to our respect for powerful women of the past? Our sensitivity to the ways all kinds of women, gay and straight, black and white, rich and poor, young and old, have in small and large ways subverted the system? But of course, there is no free choice in this world-view. Consent is an ontological impossibility. Free will is an illusion.

Being a historian my thoughts naturally fled back to the past, in this case the sixteenth century: John Calvin in the small Swiss city of Geneva. There is no free will, no free choice. Nothing you can do will save you. Everyone around you except the tiny group of the elect is irrevocably depraved and destined to burn in hell. You can know who the elect are by their certainty that they are the chosen of God and by the resolute purity of their lives. And I thought about Calvinist Geneva, policing the sex-lives of its citizens, persecuting prostitutes and fortune tellers, instituting severe judicial penalties for children who defied their parents and justifying these authoritarian policies with the argument that since people had no free choice in the great and hopeless struggle with sin (read "patriarchy"), they needed to be saved from themselves, if necessary by death.

The argument that there is no free choice in the world is never all-inclusive. It always admits of the existence of a small group which is morally superior to the corrupt mass. Typically this small group of the elect is deeply reluctant to ally with any other groups and it prefers, if possible, to separate itself off from the rest of society. It conducts periodic purges of its own ranks to ensure its continued purity. And it characteristically resorts to authoritarian measures. Because the world is so fundamentally corrupt in thought and deed, because no one is free anyway, personal liberty is meaningless and there is no necessity for respecting it on the way to the revolution. What people read, what they do in bed, how they think, are all fair game.

The conference was winding down. Sheila Jeffreys had just finished her endnote address "Eroticizing Women's Subordination: Sexology from Havelock Ellis to Gayle Rubin" and was entertaining questions from the floor. One woman asked, with an air of uncertainty, what had happened to the issue of personal freedom. Hadn't the right to choose, especially around things like sex, once been kind of basic to the feminist movement? Jeffrey's response was that once you grasp the fact that heterosexuality is pivotal to women's oppression you must also realize how irrelevant issues of free choice really are. She concluded flatly, "Personal freedom is not the sort of concept that would fit into my view of what we can do around sexuality."

At least we know where we stand, I thought. And then I thought: This is not my revolution.

Coming Out

SARAH ZOFTIG

June 1970

Marsha was my first woman lover. Our relationship was stormy, erotic and very emotionally charged. We were both married to men, she to a cop, me to a hippie. She had had many women lovers, I had had none. She was "experienced," I was "innocent." She was the butch, I was the femme. One afternoon, while her husband was out, and we were in the middle of a huge fight, she slapped me hard across the face. As my hand flew up to touch the spot on my face that tingled, I felt my whole body respond to that slap. Not in anger as I would have expected, but with a rush of sexual energy that made me unable to say or do anything.

She began to apologize profusely. How could she hit me, what a horrible thing to do, how sorry she was. I could only sit and stare, my body tingling, the spot on my cheek feeling fiery and exposed. Then, in the middle of her apologies, Marsha stopped. She looked at me, her sharp eyes taking it all in.

"Oh" she said, drawing the word out as she realized how turned on I was. And she led me into the bedroom, where we made love for the rest of the afternoon.

We never spoke about it again. We never explored it any further, but through this experience I knew something new about my sexuality and I stored it in my mind. I didn't have a label on that memory. I just kept it there, forgotten, while I left my husband and came out as a Lesbian.

June 12, 1973

I rush sex because I enjoy it real slow, so I feel guilty and rush it. Because in my experience (Steve) it all had to be done fast, or he would get annoyed and upset and tell me there's something wrong with me etc. I will slow down. I will not be embarrassed, I will be honest. I think all these things, if I can ever do them it should work.

I would like to set up a sexual rap group, maybe.

What I want sexually:

A lot of warm touching, hugging, kissing. Too general.

I would like to take a long time making love. I would like to touch and look at the other person a lot. I would like to be touched and looked at a lot. To touch and kiss all over. I like to be touched slowly and gently, harder sometimes, actually hurt sometimes.

I cannot write this any more.

May 1976

Three years after I wrote that I was at a lesbian picnic. It was near the end of the day and we were all bored. Of course, we began to talk about sex. Someone suggested that we each write down one thing about sex that we would never talk to anyone about, and read each other's messages out loud anonymously. I wrote about that afternoon of sexual pleasure with Marsha. Our papers were read out and I was surprised to hear that two other papers contained similar accounts. The other two women had given it a name. The secret that they would never reveal to anyone. It was called S/M and I knew that my secret too was called S/M. Then I buried it in the back of my mind for another year and a half.

January 1977

Two years later I found myself at a women's bar attending an informal talk about S/M given by a woman from the Society of Janus.* How I got there is both complicated and unimportant to this account, however I was there and I was interested. What I remember most about the talk was who else was there. I carefully made note of everyone who looked interesting and madly fantasized for months afterwards. It was also at this talk that I learned about safe words.

About this time I was beginning a friendship with Jan. I told her about the meeting and we giggled and teased and laughed about it for a year, during which time we became lovers. Then a friend, who knew about our interest, got us invited to an orgy, an S/M orgy.

May 1978

The first orgy that we were invited to we somehow found something else more important to do that night. The second orgy we were invited to I was going to be out of town for but Jan went. The result of that party was that we began to experiment. We went out and bought ropes for bondage. This had been a fantasy of mine for a long time. It was exciting to be tied down and to give up the power to Jan. Actually it was exciting for the ropes to lie across my body. There were no roles at that time. We each did for the other what she wanted.

Jan had an old straw broom. Not like modern brooms, this one had long wisps of soft straw. We began to use it as a whip, with and without the ropes. Then the broom began to fall apart and I made a whip out of scraps of leather. Things were progressing.

It was all terribly exciting and scary. I was alternately afraid that I was going to love S/M and Jan was going to think me depraved or that she was going to love it and be gone on a great adventure without me. You're the lesbian. No, you're the lesbian.

I began to go to meetings. First I went to a Cardea** meeting. The topic was flagellation. We got there late, just as the demonstration was ending. Barbara, the friend I was with, and I just sat there, holding on to each other, barely breathing. We listened to everything. Someone talked about where it was and was not safe to hit a person and I was impressed with her knowledge and the seriousness with which everyone discussed pain, the turn on, and the ways to be careful. They talked about trust in an S/M relationship. One woman talked about the great amount of trust it took to let her lover cut her with a razor. I hadn't thought of razors, EEK!

After the meeting a woman came on to me very strongly and I felt like a child. Fascinated, interested, yet scared to be come on to so fast, so intimately, so strongly. I fumblingly retreated.

Barbara and I went to a local gay hamburger joint to talk and to react. We both were still trying to understand the turn on. We both felt fine about bondage. We thought it gives you a chance to be sexual without any responsibility for your sexy feelings, without any control over what happens. You were being 'forced' to submit, "It's not my fault, mommy." But we didn't understand this other stuff. What was it about whipping that was a turn on? How was pain a turn on? We'd experienced biting and scratching in passionate moments, but this seemed different, deliberate.

And HUMILIATION. It scared me, the word. Only weird people would get turned on by that. How come it turned me on? What was wrong with me?

The next meeting that Barbara and I went to was the first meeting of Samois. There were about 25 women there and I knew only three of them. Barbara and I huddled close. Jan hadn't come once again. I was too paranoid to put my name on a mailing list. We talked about C-R groups, organizing the group, names to call ourselves, were we a Lesbian Feminist group and what that meant. I was bored by the organization of it and excited just by being there in that room full of dykes into S/M. An old friend came in and I was both pleased to see her and felt exposed. She now knew. I didn't come back to another meeting for three months. I was scared and needed to digest it all. What Jan and I did together felt safe and part of me, but I wasn't ready to meet and discuss and reveal myself to these new 'strange' people.

A lot of time has passed since those early meetings. I have been a member of Samois for about three years. Almost two years ago I took an acid trip with a friend. At one point she wanted to show me a piece of S/M art that she had created. In fact, I had already seen it. The S/M part was so subtle that I had missed it. She was going to point it out to me. I got extremely dizzy and slid to the bathroom floor. (One rule about tripping is that many important revelations happen on the bathroom floor.) I was scared. She sat down next to me and asked why. Because if I'm into S/M what does that mean about me? Am I therefore a depraved creature? Some cruel monster with a leering grin or some slobbering marshmallow? Those are the images. Those are the myths. In fact I am neither of those images or myths. But I am into S/M and sometimes it's frightening. That's why I've got to separate the myth from the reality, cause it's the myth that's frightening. The feelings that really happen are good and positive. I know that because I feel them and they feel good and positive.

I'm writing about me. This is not the definitive paper on Lesbian S/M. I've only just begun to explore and to feel and to analyze. In this world I seem to walk around either feeling powerless (a reality in parts of my life) or struggling to maintain what power I have. Both places take a lot of energy. It feels good (at times) to let go of the struggle to be powerful and just relax and give up all claim to that power. It also feels good to claim all my power, to feel it, to enjoy it, to express it. I get to feel incredible parts of myself. I get to use all that energy to feel me instead of to block me.

Now, you say, there are other ways to feel those parts. Probably true, and this is just one way to feel myself. I wonder what parts of myself I'll discover next.

March 27, 1979

I want to know what my sexual self is like. How I can be. How it affects the rest of me. I need to explore those parts of me and it takes a lot of time and energy. I have a sex date with a woman named Mary. To explore our sexuality, S/M—top, bottom, we will try it all. Don't know this woman very well and don't really want to know her, just to be with her sexually, not think about what it will mean...who will feel emotionally hurt, what tomorrow will bring. If I can keep myself from thinking about any of that and just get into the fantasy of my body I think it can be fun. Oh, she's shy too so we should do O.K.

March 29, 1979

Made love with Mary. Fun, some parts of it. I felt good when she made love to me and I came. But, somehow, it's all detached from my life, from who I am and I want it integrated. I want to love and care for the women I make love with.

Such a big part of me was removed from her today, held away. The feeling in my body but not my emotions. I gave her almost none of my emotional self and that's weird. Every other word out of my mouth is 'scared'. Still sex seems like an impossible mountain to climb.

April, 1979

After Samois C-R group meeting, went to Karen's house to talk about Nazis and S/M, but really just to talk. Tonight when I was

94

hitting a pillow with Mary's new riding crop and Karen was moaning in rhythm, I was turned on. No actual pain but the simulation of it. I wonder what it is (why it turns me on).

May 15, 1979

I'm into S/M, what does that mean? Wanting to let go of so much of myself. Scary. Wanting to let go and fly. Hard to be a person asking to be hurt.

I'm coming out again and once again it's scary and wonderful.

Slowly I realize that my feelings of powerlessness in this world fill me with a great desire to be powerful and being top does it in a safe way. I get to be powerful and someone loves me for it.

My struggles of continually trying to keep my power in this world tire me and sometimes I like to drop the facade and just be a helpless lump that is taken...having no will except to please.

SHOCKING!!

How can a feminist want anything but an equal relationship... but it's so liberating.

May 21, 1979

Donna. I'm turned on to her. In some ways I want to be over the part of getting to know her. It makes me uncomfortable. And in other ways I want to stay in this part forever because it's fun and I'm not yet attached.

She's got this wall around her that I don't know how to break through. It feels a lot like Jan, in control, controlling. Why do I fall for these women? Is it sick? I want to experience a real bottom space and it freaks me out.

Scared to see myself as a masochist. What does it mean? Don't want to be in any more destructive relationships. Is Donna not a giving enough person for me? Who is? Is that the turn on? Will I always put myself in positions where I don't get what I say I want and is that then the turn on? But I really don't like it. I'm ready to get what I want (I think).

I get flashes of myself trapping these women in my sick game of making impossible demands on them. Is Jan right—whatever she would give me would not be enough because that's what turns me on, to not have it. So I always find an it that I don't have. Am I a masochist? Is all of the above true? But maybe it's just that she is fucked. But I'm in the relationship for so long. I'm in it, so I'm doing it. So I'm a masochist. Like four years ago saying:

I am a Lesbian.

I *am* a Lesbian.

I am a *Lesbian.*

And now I say:

I am a masochist.

I *am* a masochist.

I am a *masochist.*

And yet—

I will not bottom out in the world.

Still not feeling that I am a masochist. Just thinking, 'I'll explore this for a while and then move on to something else,' but scared . . . maybe I'm here for good.

Call myself dual, like calling myself bisexual four years ago.

When with Jan—scared that I was into S/M and she wasn't or she was and I wasn't. Who is really depraved?

July 11, 1979

I want that total submission but I want to be made to be there. I want to give up the power, to be able to lose it. I want to be teased until I burst.

Paula and Karen tonight—read Karen's journal in the Bacchanal.*** Actually Karen read it to me.

I'm scared to allow myself to be that degraded—yet it turns me on.

I want it but I want it with love in it. It's where it connects with Jan. I know she loves me and feels tender towards me. How can I just do a scene with Ellen and Lee, who I hardly know?

There is a lot of love between Karen and Paula. A lot, and it's nice to see. Went back to Karen's house with them. They kept slipping into mini-scenes. It disturbed and fascinated me.

We talked about it. I said that I need to know that I could ask them to stop if I wanted to. Paula asked if she and Karen seem weird to me. I said no—fantasized a scene with Paula, Karen and me. I trust them in some way. Karen is real familiar to me and I identify with her. I trust Paula, for all her act she is a kind caring human being. I'm tired and I want to sleep but I also want to write about this night. I feel I'm learning something. I can be more open, I can feel more. I can allow myself pleasure and not judge.

To want someone to want me (be turned on to me) precisely because I'm submissive—my submissiveness is a gift to them. I want it. I want an S/M relationship.

Sometimes I watch Karen and Paula and I don't understand. I don't understand it and at the same time have stirrings of sexual feelings. I want those feelings and like all sexual feelings I want to disown them. Sex puts me in someone else's power. I want that and I'm terrified of it, and S/M just makes it more up front. I want to write that what I need is to be with someone who I know loves me. Who I trust. Then the sex and S/M and all of it will come together. I don't know if that's true or just more romantic stuff, but it's important in surrender, who I am surrendering to.

What I liked about being with Paula and Karen is that there was an honesty there. They were being real honest and open in their relationship and letting me see it which was very intimate. And, we were talking real personally and I could be open about stuff I've hardly talked about and it all felt real good.

Karen says she wants to be wanted for her vulnerability. That's what I go around showing to the world a lot. I think I want to be in a relationship where I can work that out with a lot of love and respect and caring.

I also love vulnerability in other people. That's the part I like in Paula, something about the contrast of her strength and vulnerability. A soft neck even on the hardest butch.

So what have we? I like to be liked for my vulnerability. I like to see that in other people. This fear of not liking S/M is just the same old fear of not liking sex. What if I'm not turned on?

I'm scared to death, not of physically getting hurt, but of. . . losing myself, liking it too much, not liking it at all. Scared of really being into S/M. What if I like it. Who am I then? I'm coming out again and this time it's scarier than before.

Sept. 1979

Sometimes I think lesbians aren't in SAMOIS just specifically

97

for S/M stuff. It's a place where sex is O.K. It's O.K. to be sexual, to feel sexual, to act sexual. I am starting to think lately about sexual oppression the way I used to think about women's oppression.

There are so many ways that "THEY" won't let us be; I don't even know about half the ways I don't get to feel who I am. And, I figure the more we talk about it and act on it, (it being sex and sexuality), the more I'll learn who I am and what I want.

This is all my recent theory and it changes every week. For the past five months or so I've been sexually experimenting, which means that I've slept with a lot of different women. (A lot means four or five.) Some of it was great and some of it was terrible, but I've learned a lot about my sexuality, about how I do or don't let myself relax and feel myself. Some of this may seem like elementary school discoveries to you, but it's been extremely important to me. It's also been clouded over by the spectre of CASUAL SEX. I've never really let myself do that before with women and let me tell you, doing sex casually with S/M is a hell of a way to start. But, S/M forces you to certain honesties and I need a little pushing. About casual sex—I think that it's fine when I can let go and be as honest as I want to be sexually, and I'm learning to be that. Also sometimes I want more caring than a chance encounter can bring (often I want more).

October 10, 1979

S/M—I want feelings—explosive—very deep—that touch me— I'm frozen—can't feel—too hurt—but I want to feel everything possible. Even to cry out feels good—what is the mystery of S/M, the fascination? And still I don't have many words for why I like it or what it means, but I have many feelings. There is some basic part of myself that I can't hide from in an S/M scene. Some way that I stand there stripped of all my disguises and open to be seen and that feels good to me.

*Janus is an S/M support group in San Francisco. Their membership is gay, straight, and bi-sexual, women and men.
**Cardea was a women's support group out of Janus.
***Bacchanal was a local women's bar.

How I Learned to Stop Worrying and Love My Dildo

SOPHIE SCHMUCKLER

I love using dildoes. I love fucking my lover with one and I love her fucking me with one. I love feeling her thighs pushing against me, I love feeling her cunt energy coming into me. . . .

Sometimes it's a slow tease: My hands are tied to the bed but my legs are free. "Wider now," she commands, "open your legs wider for me." I stretch them as far as I can feeling more and more excited. She leans over me bringing the dildo up to the lips of my cunt. I'm so wet and wanting. "Ooooh please, please," I moan. "Do you want it now?" she asks sounding so surprised. I feel the intensity of my desire and cry impatiently, "Yes, yes." "I think you can wait a little longer," she teases, "just a little longer." I feel my wanting race through me, through my body and mind, I've never been so conscious of it before. She smiles watching me. . . .

Sometimes it's just a plain old hard fuck: We're rolling around on each other wrestling and slapping and laughing. She says, "I'm going to fuck you good, and you're going to love it." I love the sureness in her and I challenge her, "Oh, yeh?" "Yeh," and she throws herself on top of me and holds me down while I push against her with all my might. I love matching energy with her. When she finally comes inside of me I am very excited and soon I'm yelling, "Oh yes, Baby, harder, fuck me harder." And she's right, I do love it.

And sometimes it's a quiet time: We're feeling very close. She is pushing into me very slowly with the dildo. I feel myself opening to her, I feel my body, my tissues, my cells welcoming her in, wanting her so close to me. She pushes deeper inside of me and opens me up more. I feel her body weight on top of me and it comforts me; she holds me and covers me with her warmth. So gently and slowly we move together, she pushes down trying to get deeper and I raise up to meet her, "Honey, I wish it was you, I wish you were really inside of me feeling me." I let this once forbidden fantasy out; it's ok with me now and with her.

And I love fucking her, filling her up. I love how our energies cross back and forth into each other's cunt. I tie her hands above her head with velvet ties and she moans with anticipation. I slowly come into her with the dildo and then speed up. She loves it and I love her loving it and wanting more. I like having my hands free to stroke and pinch and slap her and I love her sucking and biting on my fingers. I love her screaming her joy, her hips, pelvis, and cunt thrusting, twisting, jumping under me; I love how she goes with her energy and that she shares this pleasure of hers with me.

I can write that today and share it with you. Three years ago, though, I thought I was a terrible person and buried my dildoes in their brown paper bag at the bottom of my old trunk.

I started playing with dildoes in a rather innocent way. My lover at that time had a large cunt, and I, short fingers—too bad neither of us knew about fistfucking then. She suggested we try a dildo. I didn't know any other dykes who used them and had heard they were "no-no" since they were men's ideas of what lesbians did. But I was intrigued. I had liked fucking with men, something I rarely admitted out loud, and thought I would like dildoes. My lover's suggestion seemed logical, sleazy, and downright anarchical!

We got single and double headed dildoes, straps, and lots of grease and used them in as many ways and places as we could think of. Doubles have always fascinated me and I was very disappointed to find that they are not properly made for two women. However, after much research I've come up with a few new designs—see end of article. We had fun stretching our imaginations as well as our orifices.

But, alas, being the conservative, feel-guilty-if-it-feels-good person I was, I began dumping judgments, guilt, and mistrust on myself. I liked playing with dildoes so maybe I was sick! The mores of the lesbian community then, and for some they haven't changed, only supported my worst fears: dildoes were Male so I must be a Bad Lesbian, Very P.I., a Perverted Pervert, and maybe I should forget the whole thing and go back to men.

My pleasure won out a little longer until I had my "I-wish-it-were-really-your-penis" fantasy which upset both my lover and myself. But I liked being pushed into and filled up and wanted my womanlover to be able to do it to me, and sometimes fingers just weren't enough. I tried to make this desire ok by thinking that if she really did have a penis it would be quite natural just hanging there with her clit and cunt. It would be very friendly and for both our pleasure and since she was a woman she'd know just what I wanted. And we'd call it something womanly like "womber" or "cuntfills." Later, when I started fantasizing having a baby by her I felt that I had gone too far. I couldn't let myself have these thoughts so I reasoned that if I stopped playing with dildoes the fantasies and feelings would go away and I'd be fine again.

After we broke up I realized I was very confused about sex. I liked it but I thought I shouldn't. I thought it distracted me from being spiritual which I started to get into more and more. I even explained my liking dildoes and gender-change play in reincarnation terms, maybe she had been my husband in a past life or I was male and experiencing a "bleed-through" of consciousness. Whether any of that is true or not really doesn't matter, the main thing was that I felt very alienated from my self and others. I didn't feel safe to share my doubts and fears since everyone I knew seemed so "pure." I ended up walking around like an asexual zombie and flashing a very patronizing smile which meant, "Ha, ha, I'm above all that now, I'm Spiritual."

But a year later all those well-hidden fears came bursting rudely forth when I got involved with a woman who seemed pure and innocent, with just a hint of lust. She quickly shattered my fantasies our first night together when she announced that she was a member of SAMOIS. Ah, my mouth hung open, I was flabbergasted, and then upset as images of dark basements, whips, chains, and pain came to me. But, in my typically cool liberal manner I said, "Oh, really? Maybe I'll join too." (In retrospect, that was a very good idea since I actually knew nothing about S/M except what I had read in a few rather sensationalized porn books.) But, although my lover put no pressure on me, I was scared, judgmental, put-off, and fascinated, and it took me three months to finally get to my first meeting.

To my surprise, the women I met there were like other women I knew and the group had the same problems as other groups I was in. The difference was in the content. These women spent time analyzing sex and power, encouraged sexual exploration, supported me trusting my body feelings, liked having fun sexually, and openly talked about sex practices including playing with dildoes! With all of this support I realized, although I hated to admit it, that the only one in my way now was my self and all of my fear, guilt, and judgments. I could confront and take responsibility for my own likes and dislikes, no matter what anyone else thought, or I could keep hiding from myself and others. I could look at my own attitudes and ideas and claim them. And that's what I started to do. Oh, I had a few bouts of running away but I did begin to trust my body and let my head be. Eventually I had the courage to tell my lover about liking dildoes. She had never played with them and was willing to try. To her they were just another toy we could add to our repertoire and not fraught with judgments. At first I needed reassurance and would stop in the middle of a scene and ask, "Are you sure it's ok? And she'd answer, "Sure, what about you?"

Sorting through all the fears and fantasies has been a fun, hard process. For the first time now I'm beginning to feel my power and to really enjoy sex. I'm feeling much more centered and integrated as I keep accepting parts of myself I disowned for so long. Who would have thought all of this would have come about over a few inches of plastic!

Dildo Designs by Sophie

strap
c.s.
Fuckee/Fuckee

clit stimulator
flexible center
Truly Double Fuck.

c.s.
Butterfly
(dildo-assplug)

delux models have vibrating units -all models come in varying widths and lengths

Dangerous Shoes, or
What's a Nice Dyke Like Me Doing
in a Get-Up Like This?

VIRGINIA BARKER

At first, I wanted to write about my shoes—the five-inch high heels I bought the other day. I went to my closet and pulled out the box. Then I went to the bathroom to wash my feet; I wanted them to feel soft and clean. Sitting down, I slipped my foot in and criss-crossed the skinny strap at my heel and buckled it just above my ankle. That's when I felt my cunt throb.

It's called a fetish, and it works *every* time.

I teetered to standing and walked around the room. Something wasn't right. Maybe it was the frayed jeans and my rumpled "Fesbian-Leminist" t-shirt. Back to the closet: what will it be? My skin-tight disco stretch jeans and 65¢ thrift store strapless, long-line boned bra? The slinky, clingy lavender dress I wore as a bridesmaid at Jane's crazy Halloween wedding ten years ago? Or my black lace and purple satin corset with the cut-away, push up cups that hold my breasts up and expose my nipples? My stockings—yes, my black, seamed stockings—have a run in them. Humm. In another situation, I could get punished for being such a sloppy, careless dresser...

*   *   *

I like the tightness. Sitting at the kitchen table writing this, feeling the way the stretch pants and the boned bra constrict me, compress my stomach and breasts. I feel every inhale and exhale as a distinct movement. The shoes are high, precariously so, and when I'm walking or standing I have to pay attention every moment so that I don't fall. Dangerous shoes, I call them.

For as long as I can remember, there's always been something in my fantasies about costumes, especially tight, form-fitting clothes and shoes or boots with high heels. But until a year ago that's where they stayed—in my fantasies. When I was a little kid I remember running the other way when a friend wanted to play "dress-up." Even then I wouldn't let my guard down enough to play-act with costumes. There was something too threatening about taking on a different role or image, even as a game. I was a tomboy from the word "Go," hated playing with dolls and dreaded the days when my mother would dress me up in a starched, white pinafore. Me? I built the best forts of any kid in town. But I wouldn't even allow myself to dress up as a "daddy" or "brother" to play a game. Femme and frills were definitely out, but *any* costume was almost as bad.

Things always got tense around Halloween. Usually I'd just want to wear a plain mask and go out in my regular play clothes. That wasn't allowed. So for years I bored the neighbors with the next best thing: my cowgirl outfit—boots, hat, red corduroy fringed skirt and vest, gun and holster. The year my aunt's sister thoughtfully sent a fancy, handmade, ruffled flamenco dancer's dress, lace mantilla and comb all the way from Tampa just for my Halloween, I threw a tantrum and refused to go trick or treating at all.

You think I'm getting a little old to play dress-up? Listen, I do it for sex—good, exciting, never-the-same-way-twice, sex. I browse flea markets and thrift stores for lingerie, shoes and any other item that might find a place in my fantasies. And as you might suppose, I love the classics: corset, stockings, high heels. All of it, in reality, is a guaranteed turn-on for me. Sometimes I'll even dress-up to masturbate.

*　　*　　*

I play with costumes for sex, but I'm finding that I'm also playing with my image of myself and my fears of embarrassment. I've spent much of my life on guard, the original wallflower, trying to

106

make sure I wouldn't do anything that would call attention to myself. Solid walls of coolness, distance, toughness, practicality and stoicism are great attributes for the consummate butch, but sometimes it's harder to breathe inside those walls than when I wear my corset.

If I'm playing bottom and my lover and I are going to use costumes, I want to be *made* to get dressed up. I will resist. It's not *me*. Being physically naked isn't as exposing as being in costume. I'm talking about emotional exposure. Being "forced" verbally and/or physically to put on stockings, heels, garter belt, or whatever helps create my bottom space. The dressing up must be "against my will" because, surely, *I* would never, *ever* wear anything like that of my own accord. Well. . .

It's intimate sexual connection and openness that I want, and it's a certain kind of openness that I can only get to through having the most vulnerable parts of my self-image threatened or violated. This is sex with my eyes open. Many times it can scare the shit out of me. I resist, and that is part of the scene, to refuse until she gets through my defenses. Sometimes I cry from being overwhelmed at the power of that fusion of physical sensation and emotional vulnerability. The crying is a release of tension, allowing myself to be carried away from responsibility, the old feeling that I have to be the strong one all the time. And I trust my lover not to leave me in pieces, not to use the S/M that we do as an emotional weapon against me. I trust her to take care of me.

For me, S/M is about emotion, the erotic tension between my impulse toward something and my resistance against it. Every action, sensation, sound, piece of clothing, word exchanged, makes me hyper-conscious of who I am.

I like to feel both sides of S/M, the different things it requires of me, the emotions it dredges up. I like the feeling of giving up control, and I like the feeling of taking her to that edge—and holding her there. Being given such power and responsibility is as erotic to me as giving it up.

When I'm top, I want to push through her ambivalences, strain her limits, and help her experience all the feelings she's drawn to, but fears. Whatever I do, whatever I say, I listen and watch her very carefully. I look at her eyes, the way her breathing changes, the muscle tension in her stomach, the quiver of her lip and loosening of her jaw. I want raw emotion, reaction, the best possible, most heightened reaction to whatever I feel might work to break through her composure and day-to-day facade. It could be something I'd say, slapping her cheek, or perhaps a more subtle action like using my thumb to rub a circular pattern, firmly and insistently, in the soft flesh between her underarm and breast. A feather can be as important a toy as a whip.

I like costumes, here, too. I like to be dressed up and I like to dress her up. Paint her toenails bright red, get her out of that flannel shirt and make her put on her black, strapless shoes and tie her to the bed on her hands and knees. The last time I painted my lover's toenails she kept the stuff on for six weeks, even at the risk of some of her more straightlaced friends noticing. Besides, I was away and she was waiting for me to return; she wanted me to take it off for her. By the time I got back the polish was pretty well chipped—very tacky, indeed. I sat her down and kissed her and told her to take off her shoes and socks. I got the bottle of Cutex and some cotton balls. I wet them. She smiled.

Oh, she'll publicly protest that it wasn't quite that way, say I'm making too much out of it, but privately she'll admit to being intrigued—getting out of bed in the morning, looking down to see the red.

*　　*　　*

You want to know whether I'm into "heavy" S/M? What's that mean? Well, I figure it's anything I have the strongest resistances to, like dangerous shoes. Ummm, let's see. Recently I've been cruising down at the drugstore. Making surreptitious passes at the make-up counter, if you really must know. Checking out the wet-look lipstick and the rouge. Phew! I tell you, now *that's* heavy.

Marnie

DENNISE BROWN

Another yawn, and my hand wandered past my breast, drifted down against my rib cage, began to circle slowly, pressing and lifting, pressing and lifting. Arrgh, I yawned, pulling my arm up slowly over my breasts, which murmured their satisfaction. Fingers spread, my hand moved down my body, strong fingers circling my belly, reaching down to wisps of hair, burrowing in to find wetness. I traced the outer lips, dipped into the wet, used it to moisten the folds, to ease the itching heat there. Deep breaths now, down and down I settled. Then through the mists I heard the latch to my door click gently open, then closed again. That could only be Marnie. I half-opened my eyes and saw her enter, then pull the door to.

That Marnie! Such a handsome woman, with warm brown hair hanging straight nearly to her ass, and eyes of such a turquoise shade that they never failed to startle me, though I've known her for years. She didn't seem to notice me particularly, but crossed, holding a large mirror, to the dressing table, which sat in its bulkiness of light golden wood. Smiling at her reflection, she began to undress. First she shrugged out of the sleeveless tunic that was such a favorite of mine, made of five different materials, tiny prints of birds and flowers in subtle tones—a mauve, a greyed blue, a turquoise like her eyes, sunlight yellow. The different fabrics were pieced together like a quilt top, then bound around the edges with bands of cloth and ribbon. She folded this garment and laid it across the back of the chair.

Next she slinked out of her soft black sweater, pulling it up to reveal her ribs, breasts, neck, then slowly off over her head, the muscles in her arms stretching, her breasts rising with the upward pull, til the sweater joined the tunic on the chair. My heart dipped to my stomach and my fingers under the blanket felt a rush of wet warmth as she stood for a moment, the strong sculptured curves of her back revealed. My hand longed to follow the dip and swell as her rose warm skin curved into the night black of her pants, twin curves of her ass cupped closely by the fabric which touched her where I longed to, caressed her in that delicate sulcal fold where ass and legs meet. Her strong thigh muscles pushed against that fabric, and I could feel my vagina tighten and loosen, hold and release. She paused for a moment to stare boldly at her twin in the glass, turned a little to the side to appreciate the view that had already melted me. Her hands dropped to her ass, she pulled her fingers up slowly over the tight fabric and the taut skin. My breath came in gusts and pants.

Satisfied with what she saw and felt, she bent to remove shoes and stockings, causing my heart to thump and my finger to move toward my clitoris. She seemed to take an unnecessarily long time removing those socks and shoes, and I imagined she heard my heart thumps from a room's width away.

Slowly she straightens, and after running an appreciative hand over the swell of her belly, she lingers just a moment at the junction of her legs, then bends to her gold link belt, unfastens it, unzips her pants more slowly than conscious, slides her hands inside her pants and withdraws her legs from their caress. I have a full view of her bared ass and glimpse in the mirror of her secrets. Borrowing my hairbrush, she gives that long chestnut hair a full 100 strokes, and I feel every one of them. She replaces the hairbrush on the dressing table and picks up my scent bottles, one by one, until she finds the one labelled "Amber." She opens it, holds it to her nose for an appreciative moment, then quickly touches some behind each knee, under each breast, and in the crook of her elbows. Her face smiles back at her from the glass, and she steps proudly across the room to sit in my big armchair, wrapping the purple and red quilt around her. She is staring out the window at a near-full moon as she begins to speak.

"When I was a little girl in Dunedin, I went to St. Margaret's

School. I loved the uniforms we wore—red plaid skirts and red blazers with a school crest on the pocket, white cotton shirts and a red school tie. I remember the morning my father taught me to tie that tie in a perfect Windsor knot—how you start out with one end that's so long and one that's so short that it seems impossible they'll ever come out even—and how confused I got watching my hands in the mirror. But I did finally learn how to tie it and I felt so proud to be wearing a school tie like the big girls.

"The big girls were so special, how I wanted to be like them, to be as strong and athletic and good at games as Charlotte, as good a singer as Marie, to be—well, just to *be* Jackie, I guess. I loved Jackie. They called it a crush, of course, but I knew I loved her then and always would. At lunch time, she'd go to Ted's Corner Store with Darlene and they'd buy forbidden goodies and talk with their heads tilted toward each other, nearly touching, in the back booth.

"One day I talked Sheila into risking punishment by leaving the school grounds during lunch, a privilege reserved for upper-form girls. We waited until we were sure no one was watching, then we ran like anything from St. Margaret's to Ted's Store. And there they were in the back booth, just as I'd heard, drinking vanilla cokes and eating chips with vinegar.

"Oh, they were wild, Jackie and Darlene. Of course they were prefects, too, so they should have reported us when they saw us.

"We sat in the booth next to theirs and listened to them talk. What those deep tones of Jackie's voice did to my stomach! It was hard—I wanted to be near her, would risk anything to be near her—but to be near her meant seeing how close she was to Darlene, and to feel that my chances of winning her love were small. She was kind to me, and that made it even worse, because I knew she was being kind to me and I wanted her to be fierce with me, strong and ardent as I imagined—and heard rumors— she was with Darlene. Darlene had long blonde hair and breasts already, while my hair was brown and cropped and my nipples tiny buds.

"If we got out of line, we were punished at morning assembly, in front of the whole school. The headmistress only punished prefects, the prefects punished the other girls. I lived in terror of the day I would come up for punishment, for fear that not only would

Jackie see my shame, but that she might administer the strap. I had top marks and honours in drama, and I was captain of the basketball team because I was tall and fast, but one day my flair for drama did me in. I was caught imitating the games mistress, Miss Jones, who always boasted that even at her age, she could still put on her stockings standing up.

"That was on a Friday, and it meant six slaps on the bar for me, so I spent a fairly uncomfortable weekend anticipating the event.

"Monday morning assembly seemed to last forever. There were the usual prayers and hymns and then, announcements. A punishment was always the last announcement, and I nearly added to my shame by wetting my knickers before I heard Miss Blaine, the headmistress, call my name. 'Punishments—Marnerly Ashton-Smith, please come forward.'

"I went blank and cold with fear and I don't know how I got up the stage steps to where the headmistress waited for me. 'Marnerly, you were seen mocking a teacher on Friday. You're one of our best actresses, but that bit of drama will cost you the usual six. Angela.' She turned to one of the prefects who sat nearby. Angela stood. 'Will you administer the punishment?'

"The whistling of fear in my chest eased as I learned it would not be Jackie, and my groan was more of shame that she would see me so than fear of the pain to come. I know I blushed to my finger and toe tips but there was nothing to be done for it.

"Angela came to the center of the stage and sat on a chair. 'Right over, Marn, there's a good chum. Grip the legs of the chair with both hands and don't let go 'til I say.'

"She must have felt my heart pounding against her knee as I upended myself over her lap. I squeezed my eyes tight shut as I felt her pull my blue serge knickers down to my knees, and knew my bare bum glistened pink for all to see. 'Ready, then,' said Angela, and it began.

"One, two, my skin began to tingle; three, four, a definite glow; five and six were real stingers, but I never cried out. 'Good show, Marnie,' Angela said, and pulled the elastic of my knickers back up to my middle. 'You can go now.' I did, stumbling a bit on the steps because tears blurred my vision, hastening back to my place on the long bench, where my form sat in solemn array, tallest girl on the left to the smallest on the right.

"I couldn't look at any of them, I was trying so hard not to cry. That was the day when Jackie came up to me at lunchtime, and asked me to walk on Willows Beach with her after school, the day she first kissed me . . ."

Her story was an exciting one to me. I could see each scene, and I was still at St. Margaret's in my mind when she addressed me sharply, "Julia! What are you up to, with your hands under the covers?" She was on her feet so quickly I had no time to change my position, and I felt cold air on my bare skin as she flung the covers off me.

"What are you *doing?*"

It was only too obvious what I'd been doing, and hot scarlet crept across my cheeks and I looked away from her, out the window to the bay beyond. I remember noting a fishing boat passing at that moment. Time seemed very long to me then.

My heart pounded and my hands reached for the covers she'd pulled away, but she was too fast for me. "You naughty girl, you must be spanked."

I don't know how she got my hairbrush in her hand again, but that was not her palm I felt on my bare skin as she knelt above me, her knees like a vise around my body.

As my skin warmed and softened, I felt her strokes more and more. They stung like bees but a deeper, sweeter fire drew my attention, one that flamed deep inside me. I wriggled to ease the double heat, but she clasped her knees tighter until I couldn't squirm.

The spanking ended as I was sinking into a warm wet voluptuousness. I reached up an arm and pulled her down beside me, my hand behind her head, drawing her lips to mine.

DB
10/80

Demon

DOROTHY ALLISON

Some there are
found in the hands of a demon
a demon who tears and takes and makes you
something you were not before.
No matter the nature of the demon
the details of what was done or when or how.
No matter, in fact, if you escape.
　　No one escapes.

The Demon is always there.
Years later, so far after the fact
that there are no facts left
no memories that can be trusted
– and it is the nature of the demon
that trust is the first eaten
the possibility of trust,
the hope of anything at all –
Years later, the demon turns around
grins from the inside
that wounded place.

And Oh!
the demon is clever.
The demon is beautiful.
The demon is much lusted after, much denied
and when, in time, he recedes

it is the dream of the demon that grips and tears
while only the audience remains,
the audience that whispers

    "Tell us about the demon."
    "Tell us how he touched you."
    "Tell us about his belt, his teeth, his cock."
    "Tell us about your blood, how hot it was
     and how it ran down."
    "Tell us about you,
      though, we know of course,
      the only notable thing about you
      is that once a demon wanted you."

    "Once."

The audience grows teeth
takes up a belt, becomes beautiful
The audience looks down
    sees itself
    sees the demon.

You see the demon.
You are not alone anymore.
You have it back – all you wanted.
Now all you want is to be free of it.

But didn't I tell you?
It does not matter what you want.
The demon does not care.
The demon does not even notice.
The demon is filing its nails
    bending over
    waiting.

    Like I said,
        No one escapes.

Mirel

A. J. SAGAN

To others it may have been an insignificant village inn near a spaceport on a backward planet, but to me it was the first place I saw Mirel. The Inn always provided a good meal, nothing fancy, and usually some fine local music which was a very refreshing change from what was popular in trade cities and on board ship. The ship's computer had a few tapes of music of the First Renaissance on Ancient Earth. The music of Rrawrh was similar. In fact, Rrawrh looked a lot like pictures I had seen of the Renaissance period. But for all their relative technological simplicity, the Rrawrh were free from religion and other forms of superstition. After generation upon generation this still cannot be said of Earth people and their space warping offspring.

I had a pleasant walk to the inn. The cool evening air was alive with bird and insect songs different from those I was used to in the ship's botanical gardens. I walked with the pleasing knowledge that under me was a solid planet with a self-sustaining climate, a planet that could not run out of fuel in some cold empty sector of space.

When I stepped into the inn and pulled the wooden door shut behind me a brief silence broke the hum of voices. All eyes were on me for a second or two, then everything returned to normal. The inn was low-ceilinged and dimly lit by glass-enclosed candles set on the low tables. A hearth fire glowed behind dark grillwork at the kitchen end of the room. One musician plucked at a large pear-shaped instrument producing a soothing unobtrusive melody. I picked an empty table and lowered myself into the seating of thick resilient cushioning and soft fur. Tables were occupied about equally by small groups and by solitary Rrawrh.

A young female waiter came to my table. I noted with silent appreciation her beautiful black and gray striping and smooth, cream-colored ventral fur. "Good evening, sister-friend. How may we serve you tonight?" She used a comradely casual expression for "sister-friend."

"Good evening, sister-friend. What do you recommend for dinner tonight?" My faithfully cultivated command of simple Rrawrh gave me a sense of security and usually pleased those I spoke with.

"The roast fowl is very good tonight. I think you'll like it. And we have fresh wild greens in abundance."

"Sounds good. Please bring a serving of each. I would also like a carafe of u'ul." U'ul was a euphoriant beverage infused from a hardy native herb. It was at its best freshly brewed and cooled. It would remain flavourful and effective for about a week if stored in a cool place. "Your best u'ul." For the Rrawrh it was a stimulant and aphrodisiac. I felt its sexual effects but it also acted as a mild sedative on me.

"Yes, of course. I'll be just a few minutes."

When I made my visits to the village, which were as often as my ship came to Rrawh, a regular stop on our circuit, I was frequently the only off-worlder to be seen. Occasionally I ran into someone from the local unit of Galactic Cultural Survey. Most humanoids of Earth type were extremely uncomfortable around Rrawrh. They were, and *are*, feline humanioids having just that mixture of similarity and difference as to seem grotesque to many humans. I was rather taken with them myself; moreover, I was erotically fascinated by Rrawrh females. Why didn't someone back at Galactic Central see that people who love cats were sent here? I wondered. Perhaps I should suggest it.

The Rrawrh found us equally grotesque. It was a select and well-trained group who had dealings with us regularly in the trade city. My friendly treatment led me to believe that their dislike of us was not a question of species or race but of manners and attitudes. My gray friend brought my carafe of u'ul. I sipped a glass as I waited. Gentle tingling vibrations crept through my body with each swallow. I began to relax and noticed that I was smiling effortlessly. I looked around the room. I felt good here even though I did not know anyone personally. I don't think I ever felt quite so good on New Earth where I was born and raised except when I was very, very young.

I continued to sip u'ul. Tonight my sex drives greedily sucked up the magic energy of u'ul. All the sensitive sexual folds and tunnels of my body tickled and convulsed. Tiny maddening ripples of pleasure and desire danced through me freely. While I was caught up in this delicate state my gaze crossed someone's and for a moment we seemed locked together. When the linkage abruptly broke I felt a palpable shock. Who was this? She sat alone, apparently absorbed in the music and indifferent to my presence. This was Mirel. I saw a glint of green from her eyes. Her fur was mostly black with white on the throat, belly and hands, and a tiny white spot next to a pebbly black nose.

The waiter brought my meal. Food took precedence over all for a while. I ate hungrily until the edge of my appetite was blunted. As I finished my meal in a more leisurely fashion, a small ensemble of musicians playing wooden flutes of different sizes and a couple of hand held drums began to play. As tune followed tune they played from a slow solemnity to lively, rollicking rhythms. The musicians encouraged dancing and I was treated to an impromptu program of Rrawrh dances, some dignified, others rather frantic. Nearly everyone joined in at some point. Good feelings filled the inn. I had just a small twinge of feeling left out. I finished off the last of my u'ul and motioned to the waiter that I was leaving. As I counted coins I remarked, "Everything was lovely! The food was delicious. And the music and dancing—delightful!" She smiled at me.

"Your happiness increases our own, sister-friend. Please return." I gave her a few extra coins which was quite proper and even expected since I was so obviously pleased. I bid her goodnight and turned to leave. I saw her glance nervously at two young Rrawrh reclining at a near table. They glanced at me several times and whispered and nodded vigorously. I made nothing of it what with the u'ul and the inn's air of good will and cheerfulness. A trace too much u'ul perhaps. I bet I could fall asleep standing up. Scant steps outside the inn I did just that.

When I came to my head was throbbing painfully in the area of one nasty lump. This was no u'ul hangover. I could not move. I was bound, hands behind me, and lying on the ground. I was blindfolded. I heard three distinct voices speaking rapidly in Rrawrh. The conversation sounded very angry and excited. I concentrated and slowly was able to pick out words and phrases: our chance, revenge, stinking offworlder, violated, justice my ass, debt of honor, obviously in her season. The voices stopped. Off came my blindfold, then my bonds. I sat up and looked into three very angry Rrawrh faces, eyes blazing, ears twitching. Claws on several hands flexed in and out continuously. A pang of helplessness bolted through me. I struggled quietly to be calm and alert.

Now they spoke to me, or at least at me. "You thieving offworlders think you own the universe! You don't own us. You'll pay. You'll all pay!"

"I don't know what you're talking about. Look, I haven't done you any harm. Let me go."

"You speak well for a furless, scabby offworlder, but it won't help you. My sister didn't do anything but one of your filthy spaceboys didn't care! And you have the nerve tonight to say sisterfriend! Now we pay the debt of honor!"

I opened my mouth to speak and one of my captors slapped me hard. Fortunately her claws were tucked in. I was afraid to move, afraid to stay still. They ripped through my clothes. I stood before them naked and shivering, sure of being killed or maimed. We were in a dark quiet room with a hard dirt floor. Light flickered from several glass-windowed metal lanterns. The three Rrawrh forced me to a kneeling position over a wooden crate. My legs were tied to the crate and my hands to a ceiling support post.

"You can make all the noise you want. No one will hear you. There will be no rescuer for you!"

"I'll make sure you make a lot of noise. Feel that?" She dragged something smooth over my skin. Then she struck me with it. A whip of several tough leather strands. "You will pay! Scream! Your filthy scum will never try to violate any of us again!" She whipped me furiously. My flesh was soon aflame with her efforts. For a long time I only groaned under my breath. Eventually I cried; at times crying gave way to hoarse screams. When one tormentor tired another took up the whip.

"Please don't. Ohh, please! No, no, nooo-oh!" I begged. I pleaded shamelessly. I vowed that I would sooner die than violate a Rrawrh, that I would kill anyone who did. They only laughed. I still wasn't sure what we were talking about. Desperation fueled my creativity. Finally they stopped. I stayed still and quiet as if doing so would protect me from further beating.

"What an ugly furless animal you are! You've had better treatment than you deserve, understand? What should be done is you should be taken out of season over and over until you are torn and ruined. But you're obviously in your season! You think any of us wants you? Do you think that any of our males wants you? Not one! Not even one!" She exhaled a loud and obvious sign of disgust.

There was a jarring blow to my shoulder. Several deep sharp hot pains persisted. The wet of blood seeped from where her claws had ripped me. I wept, shuddering silently. I waited.

"Get the barbed whip," someone urged excitedly, "or a thorn twig."

"Well, cousins, have you found a new pastime?" This was a new voice.

"Mirel! We were just paying the debt. When the offworlders see what has happened to this one they will walk more lightly. Maybe we will be rid of them." With some difficulty I saw that the newcomer was she whose gaze had locked mine at the inn.

"Eryl! I am shocked. She is innocent. They were all males. There is nothing honorable about this. The incident has been handled. Would you risk a blood feud? Debt of honor, indeed! You toy with her! Offworlder or no, you wanted her! Can you deny it to me? I saw what you were doing, all of you!"

"Mirel, she's just a slimy offworlder!"

"I don't want to hear it. Understand? Get out!" Together the trio hissed and then left without a word.

Mirel came over to me. "I really must apologize for their treatment of you. This was totally inexcusable." She slashed the cords that bound me. "Your bottom looks sore but not really damaged. This claw wound on your shoulder is a bit nasty, though. I can help. Lie still and relax. No one will hurt you now." Without thinking I trusted her. I lay quietly. Mirel touched my shoulder, then

cried out in pain and broke the contact. A few moments passed
and she touched me again, now maintaining contact. A subtle
vibration flowed from Mirel to me. There was an itchy tingling
sensation in my shoulder. When Mirel took her hand from me I
glanced around at my shoulder. There were three tiny pink scars
on the skin.

"Thank you, . . ."

"Mirel. Mirel is my name."

"Thank you, Mirel. I am Kiri. You are a healer?"

"Yes. And empath." She seemed to be holding herself back
from me. "But some things are, perhaps, beyond me."

This last statement made no sense to me but I felt no energy to
question it. Now the strain of the ordeal caught up with me, "I . . .
I . . ." I cried and Mirel held me and murmured soothingly.

"Everything's going to be all right now. My home is nearby.
You will stay with me tonight. You should not be walking about
alone until you feel stronger." I acquiesced gladly. Mirel helped
me to my feet. She put one arm about my waist and we left that
large silent room, one of the inn's unused storage rooms. Outside
I shivered and realized that I was naked. I leaned on Mirel. Where
our bodies met I was warmed. Shortly we arrived at a small wood
and earthen cottage.

Inside, Mirel laid me down on a soft bed; she lay down beside
me and pulled a warm soft fur cover over both of us. What was
the cover and what was Mirel? We slept.

I awoke once, early, to the sound of birds. Mirel got up. I drifted
back to sleep, exhausted. Later, much later, I awoke to Mirel's
touch.

"Kiri."

"Mmmm?"

Mirel pulled the cover slowly from me and lay beside me. A
light lick from her raspy tongue sent tickly currents up and down
my body.

"Hungry?"

"Mmmm. Still tired."

"Come on. Get up. Before you know it the sun will be setting!
I've got some food outside for us."

I got up. There were still no clothes for me to put on. I must have looked self-conscious. Mirel smiled at me, a smile I took to be a sly smile, and pulled me outside. Late as it was the air was pleasantly warm. We sat in thick short grass. Mirel had set out a meal of grain and meat and water. She nibbled while I dug in hungrily.

"So, how are you feeling today?"

"Good, very good, Mirel. My bottom's a little sore. Ehh! . . .I feel very. . .lucky. You may have saved my *life* last night. I don't know how I can ever thank you enough."

Mirel regarded me quietly for some moments. "I doubt they would have killed you but you could have been cut up more if I hadn't caught wind of their plan. Your thanks are sufficient but if you would accept my friendship it would please me greatly." Tiny needly rainbows gleamed here and there on Mirel's fur in the sunlight.

"Mirel, I am honored to be your friend." She hugged me lightly and rubbed my hair. "What was all that, anyway? I picked up a little but the total picture escapes me." I recounted last night's events as I understood them. "So they are your cousins?"

"Yes. It both angers and saddens me that they should behave so. Nothing more will happen, though, I assure you. Some time ago three offworlder males ventured out of the trade city. They were totally ill-mannered and unruly but worse—they became violent. We had not seen your people behave so badly up until that day. They attacked a lone young female at a short distance from the village. She could not understand their words but their feelings were clear. I was walking nearby and heard the disturbance. When I got there they were attempting to mount her! Even if she had been in her season I doubt that she would have accepted *their* advances—but they ignored the fact that she was not in her season!"

"Mirel, we don't have sexual seasons, at least not as definite as yours. But we do not condone forced sex either. It is a crime!"

"Mm. Yes. Well, I found that out—eventually," Mirel paused. She was obviously reliving the incident as she spoke. "I attacked them—and with surprise and fury in my favor I killed one. I wounded the other two but they ran and I stayed to help the young one.

"It stirred up some diplomatic dust but once your Galactic authorities understood exactly what had happened they assured us there would be no further trouble. The two surviving offenders were caught and punished and sent from Rrawrh never to return." She exhaled noisily.

"Well that explains it then. Your cousins wanted to be heroes, too."

"But they've got it all wrong. Revenge on innocent people. Nursing irrational hatred. We don't want this kind of thing to be blown up all out of proportion. You offworlders have always been respectful."

"There is this species revulsion problem."

"Mm. Yes. But it's manageable. I think it will gradually change . . . I don't want to get into that right now, though. Tell me something about you. Tell me about Kiri."

I laughed nervously. "I'm Kiri Ad'ara, ship's officer in charge of botanical gardens on board the Space Cargo Carrier Roc. Originally from the colony planet New Earth. I've been in the space service ten years. You could say my destiny is in the stars. . . Rrawrh is my favorite place. Very seriously." I was unsure what to say next.

"Do you like space, then?"

"Not exactly. But the gardens suit me. I take care of some small animals, too. I probably wouldn't be in space anymore except for ships' gardens. A lot of people have gone crazy in space. Couldn't be predicted, either. Finally, someone thought to take along a piece of the planet on ship. It really cut the percentage of mental and emotional problems in space. I came out of a really heavy depression in one of the first space station gardens."

"So you went back to space rather than live on a planet?"

"Yeah. I'd like to stay somewhere but. . .I never felt that I really belonged anywhere, even on New Earth. I don't belong in space either. But everybody has to live *somewhere*."

"Yes." Mirel had been rubbing my body as we talked. I felt safe and relaxed into it. "You are very lonely, are you not?"

I hesitated. "Yes." I began to feel guarded and still continued to talk. "I seem to miss connections with the people I know. The animals I care for are some company. Especially the cats, you know, the ones that look like you." I smiled.

"Cats are special for you?"

"Un-huh."

"And Rrawrh is also special?"

"Yes."

Mirel stopped rubbing and just held me. "You feel special to me, Kiri." She held me tight for a moment, "You could let the sun of Rrawrh be the star of your destiny." She slowly rubbed her face all over mine.

"Mmmmmm. Mirel. I feel so good with you. I don't feel alone. Maybe. Maybe I could."

Mirel kissed me gently. "When I first touched you last night I did not shield my empathy. I had not thought it necessary. When I cried out, I had been only touched by your loneliness. The loneliness of an entire lifetime sitting all in one place in you. I could not bear it. How do you?"

"I don't know." I didn't. We were quiet together for a while.

"Kiri, stay with me. Just for a while. I promise you won't feel so lonely. And it would make me happy."

"I would like to, Mirel."

"Then stay. For a while. If you must leave you will know when." There was a deep rhythmic hum below her words. I could feel her body vibrating. "I *want* you, Kiri. I *know* that you are in your season. I felt it last night at the inn and later on, too. And I am in my season, too!"

I looked deep into her fiery green eyes. Mirel. Reminding me of precious cat desires that seemed so fanciful. Now I was touching the dreams. What foolishness it would be to pass up such a chance!

"I want you, Mirel." Saying it rekindled my desires. Mirel kissed me again. I cuddled secure in her arms.

"Kiri, do you *own* your cats?" This seemingly unrelated question put me off balance for a moment.

"No...I care for them. There's an old joke that the cats own the people who care for them." A long silence followed my answer. Mirel kept stroking my body with slow, continuous motions.

"Kiri, I want to own you." An erotic shudder took me. Mirel felt it, I knew.

"Rrawrh desires are fierce, Kiri. That whipping you had last night? Love taps. Child's play. They wanted you, though they denied it. I stopped them before they used a barbed whip on you. Are you frightened?"

"A little. But you know how I'm feeling, don't you, Mirel. I would...I would do anything for you, Mirel. I'm a shameless crawling masochist."

"I just needed to hear you say it, Kiri." She grinned and stroked my hair with her claws just barely out. I lay with my head in Mirel's lap luxuriating in her fur and beginning to hunger now for things beyond food.

Mirel changed our positions. She got her head in under my arm. Her claws kneaded teasingly at my skin. The points of her teeth touched me; I tensed. She licked greedily at the small tuft of wiry hair and I began to relax again. When she bit hard into my tender flesh, I let go, accepting the pain and it slipped through me leaving a trail of excitation. An easy submissive reverie fell over me like a warm weightless blanket. Now Mirel dug claws into my smooth naked bottom. I cringed and clenched my pelvic muscles. She reached a hand between my legs. "You're wet." She smelled the wetness and then had me smell it and lick my own fluid from her hand.

"What does Kiri want?"

"To play, Mirel."

"You will address me as Mistress."

"Yes, Mistress." I quivered, not in fear but in awe.

"You will serve me, Kiri. You will obey me. I am a harsh mistress. You need hard discipline to be a good slave to me. Kneel." She pushed my head to her feet. The last rays of sunshine had long since faded and given way to a soft darkening. A crescent moon shone silvery as a newly honed and polished blade. "I think you need to be whipped."

"Yes, Mistress." Oh, whip me, Mirel. Please whip me.

Mirel gathered several stout switches. "Pick up the remaining food and dishes and go into the cottage." I did so. Mirel walked beside me, urging me on with little strokes of a switch.

Inside the cottage, Mirel bound my hands and had me lie over some piled up covers on the bed. She also blindfolded me. "Do you know why you're being whipped, slave?"

"Because I need it, Mistress?"

"Because I *want* to whip you. And because you *want to be whipped.*" She emphasized with hard strokes to my ass.

"Yes. Mistress." I whimpered.

"Poor Kiri! Poor slave! Poor slave must suffer." She steadily whipped my already sore ass. Oooh, it hurt! It burned! My ass clenched and my clit tickled. Oooh, I want you to fuck me.

At first I only moaned. After awhile I began to cry out loud, "Nooo, noo, noo."

Mirel stopped abruptly. "Do you really mean no, Kiri?"

"No, Mirel. I mean I like it, I want it."

"Well, if you really want me to stop, even if only for a little while, just say 'moonrise.' Understand?"

"Yes, Mistress. I understand. 'Moonrise' means 'stop.'" Mirel resumed whipping me. I got hotter and hotter. Use me, Mirel. Take me. She alternated whipping with tickling and rubbing and squeezing. She was so good to me! Finally, after a number of strokes with a thorn switch I had had enough. "Moonrise!"

"Had enough, eh? Well, I'm not *all* done with you! Tell me, slave, and be truthful, what is it that you want now more than anything else?"

A poignant question, to be sure. All through the whipping I kept slipping ahead in fantasy to my orgasm. Fuck me, Mirel, please, fuck me. Okay. So move the lips and say it out loud. I hesitated. "Please, Mistress. I want... I want for you to f-fuck me!" I teetered near the edge of orgasm.

"You want me to fuck you." My crotch ached to hear her echo the wish. "I'm not sure you deserve to be fucked yet. Do you think you deserve to be fucked yet?"

"Oh, yes! Please, Mistress!"

"No. First you must please me." Mirel untied me and took off the blindfold. Then she lay down and pulled me to her. "Make love to me, slave. Show me how devoted you are to pleasing your Mistress!"

I kissed Mirel, tentatively at first. She pulled my tongue into her mouth hard. Gradually, my tongue slid over every smooth and slippery surface of her mouth. I bit at her lips. Her breath rasped in her throat. Her body pulsed against mine. Through all my frenzied attentions I remained delightfully aware of her fur on my flesh. I sucked at each of her eight tiny nipples and fingered ones I was not sucking. Her hands moved over my body, the claws digging into me with pleasure and abandon.

Mirel pushed my head down between her legs. With both eagerness and care I licked her soft wet swollen sex. "Put fingers inside me." So I did. First one, then two, then three fingers moving with her cunt's rhythmic squeezing. She moaned and growled and when she came her claws dug painfully into my shoulders and held me there. When she came, I almost came. Almost. Mirel let out one last long moan, like a baby crying. Her claws relaxed back into their hidden sheaths. I shook with unreleased sexual tension.

Without warning, Mirel sat up and pinned me to the bed. "That was very good, Kiri. You've been a very good slave so far." Her breathing was still labored. "You deserve to be fucked, my hot little slave. How do you like it?"

"Please Mistress. In my ass. I like it best in my ass."

Mirel got up. She brought back to the bed a glove of tough leather, a container of grease, and a switch. She warmed up my ass some more. Not that it had really cooled off. Mirel became more and more excited as she whipped me. "Want to be fucked, do you? I'll fuck you good. But first I'll see that you're properly whipped."

"Please, Mistress! Please fuck me! Please." Mostly I just moaned.

"That'll do. All right. Keep your ass up." With a gloved hand she worked grease into my ass. Slowly, steadily, a finger at a time, with an easy rocking rhythm, Mirel eventually, incredibly, deliciously worked her entire hand into my ass. Her other hand helped us along, continually pressing against my tender clitoris. She talked to me the whole time. "Mmmm, yes, easy, easy. Take it, take it. Feels good? Yes. Mmmm. I *like* fucking you. You're a hot little cunt with a *talented* asshole!" And so on. I kept up a steady stream of wordless sound. Inside my head was a boundless universe full of diving, dancing changing lights colors shapes, Mirel's voice guiding everything. I was going somewhere; wherever was fine with me.

At some point in all this Mirel started pinching on one of my nipples with her other hand. She slowly dug the claws into me, piercing the nipple. I thought I could not bear it without saying 'moonrise'; but I did bear it. "Ohh, ohh, ohh, noo! Oohh! Mirel! Ohh, Mirel. Fuck me! Oh, yeah! F-f-fuck mee!" I barely knew who I was. Oh, she fucked me so nice!

"Come on, Kiri. Come on! You want it. You're almost there, almost there. Take it! Reach for it!"

I teetered on the brink of coming for so long! I began to think that I would not make it and started to cry. The pulsing in my ass and cunt became more rapid and stronger. Suddenly, I could not *not* come! I moaned and groaned and grunted deep in my throat. My pelvis thrust continuously of its own accord against Mirel's motion, my whole body heaving and shaking uncontrollably, tears streaming down my face. I cried gratefully, a smile possessing my lips. Mirel hugged me and rubbed me all over, murmuring all the while. "Yes, yes, yes. It's so good. My lovely Kiri. You deserve to feel so good! Yes. Precious. You are *so* precious!"

Very gradually and carefully Mirel pulled her hand from inside me. At the last it slipped out easily. She removed the glove. I fell asleep in her arms, all problems and decisions placed aside for another time.

The Seduction of Earth and Rain

HOLLY DREW

"Would you come with me? There's a favorite glen I'd like to bring you to," Elura asked.

I saw her neck-thong rise from the moss soft flesh of her throat. How is it that she sees in me the courage to take on the role she leaves me? I, who so recently fled the strangling morals and ethics of the Bureaucra-Biz Sector, my birthplace and home—so alien to me. I, who am even in body different from these Outwomen, living wild in the welcoming hills, for I cannot grow those long strands of flesh her people raise in their passion. I cannot answer the collar forming at her throat with whips emerging from my knuckles.

Today she wants to be Earth. More often Elura desires to be Rain, and so flaunt her finger-whips.

All I have are brief remembrances of shadowy stunted fantasies, desires I'd buried deep down inside me. So hard it is for me to release myself to these women who hold their passions so firmly, joyously, so sure and proud. So unafraid to mirror the intense interplay between the land's moods and cycles in their sexual love and play.

"Come, Kurisa, I know your fela is not lame, and I know you are free today. Mount Heloa and I will show you this sacred hiding place of mine. It is not far, and though you are unable to grow finger-whips, I can sense your cautious desire."

"Elura, you have watched me long, respecting my fear, you have not come near me. You know I have courted you in my dreams. It is so easy for me to take and be taken in my sleep.

129

But now I am awake, and barriered. I would like to postpone this invitation of yours. I would like to escape on Heloa for a gallop and swim. We have many estuaries and peninsulas to cross, my high-headed fela and I."

Elura looks down at me from her perch. Her blue-grey fela fans her fins slowly to shoo away insects, and stretches slowly one webbed foot, bored by our encounter.

Elura wonders how I can understand the open sea's high waves, how I can comprehend rise and swell, ebb and flow, the fair weather and the stormy, if I am unexposed to these power roles, these exchanges, within myself.

I am so busy shaking off layers, skins, rings. Like the shattered concentric reflections in a pond after the pebble is thrown in. The pebble is that instant of change—when I left my home place to come here. And Here has so upset the surface of my being, I am fragmented, tangled. New pebbles, those unforeseen barriers, keep falling into the pool. When will they cease? Perhaps not until I reach my hand into the pool to set my own rhythm in the water.

I stroke Heloa's shoulder, she nudges me. She knows that I have come to take her on a joyride, not some mundane errand.

I am tense, nervous, aroused before Elura. I would slight myself if I left her now. But I am shaky, too scared to move on her offer to play in her glen.

"Elura, would you and your fela join us on our gallop and swim?" I gesture off towards the lowlands, and lift myself onto Heloa's back.

Her face split by a broad smile, neck thong still banding her neck, she cues her mount to leap forward. They race by me. Heloa lunges after her, her horny webber pads thudding soft and firm on the spongy humus edging the narrow bay.

Side by side we race, swimming our amphibious mounts through bays, canals, sharing the snakelike writhing of their bodies churning between our legs, responding, drinking the wind, sharing the exhilaration of their powerful strokes of leg and fins, sharing their headlong gallop across marsh, prairie, low hills. Spirits fly, thunder and wind. Tears fly back into our hair, and our dancers tire as we approach the forested sector of the hills.

Elura laughs. Buoyant and hearty, I join her. Dizzy from our dash, thighs tired and clit erect from gripping Heloa, my laugh is low and throaty.

"You have brought us straight to my glen," cries Elura, and then gently, "You are silly to try and avoid your desires, Kurisa, for your body will bring you to your finest passionplay even though your hesitating mind says no. You are a powerful rider, you master and merge with your fela so completely. Do you not think there are other areas where this skill might benefit? My throat collar," she says grinning, "is engorged near to bursting, Kurisa my friend, and you are drunk now from our race. I will lead the way."

Yes, I have this haunting sensation that I have been here before, that I have known the roles of Earth and Rain to their raw core. I am being urged to let go, to do something new, something innately old.

Yes, I do feel like rain today, like showering down welcomed blows, like cutting chasms with abrading rivulets, like marking a defenseless and vulnerable waiting and pleading earth. The evil mischievousness of building storms.

Truly a fine retreat, this glen. All light diffused and misted. Trees tower around us, guardians. From them dangle the pliable vines so valued by Elura's Outwomen, strong, soft and everywhere available. Thunderheads gather in the afternoon sky, bringing to this forest and the waters below its daily precipitation. Never could this countryside forget its dominance by the rain, this severe and mirthful jesting game.

Watching those clouds, as Elura and I dismount and hobble our felas, those muscular and arrogant clouds. They challenge, gathering water from earth and sky.

So close these women are to the ebb and flow, the dominance and submission acted out in this ecology. The two roles overlap, intermix—and all at once I see—that there is no grass without rain, no rain without the moisture drawn from plants and waters by the day's heat. This most basic of cycles, this most perfect powerplay, gentle, generous, yet unyielding. So. I grasp. Cognition.

"Elura," I turn to her, "gather me vines, four lengths, no, five, and fray one, tying knots at the strand's ends."

She looks at me. For a moment playfully defiant, haughty, testing. A wild thing, yearling fela.

"And Elura," I say, "remove your breeches and tunic." She looks me in the eyes, fighting and blushing and asking for more, for harshness, looking for the priestess of the Rain in me, for my voice to crack her like thunder splitting sky. So it is lightning that slaps her across the cheek, bringing sting to the back of my hand and a gasp from her lips, now parted and moist.

"Remove your clothes," I say, welcoming my role like hands welcome gloves on the mornings when the canals freeze over, "or I shall unhobble Heloa and leave you here gasping, parched."

Elura complies, lifting her tunic over her shoulders, lifting her hair back from her face, and on her cheek the red print of my hand. She slips from her loose breeches. I draw her to me curling my index finger. Now she comes to me humble, tamed, her neck-thong willingly crimson. I draw my finger along her cleft. She is warm, seeping, fragrant. I taste her, then have her lick clean my finger. I can feel my own thighs moistened. I drool, I crave, my canal open, begging.

I will have her do my bidding. "Elura, undress me, enter me sweet woman."

So she kneels. Drives her fingers up into me. I crumble, erode, say "harder, faster, do not stop," such lover's cliches. Through lazy slits of my eyes I see the thunderheads gathering in mighty clumps, darkening. I feel the grass and soil stain and scrape my back as Elura plunges into me, rocking my body, pounding me, waves upon a beach, storm, thunder, white biting lights of pain, surges. All of my being desiring to push out through that orifice now filled with Elura's obedient hand, like a birth, I will my existence to spring from my womb. I ache. Can no longer see the clouds. I forget form, color, speech. I am shaking, quaking, splitting, oh, do not stop, oh Elura—fling me apart, destroy me, breathless. I am the earth parting—no, I am the lightning striking—which one?

I am lost. I am a victim. I have no memory, only, yes, that I am parting, that from my clit and her plunging, rasping hand I am melting, burning—I am overcome, I am washed over, am floating...and Elura squats at my hip, her hands flowing over me like slow water. "Lover," she whispers, "I'll gather vines while you drift."

"Yes." I respond, shadowy. Then from my purging comes a strength so clean, so raw and unadulterated. My head lolling to one side, I watch Elura deftly shinny up gangly trees to cut off vines . . . roles become so diffused. She is fraying and knotting one short vine. She focuses so totally on her obedience to me. It is her purging. She forgets all else. So I turn the thrill of my climax into my role, I say, "Earth, come before me and kneel."

I see that I will have nothing if I do not grasp my role with both hands, letting it become me, becoming Rain. Drawing chasms up a smooth prairie, I draw my fingernails up her smooth back, and in my bending bring my pubis to her face so that she breathes my scent. That strong back arches. I see her toes curl. Such power I have! It is I who dictates how my lover shall feel.

Brief flashes of the ugly authority of my parents over me, trying to force me to conform to their restrictive culture, in the city where one flees the rain as it splatters down on asphalt, and one never feels the earth except in greenhouses, then only feeling the treated soil with hands encased in gloves. So contrived. They are so afraid of the dirtiness of the earth. Their sexuality so sterile, so product oriented—did we produce offspring? And how many orgasms this time? Dull and decaying, no light for spirit's fire, sexplay steeped in the fear that some lusted urge might be wrong, perverse—*unclean*. Unclean like the earth, like the sweat off my fela, like these fresh grass stains down my back, like these vines dusty and bluelichen coated—no!—not unclean, *not* unclean, *not* separate, how was it that I was raised to worship such dualities? Welcome the soil now, welcome the sticky moisture slicking my thighs, as my lover welcomes the red tracks down her back, welcomes that intense knowledge that there is no split, no duality. In our play we bring on the roles, Rain the mistress over passive, servile Earth, only that we may know afresh that pain and pleasure, give and take, submission and dominance are so intertwined that they can never be separate, and so we who play with the roles find that the duality is a convenient illusion, realizing all is one.

Above Elura and I the thunderheads run into each other, quiet thunders roll down around us, and today's warm rain begins. So I begin. I take from her limp hand the whip saying, "Elura, expose yourself to me, on your hands and knees," and I satisfy her, I rain down lashes, I become drunk again, drunk on this power, this force. I become cruel, I have no mercy, I whip her until she trembles into a heap, and then I turn my lover's body over, I lick her erect nipples, I lick her throat-thong, I sink my tongue into her gaping mouth, her lips so red and filled. I pause for a moment in her eyes, to check in, her eyes say yes, yes, I am entrusted to you, take me, disintegrate me, I am yours, we are one, without divisions. I caress her soft body with tongue, with fingertips, until she remembers that she is wanting, until her body writhes, her throat moans. She moves to hold me, silly woman. I pinion her down. Lashing vines to wrist and ankle, I tie her wide open for me. I stand back to watch her, I remember my cruelty, I go over to Heloa to scratch her favorite places. I stroke her vulva, she lifts her tail and flops her ears akilter, enjoying. Returning to Elura, who has watched me helplessly, I slap her again, throwing her head aside and taking a nipple between thumb and forefinger, twisting, pinching, squeezing. Elura has lifted her pelvis, is thrusting it toward me, asking, pleading, how much longer will I tease before I give her what she loves best? With my free hand I draw the knotted strands of my whip up her thighs, through her cleft, alongside her clit, then it is my fingernails swiftly scratching thighs, my hand slapping, bringing all her awareness to the entrance of her womb. I straddle her thigh and rub my again swollen clit along her tense muscle. I remind her this way that it is only by my whim that she shall have pleasure beyond what I have already given her, but I realize that I am her slave also, it is that which pleases her most that I will ultimately do. So I enter her canal, two fingers, I release her nipple and stretch back her mons, exposing her clit, encircling this fine berry with my tongue for a while.

Just when Elura has relaxed into this soothing caress I plunge full up into her, four fingers and thumb also as she rises and opens her canal to me. I curl my fingers up so that with each thrust I prod her clit from the inside. I know that stinging silver pain, I bring it to her in swift waves, I allow her no pause, indeed, she asks for more. I am harsh, unrelenting, I am her Goddess, I give her all I have, when my arms tire I continue. When I see my hand becoming earthbrown and I fear injuring her I continue. I continue until she is almost gone, groans become dry sobs and she does not strain against her bondage. Her breathing falls away, her eyes are rolled back in their sockets, I ease off my rhythm, bringing her empty body to limp stillness, running my hand down her torso, forehead to cleft, our sweat mixing with the rain. I quickly untie her. I am again purged, entranced, as is Elura, faintly smiling, sailing away on some mind's sea, I draw her body around mine, she plants soft kisses at my throat, we drift off into free dreaming, soaring.

Give and Take

HOLLY DREW

For Lydia

Quick glance. Yup. Table seven's ready for salad, and numero tres is waiting for dessert, and here comes Mr. Big Eyes on the hunt. What flaws will he find this round? Carie flies by arms armored with main courses. Focusing on me she asks, "What's on your mind? How's the love life?" This brisk shorthand our means of on-the-job communication.

She means Rima. Rima scheming no doubt, Rima contriving scenes, lioness in her lair—"Where are you today, Miss Cratner? I want those rolls on at the same time as you set down the main course—I thought we went over this enough last week." "Yes sir. . ." He struts off to accost another played-out waitress. Our manager Mr. Big Eyes Young Buck, head man, to be tolerated, part of my job's compromises. That bastard who never totes a dish, or burns fingers on hot plates—but still we must set the plate down with grace or face humiliation and no tip.

Dinner over. We reset tables, casual conversation. This strength we own—our ability to do this, day after day—and still have beauty. Beauty in a face lined with pain and struggle that lights up in a smile, strength in our ability to lift each other's hearts.

Carie asks, "Do you go to Rima after work?" I nod. She adds, "You be a good girl then, behave." Light in her eye, fleeting grin. She brushes my hip with her fingers, silent hidden touches that sustain us here.

*　　*　　*

Rima like the tower card in the deck, my values and perceptions falling to ruin, to revolution, the Tower all aflame—I can't stay here, yet I still perceive survival as necessitating these compromises. I need money to live in the city, in the city I live by the job. Rima, you are the fire in the Tower, and I run, a fool, straight toward you as crazed horses do in a stable ablaze.

Curious as it is I walk now up the stairs to the house of desert, to my place of honing down, to my letting go, to Rima.

And oh, my mind's images always hold so much less challenge than the real. Rima ready for me, welcoming me by her obvious desire. Her dwelling is red, burnt sienna cloth hung in drapes and gathers from the walls, in the shadows deep accents of black. She is proud of her craft. She has ornate altars in cubbyholes, has herbs drying. Rima who moved here from a rural town, moved to the city for its women, and on her walls she hangs whips, crops, satin sashes and oiled leather thongs, she an eagle displaying beak and claws, she ruffles her plumage righteously.

I want to crumble at her feet, to be her slave now and worry about equality later, but Rima will not let me have my pleasure so easily.

"Sharra," she speaks, raising her voice on the ra. It is our password, my name spoken to imitate the whip's lash. "You look beaten."

"I wish!" I respond, and we laugh at this old joke. "Same old grind, Rima. Mr. Big Eyes Young Buck being his horrid lecherous self, ah I grind my teeth in his presence. You are such a haven, Rima. I am such a damned perfect slave to my job, to Mr. Big Eyes. I hate it with all my gut—but if I ain't waitressing then what else? Secretary, salesgirl, or should I struggle to learn a man's trade to then find myself with a full time job working with young-bucks and World War II veterans, cut off from women? Goddess, Rima, I need some clarity, some sign or hint. How're you?"

"Hum, sweet Sharra, I've had nothing better to do today than create scenes, I'm nearly wasted by the effort. Lie down on the bed, I'll clear you."

She runs her fingertips slowly down my entire length, again and again cleansing and preparing, connecting us firmly through this gentleness. I really must be crazy, schizy. I come here for the healing and the enlivening of my submission to Rima—how, *how* can I tolerate the humiliating degradation of my job? I want out. Today. "Rima?"

"What is it? Then silence."

"Help me find the path to the mountains . . ."

"Is it that you are not satisfied with me? You want to leave me?" I can feel her becoming sinister in the fingers, so I moan, and she answers with a long piercing scratch. Moaning more I say, "No, you know you are—"

"Shush, lover." It is Rima becoming animate, we release humanness, such as society sees it, and it is slaps on skin, cries, grunts, gut pleadings that fill this room now.

I see that Rima has taken a whip in her hand. Lying on my belly, my ass raised in want, I hear the whip slice air, I roll onto my side cringing, evading, fighting the inborn fear of being struck. It is a reflex only trust can alter.

"If you don't lie still. . ." Rima says threateningly. I know what she means. She refuses to whip me if I tense; I am not allowed to anticipate. All of my awareness pours into being submissive. I am so distracted by my efforts that the lash surprises me, I, so open to this, all my body's sensations swarm through my womb and clit. Lash after lash comes down. I am transferred beneath the sexual. I am dealing with pain, am challenged, am challenging. It is always a focusing and a purging beyond my perceptions. I do not understand it. There is no room for understanding. There is only the pain, the repeating blows, driving me higher, squirming, trapped there on the floor beneath my Rima. Can I take more? Do I even have the spare energy to cry mercy? My body contracts with each blow, each muscle spasm—then my awareness of my desire returns, the surges flowing through my birth canal—as fire, as blood, all my being desiring to burst from my womb.

Rima stops, and I lie there remembering how to breathe. Remembering each muscle and tendon as they let my bones settle, loosening that clenched grip.

Rima says, "I will have you wash my hair, now that I've got you in the proper frame of mind." Whispery smile gracing her full lips.

I go to make preparations. From the rosebush I gather petals which I let float in the bath water. I light candles. I let droplets of amber oil mix with the water and scent the room. My hands are unsteady as I unbutton her blouse, unsteady as I reveal all that apricot skin, skin I would lick, caress, be lost in, lost in folds of labia. I venture a stroke, a finger trace, hip to groin, I see the electricity of my touch shimmer through Rima, see her almost swoon, tempted to succumb. But no—she sets the roles straight now, handful of my hair twisted in her hand. She pulls down so that my face is exposed. Through pinched eyes I see undersides of breasts, see nostrils flared. I arch my head back, falling forward—Rima holds me silent there for a moment, sweet ecstacy, I would stay there hours—long arch of my throat pressed into her moist hair, her scent...

Squatting before Rima. Pouring water over her shaggy brown hair, feeling her fingers sneaking up my thigh—ah, she is going to torture me here, one of her favorite turn-ons, to tease me, to see me beg her for deep plunges, she with so much power, power over me while I moan and beg. Odd that I will grovel before Rima, feel so clean doing it—yet back there under the absolute insensitive and cruel power of Mr. Big Eyes the Manager it is true out of my control torture to allow myself to be so consistently squashed beneath his thumb. All I have to do is not return. Yes. Then what? To where? A void to fill...mountains, smell of sage... solitu—ewe—ey— Rima please, I am so faint. With your fingers crawling in and out of me, and your thumb whirling suds from the soap at my clit...

    floating
    Ah Rima, yes, Rima, yes.
    Look at you,
      you are smiling
    caught up in my pleasure
    my body arched back
    jerking as I rise and fall
    your hand and arm a piston
    and you are laughing.
    Clear waves, songs,
    gathering me into your embrace
      bringing me down

light feather
on top of you—
Rose petals and water
  a tsunami taking over
    our bathroom.
We laugh and laugh.
We slither over eachother
hungry snakes
biting and sucking
entwined
oblivious.

*   *   *

Coral and salmon, and aquamarine where night gives way to
sun. Peering from my loft, my mountain dropping down, steep
scarp, leveling into bluegreen and sandy desert blurring into the
eastern horizon. Blurring where the earth meets sky at dawn,
my body fluid from another memory lived again. Rima I return
to you at first light, I bring back all our ways of loving. Never
have I known such unabashed creativity and variation, such vulnerability. But you are in the city, over the Sierras on the Bay,
and I bask in my mountain home, this humble shack, cat on lap,
working out the nuances of my existence.

I was locked into the city, into my job and expensive living,
Rima you catalyzed me to take the leap. . . now I have my sweet
solitude. . . and also loneliness, and a gnawing desire to have a
change from sex as one, to hold another woman, to roll and play
as intensely as we once did. . . So few women come here who
embrace the power plays of roles, pain and its pleasure. It's those
nagging compromises again. I will never live in the city again. . .
it is give and take. While living alone I soothe my own hurts, I
stare much into mirrors, I cry for lovers who feared what I feared,
to make the break when wilderness tugs on the soul. And Rima,
sometimes tears roll down for our dances locked in memory,
relived only in my fantasies as the day slithers onto the land. And
I lie vulnerable to the rawness of the dawn.

Girl Gang

CRYSTAL BAILEY

I met Benta on a Thursday evening at a friend's house; I was having a cup of coffee and she walked in through the door, not even bothering to knock. My friend gave her a very warm hug. I watched the reddish brown glints in her hair and then the narrow beauty of her face; I liked the green shadows of her eyes and I couldn't help but linger on her lips—full, slightly moody looking and sweeping up at the corners. We were introduced and she gave me her hand in way of greeting. It was surprisingly strong—surprising because she seemed so slight and feminine—and I wanted our grasp to pull us together. Her eyes told me that she had similar interests. Throughout the evening, over a span of a couple of hours, we traded side glances, a few heart beating stares and then, when she got up to leave, giving me a beckoning glance, I got up too, and asked her if she wanted a ride home. Yes, she did, she said, and I followed her rounded ass, her purposeful, narrow shoulders, the swing of her hair, out the door.

We began to spend time together, drawn by the sexuality that licked at our veins. One evening I asked her to go with me to Lima's. She had heard of it and agreed. We entered the bar, a cavernous place on a dark San Francisco street corner. I had picked her up in my shiny blue MG; just as I had requested, she was waiting outside her place, dressed in rose and black—shoes, pants and light sweater. I paid for us both; the cover charge was minimal. I took her past a dance floor glittering with lights and studded with outfits of leather, up a sweep of stairs and through an ancient door into a room generally used for dressing. A few comfortable chairs—red and lush—skirted the edges of the room. Seated there were a small number of women. Two of them wore black leather. One had a beautiful whip hanging from her belt.

"Take your clothes off and pile them on this chair," I told Benta, looking firmly into her eyes.

She watched my face, her eyes flickered with arousal. She bent her head to her buttons and undid them with slightly clumsy fingers. The women watched as she removed her shirt, her large slow breasts swinging heavily as she bent then to the removal of her pants. Her dark patch, so neatly triangular between her legs, was inviting. She stood naked. I gave her a pair of black leather pants with a zipper that unzipped to the bottom of the crotch.

"Put these on, Benta."

She did, having to wiggle her sumptuous ass to fit. I zipped them for her, sealing her goods for later tasting. I gave her an unusually soft, black leather bra that, when she put it on, let her nipples stand open and uncovered.

"I want you available to me, Benta."

She showed her willingness by rubbing her very erect nipples against my shirt front: very titillating. I had a long leather thong, very supple without any stiff cutting edges.

"Pass this thong between your legs, inside your pants; one end should come from the back, the other from the front."

With some effort, having to partially unzip herself from the grip of her pants, she accomplished this, feeling the taste of the leather along her ass, through her tangled wetness. I imagined that her vagina was beginning to throb. All the women watched hungrily and silently. When she was rezipped, I turned her around and with the rear thong end tied her wrists together—tightly. Then I turned her about once again; her breath was getting slightly thick, her eyes were closed. I took a collar, a studded leather affair, and fitted it about her neck, roughly tightening it, making sure it wasn't choking tight, and then decisively snapped the front thong end to the collar. I knew the leather was rubbing the heat of her vagina into sticky wetness.

"Benta, I want you, I want your lips—baby—to go down on me, to suck my cunt." I pushed her firmly down onto her knees so that her mouth met the unzipping of my pants, met the lush of my wet dipped tangle. I pushed myself onto her. Her hungry tongue, hungry to please, eager to suck cunt, came down on me. I let her, I opened myself to her, I wanted the loving of her tongue and those wonderfully talented lips. She brought me coming with my hands stroking her hair and my voice calling out and out. For a moment she rested her face against my thigh. I was throbbing, rezipped my pants and pulled her to her feet.

With one hand on her elbow, I took her from that room, my own slim leather whip swinging from my belt. We went down the stairs, down yet another flight and into a dimly lit room where music played. A few couples danced, others crowded about tables laughing and drinking, and yet others played with one another, nipples becoming hard between fingers, vaginas being filled; women seeking arousal and pleasure. Benta and I danced. First I untied her hands, unsnapped the leather thong from her collar and slowly, teasingly, pulled the length through ass and cunt. She gripped my hand, indicating that I should go real slow, liking the slight bite of leather. I played around with her zipper, slid it down, exposing her cunt and then gripped her ass with my left hand, pressing her onto my leg. With my right hand I gently flicked the thong across her face; she flung back her head, rubbing her cunt on my leg with an abandon that I liked and encouraged with the tiny slaps of leather against her cheeks; she entered into the huge sweep of arousal. I knew her clitoris was swelling and swelling from the rubbing and soon she was jerking with orgasm, her lips pouting with gasps.

I unsnapped her collar and tossed it. I let my lips down onto her neck, softly biting her. My breath thickened, my heart stamped, with strong arms I pressed her into me. She moaned as I bore down, I flushed with wanting her, I rushed with wanting her and grabbed with strength, roaming her body as I bruised her neck. Each of us somewhat faint, we gyrated our hips together, turned in and out of each other's circling arms. Her movements invited me to take; my hands grazed her standing nipples. Then we were close, real close, dancing with aching crotch onto strong leg, hands coming down on hips, nipples, crushing her lips to mine. I pinched her nipples and, swamped by a rush of sensation, she stopped dancing, her eyes slightly glazed. Harder I pinched, she gasped,

143

gave little trembling moans, sending my fingers along the fine leather ribbing of her bra. The straps turned me on the way they delicately touched her handsome shoulders. My mouth took those straps down to her breasts, my hands freed the catch and as I slowly pulled the garment from her, I sank to my knees. My large hands pulled her breasts into my mouth, I sucked, she moaned, pressed my head, told me, "yes, baby, yes, harder, oh suck them, baby." I did, I bit and rubbed, took what I could into my mouth without choking.

Eventually I stood up and we danced a bit more, apart from one another, gaining our breath again. Then I took Benta into another room where seven friends of mine waited. I had requested that they meet us about eleven. Benta was stunning, she strode bare chested and with the sinuosity of a cat into the room and my friends looked at her, damp heat in their eyes. Her legs and ass were un- doubtedly hot in her leathers.

"Benta, come here." I motioned to where I had sat down. She crossed the room and stood before me, waiting. My hand reached out and rested on her hip, lightly my thumb wandered, curving towards her crotch. I felt her wanting me. Subtly she shifted her weight to open her thighs more. "You want it, Benta?"

She glanced around quickly at my friends, each of them watching her, their tensile hands poised and ready; her gaze returned to me. "Yes." Her voice was breathy, probably affected by the throb of her vagina.

"You ever heard of a gang bang, Benta?"

"Yes." She lowered her eyes. We could hear her swallow in the tense silence of the room.

"You want to get fucked like that, Benta?"

"Yes, yes, yes." She was melting fast, her pelvis pulsing and gyrating; she wanted to be taken.

"I asked these women, they're my friends, if they wanted to get involved in a girl gang fuck. I told them I was bringing a hot woman here, Benta. They were more than eager to come. Are you hot, Benta?"

She was softly moaning. Her hand moved to her crotch; my heart ran jagged and crazy watching her hand toy with her zipper. I wanted to spurt past this tease, to lunge upon her, to tear her pants from her, lay her open and take her myself—but I waited.

"Are you hot, Benta?" I repeated.

"Yes. I want to be fucked. Fuck me. I want all of you, I want to be taken. I want you, I want you!"

I grabbed her and laid her across my lap. Quickly two women tied her hands and her legs to the chair. She was writhing now; the scent of her was hugely strong and exciting to all of us. We were a girl gang lusting after a bitch in heat, and Benta was fully that. She flung her ass into the air, arching against her restraints.

"Fuck me, come on you cunts, fuck me!" Her words rose and the first woman tore Benta's zipper open and plunged in. No playing around, just a deep thrust. Benta screamed a welcome. The woman plunged, her face leaping with the fury of lust. I motioned the woman away with Benta only having a taste. The second woman stepped up. She came on slower, teasing, causing Benta to beg. We all watched the woman lay open Benta's lips, wet with ooze. Each of us felt that sight in our own cunts, it whipped us into a kind of animal lust. Silently I handed the woman my whip. We were heaving at the chests now. She flicked Benta's ass, Benta came. She flicked again, a little harder, her other hand playing at Benta's vagina mouth; then a series of sound slaps, the leather marking her skin. Her cries tattooed our ears. The next woman took over the whip and without warning came inside Benta with the soft, slender handle. Heatedly, crying with Benta, the woman fucked her. We watched, played with ourselves, some of us unzipped, others not.

"Oh! Uh! Cunts!" Benta opened, we could hear her vagina gulping and swishing around the whip handle.

The next two women came in and out of Benta softly, moving with ease and care. She felt it no less intensely but it was a slower rising, not quite so hurtling. We untied her, pulled her up and then I kissed her face, her lips, supporting her in my arms. The kisses wandered to her neck where I nipped then bit; one hand wandered to a breast, flicked her nipple then pinched. Her entire body quivered. Someone brought me two clamps covered with a soft, black leather. I put one on each of Benta's nipples. They not only pinched, but their weight dragged on her breasts; she loved it. The pressure wasn't a harsh one and when I swung one of the clamps with my finger, her upper body shuddered.

She was ready again. This time I had her put a shirt on. I gave her mine. Then I took her by the lapels. My strong arms commanded her stay. By now her pants had been fully removed. While I held her in one hand I began lightly slapping her face with the other. The sixth woman approached Benta from behind and entered her.

"Bitch, Benta, take it, take it." I whispered fiercely into her ear.

She was fucked, I slapped her repeatedly, sometimes hard, mostly for the light sting, but several times ferociously, tightening my hand in her shirt. I motioned the woman away and the last of the girl gang came up from behind. I took off slapping Benta and entered her cunt slow, sliding into the red wet. Very slow; I took my time, letting her come down a bit. She didn't want to come down, she shoved herself onto my fingers and tried to bite my shoulder.

"Fuck me, please, please. I want you. I've been waiting for you."

I obliged and entered her hard. At the same time the last woman entered her ass and the cries from Benta's mouth tore at our frenzy, pulled us into her, pulled the watching women's hands into the touching and taking. Heat, lust, our pleasure, spilled and bubbled, we dabbled, plunged, bit and sucked. Benta sagged in our arms and we slowed, all of us suddenly spent. We lowered her to the floor, removed my shirt from her torso. She was in a space all her own, barely aware of us.

We were her servants then. Blankets were brought, a pillow, and very slowly, bringing ourselves down too, we rubbed her, offering soothing caresses along this woman's body who had opened so far for us. We loved one another for sharing together. We began to sing a soft lullaby:

"We have traveled a long way into places we had not known. We found pleasure there, we went together, we came on home."

Dear Aunt Sadie:

Aunt Sadie's columns appear in the SAMOIS newsletter, offering advice, humor, gossip and miscellaneous information. We have collected some of the best items here for your enjoyment.

Dear Aunt Sadie,

I have a handsome pair of combat boots that I enjoy wearing but all that tight lacing makes it hard to remain dignified while taking them off during a scene. What do you suggest?

Sincerely, Butch Top

Dear Sir or Madam,

The answer, as usual, is simple. Require your slave to bring you a comfortable chair and then to prostrate herself at your feet. Using either her hands or her teeth, she should unlace and remove your boots both gracefully and efficiently. Any lapses in style or rhythm might be cause for reprimands on her shoulders or buttocks. Have fun.

Love, Aunt Sadie.

Riddle: How many S/M dykes does it take to change a light bulb?

Answer: Two—one bottom to do it and one top to tell her what to do.

Riddle: How many anti-S/M feminists does it take to screw in a light bulb?

Answer: At least four. One to handle the bulb, one to critique the word "screw," one to lend professional credentials to the operation, and one to find common ground with the utility company.

Dear Aunt Sadie,

Here is "What S/M Means to Me" with gratuitous *pun*ishment, compliments of the Phantom Punster.

Sadism and Masochism	Sex Maniac
Sensual and Mutual (the basics)	Southern Methodist
Simply Magnificent	Send Money
Sensory Memory	Sue Me
Sensual Magic	Service Manual
Sexual Magic	SM is the last word in feminiSM
South of Market	

Dear Aunt Sadie,

In yesterday's *Chronicle* The Question Man printed answers to the question "What did you do on your last date?" Here are some answers that never made it into the paper.

Lisa Athena, social worker, San Francisco: My lover was hot and impatient. Our dinner plans would have been ruined if I hadn't taken her out in a collar and leash. Later she apologized for her behavior and begged to be punished. Of course she really got it that night. It was a wonderful evening for both of us.

Lilith Deborahchild, carpenter, Berkeley: We met some friends at the Ramrod for a drink. Later at a women's sex party I got the best whipping I've had in a long time. And we fucked all night—with everybody. Just fantastic.

Jean Harker, office worker, Oakland: It was quiet, intense, sensual. My mistress had me serve her dinner. I was also permitted to eat. Later we continued with my training, especially in whipping, nipple torture, golden showers and sexual service. I am extremely grateful to my mistress and she wishes me to express this to you.

Aunt Sadie's Quiz: Where can you get tops for $4.95 and bottoms for the same price? Answer: at Bargain Surplus (come, come, who ever heard of a surplus of tops?) Of course, what you're getting is thermal underwear.

Dear Aunt Sadie,

Is masturbation S/M?

Hopefully yours, Jaynee "J.O." Offenbach

Dear J.O.,

It's all in your head. If you feel it is S/M then it is. By the way here is a helpful hint for women into tits and clits when they are alone. Attach your nipple clamps to an 18-inch string. Fasten the clamps to your nipples and with the string clenched between your teeth and a quick twist of your head you can jerk yourself off at both ends at once.

Love, Aunt Sadie

Dear Aunt Sadie,

She claims to love me dearly but all she ever does is whip me and fuck me. I dare not mention my desire to be bound, for milady is unable to tie a proper knot. What should I do?

Signed: At Loose Ends.

Dear Lucy:

This indeed is a knotty situation. Perhaps as you sit at her feet at night you could read to her from the Boy Scout handbook. There are also many adult books on ropecraft and knot tying although none of them are "strictly adult." Do not attempt to learn from commercial bondage magazines. Those shots are often posed for drama or effect and show positions that are impossible or unsafe. Rope bondage that does not rely on knots can be contrived with a variety of mechanical devices for securing ropes and chains, to be found in hardware stores, mountaineering shops and at the marine supply house. Happy shopping!

Love, Aunt Sadie

Dear Aunt Sadie,

Perhaps you remember me from the last soiree. I am the tall, elegant Victorian mistress in rich, dark brown. I want to solicit your advice on one slight problem I am having with my wardrobe. In order to keep my submissives in their proper places, I find myself having to keep track of a large number of keys and I begin to feel more like an ordinary jailer than the great and dark lady that I am. What can I do to relieve myself of the odious burden of so much hardware?

Most Sincerely, Aristo

Dear Aristo,

It is a pleasure to hear from a peer of your caliber. The solution to the key problem is a simple and elegant one. When your servants purchase padlocks, instruct them to buy locks of the same size and to look for the key number stamped on the right side of the bottom, not back, of each lock. Don't confuse it with the model number of the lock. You will then need only one, perhaps two, keys on your person and they can be displayed or concealed in leather, lace, or velvet according to your tastes.

Sincerely, Sadie

The Ministry of Truth provided Aunt Sadie with this bit of wisdom: Calling an S/M person sexist is like calling someone who plays Monopoly a capitalist.

Aunt Sadie asked readers to tell how they used S/M to eroticize situations in their daily lives. Here are some replies.

Dear Aunt Sadie:

When it became clear to both of us that I was becoming too dependent on my vibrator, my Mistress forbade me to use it without her express permission and required me to keep it tied up in a shoebox under the bed. Now when I vibrate it is a special treat instead of a mundane habit.

Dear Aunt Sadie:

As you know, even tops feel guilty about their behavior sometimes. I used to feel guilty if I didn't want to make love or even cuddle with my lover when she was crawling all over me. Sometimes we'd snarl at each other playing chase games in bed and believe me it was no fun. Now, if she gets too feisty when I feel down I have her sleep on a mat on the floor by the bed. She knows that emotionally I am paying very close attention to her and I know that I can have the physical space I need.

Dear Aunt Sadie:

I get home from work first, bring in the mail, and rush around the house doing dinner and organizing the evening. In the rush I used to scatter the mail about the house, reading it as I went from one activity to the next. My lover would be furious when she got home and couldn't tell if there were any letters for her. Now we have a little ritual every night in which I play "doggie delivery" and go about the house on all fours, collecting the mail and one by one laying the envelopes at her feet. She reads her mail, pats my head lovingly, we look into each other's eyes and get on with the evening.

Dear Aunt Sadie:

I had been moping around the house for days not wanting to type up my resume when my lover, finally exasperated, pulled me by the hair over to the typewriter and told me to sit. "You have until I get home from work tonight to finish that," she ordered. "Take your pants off, then start." I was very excited but puzzled. A few minutes later, as I was typing, I could feel her playing with my behind and then ooooh, she had slipped in an assplug! "And that does not come out until I take it out tonight." "Yes mistress," I answered, trying to keep my demure manner while being overcome with rushes of pleasure as I settled down to serious business. Ahh, if I only had known how fun typing could be when I worked downtown.

Handkerchief Codes: Interlude II

B R O W N (Shit)

"Shit! Oh no! Shit—I'd never touch that!" my lady protested.
I'm telling her that not only would I like it if she ate my asshole, but I might require her to savor the contents.

She's fascinated and horrified. Over a rather "special" dinner,
I tell her I've been watching my own shit for weeks to see what
foods produce various textures and odors. Suddenly, her eyes
cloud over, she looks at me again in that combination of fascination and horror and she realizes that this is indeed, a "special"
dinner. For the rest of the meal she exceeds her usual zeal in
seducing me with her charm and admiration, always trying to dis-
tract me from what is obviously on my mind.

After a delightful meal, I order her to fetch me a large china
bowl in which I deposit a tidy pile of after-dinner turds. "No,
no" is in her eyes as she also begs for my love. "Eat them or eat
me," I tell her. Her choice is obvious. "Kiss my sweet smelling
turds or you will spend half an hour tonguing my asshole." Her
choice is obvious. After I come and she pants some more I say,
"Eat them or I'll whip you to punish you for your lack of
enthusiasm." Her choice is obvious.

My fresh shit stays by the bed all evening, stays in my mind,
stays in her mind; proving that a lady can say, "Shit! Oh no! I'd
never touch that!" and still be very moved by it.

Y E L L O W (Golden Showers)
The orgy room is dark, full of grease and sex. My little pet has

been waiting all night for the treat I have arranged for her. In fact, we have been talking about it for weeks. She, sweetly complaining that I never give her enough warm, fragrant piss to cover her entire body; I drinking more beer and coffee than I really want in an attempt to satisfy my ever hungry—and thirsty—bottom. Our friends know of our "problem" and every now and then my little one would be reprimanded for sassing me with comments like "I bet Corrine could get me wet at least to the waist," or "Maybe the whole softball team could pee on me after a long Sunday afternoon celebration."

Well, now is her chance and since she is such an active little thing in seeking her own pleasure, I have instructed her to station herself at the bathroom door where she politely greets each party-goer in need of the facilities. She'll be there from midnight on, begging, asking, cajoling each top or bottom not to piss yet but to save her golden showers for a 2 a.m. special.

At the appointed hour I take all these lovely ladies and line them up, one behind the other, ass to belly. I caress my pet and find that her own moisture is barely contained as I give her permission to drop to her knees and crawl between the legs of our understanding friends. She receives piss from each of the twelve dripping lesbians. At the end of this tunnel of love she stops to savor her drenching, but the woman at the head of the line demands that the drops of wet, stinging urine be licked from the inside of her thighs. Immediately my lover turns around and goes through the entire line, licking up the mess that has been made on her behalf and totally thrilling us all.

KHAKI (Uniforms and Military)

I'm wearing army fatigues and a form fitting black military shirt. I apply a gash of cruel red lipstick to remind her that I am all woman within my command outfit.

I put her through her paces, watching her tits jiggle, her ass sweat, her cunt drip.

Yet she's not quite sexy enough for me. Nor, really, for her own pleasure. So I put her in the cage and allow her to lick my big black boots through the bars.

When we are both thoroughly aroused I return to my bed and we listen to each other masturbate.

Later, I punish her for experiencing pleasure unsuitable for a prisoner and for spying on an officer.

When I take her across my lap for her punishment she follows instructions to keep her fist in my cunt as I paddle her. She comes just seconds before I do and she is punished for preceding an officer...

FISTFUCK
yea, some
women
really do
like it.
MORE, MORE.

From *Jessie*

PAT CALIFIA

I wandered around the huge loft, dodging elbows in blue cotton and carelessly held cigarettes. Small knots of women sprawled in chairs, doing more laughing than talking, unaware of how raucous they had become. "What was this, a benefit or something?" I heard someone ask behind me. No one answered her.

The party had gone on until the floor was littered and the room almost empty. It was past midnight. Women who had to work in the morning and the tight, fledgling couples and the militant non-smokers had picked up their jackets and gone home. The rest of us would probably have to be asked to leave one at a time, and helped out with a hand on the elbow. In the meantime, it was still possible to convince yourself you had a chance to pick somebody up, and there were enough dancers to attract a small ring of voyeurs, all of whom seemed to have their arms around each other.

The women selling beer were harassed and impatient. "We're going to close," one of them told me over an ice chest full of beer and cold water. Her black hair was stringy with perspiration. "Oh," I said. "Can I have a Bud." She sighed with exasperation and fished me out a can. "Eighty," she grunted. I dug up exact change. She tossed my dimes and nickels into a little cardboard box and hustled over to her comrades, who were sharing a joint in a not-too-dark corner. "You're welcome," I politely informed her scapula.

"Bad service is politically correct at women's events," someone said at my elbow. While I was laughing I checked her out. She was tall and blonde, with the shoulders of a swimmer. I love butch-looking women. They are disconcerted by my admiration, my willingness to be flattered into bed and ordered around. I blithely ignore their suspicion, continuing to give them what they like without talking about it. I'm not looking for a husband or a daddy, and I don't consider myself a femme—I just turn on to aggressive and strong women. I love french kissing and finger fucking, and I could very easily imagine this woman probing my mouth with her tongue, arranging me on her bed to allow her to penetrate me still more deeply, more fully.

"Hey, Maxine!" somebody yelled. "Get your ass over here and DANCE with me!"

Her eyebrows, which had begun to frame a question, shot back to home base. " 'Scuse," she said, and shouldered by. I sighed wistfully, shreds of fantasy trailing uselessly around me. Tomorrow, as I salted my scrambled eggs, it would come to me in a sudden burst of inspiration—what I should have said to hook her attention. Alas and damn.

I reminded myself sternly that masturbation is the foundation of female sexuality, and a mode of gratification that is every bit as valid as getting it on with a partner. I tried strenuously to work up a little enthusiasm for the new $40 vibrator a friend had brought me from Japan. It was only a week old, and bright orange. I asked myself, what would Betty Dodson think if she could see me standing here, practically in tears because I can't get some woman who doesn't even know my name to seduce me? She would hit me over the head with my own cunt portrait and send me back to Remedial Sexuality with my finger taped to my clit.

I could make myself laugh, but I couldn't make myself any less horny. I started thinking about Jessie, lovingly enumerating all those things about her that made my toes curl.

One of my more verbal lovers once told me I was a starfucker. She was as accurate as she was hostile. Oh, my, yes, Jessie was a celebrity. She played bass for a women's band that performed regularly in the city. And she was good. In fact, The Bitch had been playing for the dance tonight—which is why I showed up.

There wasn't a woman in town who didn't want to be held the

way Jessie held that bass guitar, and she knew it.

At every performance, Jessie had this little ritual she went through. She always started off behind the rest of the band, in the shadows where you could hardly see her. While the rest of the band was still playing around with high C, Jessie would slip off her leather jacket and hand it to her current lover, who would accept it, carefully fold it, and carry it offstage, to jeers and cheers from the audience. We all thought it was humiliating as hell, but none of us would have refused to do it.

Just when you were ready to bet they wouldn't get started for another half hour, Jessie would hit a chord and they'd be on. They nearly always opened with the Stones' song, "Bitch" (what else?). She didn't sing on that one, but if you sat in the first two rows, you could catch her cynical smile at the crucial lines.

As the set progressed, she would move closer and closer to the audience until she had assumed front center stage. By this time, they were playing some of their own music—Snake Goddess, Boxcar Bertha, Liberated Lady—and Jessie had kicked out all the stops.

They never did encores. After they disappeared from the stage, a lot of leftover energy would be flying around, and sometimes it would do strange things. One post-concert crowd was treated to a knife fight in the best tradition of West Side Story. When members of The Bitch were confronted about this in the feminist press and asked to comment, they all disclaimed responsibility and shuffled and apologized—all of them, that is, except Jessie. She scowled and announced that it was time for women to reclaim their heritage of violence. Then she offered the interviewer a hit of coke.

There was a little stir at the head of the stairs. I looked over crossly, unwilling to break my introspection. Then I saw who was causing the commotion. She had come back. It was Jessie.

I had an immediate physical reaction to her presence: my clit jumped. Then it started throbbing in time with my heartbeat. As I watched her speak to acquaintances here and there, moving on before a greeting could turn into a conversation, I began to shake a little—an erotic attack of fear.

The party picked up. There was a last minute rush on the

refreshment table. More couples started dancing.

Jessie found her spot on the stair railing and leaned there, not moving. I ran my eyes up and down the slim, well-muscled lines of her body, teasing myself with estimates of her strength, wondering what she would feel like pressed down against me, her arms wrapped around me.

She was taller than me by six or seven inches. Her dark hair was clipped short and neat. She was wearing a black velvet jacket that showed off her shoulders and lean build to perfection. A long, white scarf was knotted around her throat. Whenever she moved, the fringes floated behind her.

Perched in my window, I wondered about Jessie. A friend of mine told me that her last lover left her because "she was tired of being pushed around." Pushed around? How? I asked. My friend smiled mysteriously and began to roll another joint. It was the kind of remark that was calculated to set all my fantasy movie machinery in gear, and it had.

My fantasies have a way of turning into challenges. I started to frighten myself with the idea of going up to her. What the hell—she was a woman, like me. Puts on her pants one leg at a time like the rest of the Lesbian Nation. Wouldn't it be enough to just talk to her for five minutes, introduce myself, even if she snubbed me?

I found myself transported to her side. She turned her head to stare at me, and all the beer I had drunk ran straight into my kidneys. We were too close. If I puffed out my breath, it would disturb the downy hairs along the sides of her neck.

She did not back away, just gave me a cold little once-over. I forced myself to stand my ground, keeping my feet apart and my hands unclenched at my sides, while she took in my tousled gold-brown hair, the embroidered, gauzy blouse, and my faded button-fly levis. But I could only bear to look her in the eye for a few seconds before I had to drop my gaze to the toes of her boots. I was in agony. I had no alibi, no catchy opening line, no excuse. I needed a haircut. One of the buttons was missing from my fly. I tried not to pant, knowing that would expand my cleavage, and wound up hyperventilating. When I glanced up, she was, indeed staring at my breasts. . .or was she looking at my throat? Then

159

her eyes flicked to my wrists, and back to my neck, and I knew what had caught her attention.

I was wearing, as I always do, two braided leather bracelets and matching collar. It sounds dramatic, but most people don't notice them unless they're looking for them.

If she read me, it didn't show on her face. "What's your name?" she demanded.

"Liz."

She nodded, and continued to stare at me while she finished her beer. "Dance?" she said finally, and walked toward the music without looking back to see if I would follow.

I was there when she turned around. Her arms accepted me, fit me to her, and we began to duel with one another. I wondered how many women had been settled against her hip. How many eager cunts had pressed just where mine was pressed? More than she could remember, to judge from the practiced, almost automatic rhythm of her dance.

At first, we stared over each other's shoulders, our faces expressionless. This dance is so intimate that some formality must be maintained, even as one of her breasts fits between yours and you feel your own breasts similarly nestled. You must pretend there is no flame between you, no erotic friction, no liquid silk sliding between your thighs. It wasn't easy for me to feign nonchalance. She was damnably competent. I finally quit wondering whether I was having hot flashes or cold chills and just let waves of excitement flicker up and down me, praying I wouldn't shiver in her arms. Her own smell (the salt of perspiration, the secret hollows and folds of her skin, the musk and wild onion of her sex) was mixed with tobacco and booze, and it aroused me so painfully that I wanted to bury my nose in her hair, her armpits, the folds of her labia.

She started playing with the leather band around my throat. "You have interesting taste in jewelry," she said casually. "What is this, a choker or something?"

"It's a collar," I said.

She was looking for a snap or a knot. "Doesn't it come off?" she asked, turning it. I smiled. "Well," she shrugged, "*I'm* impressed."

She let me snuggle up to her, and rested her chin on the top of my head. "You're very sensitive," she drawled, stroking my neck. Goosebumps covered me in a flash. "Just the lightest touch...and your skin is so pale." She pretended to take a professional interest in my health—"I hope you're not anemic?"

"No, but I bruise easily."

"Aah." Her nostrils quivered.

My inner lips had begun to swell, unfurling themselves until they were in full bloom. I was slippery with hot vaginal oils. She continued to tease me, shifting suddenly to apply pressure when I least expected it, clinging and grinding against me when I tried to move away. I threw back my head and looked at her, letting her see the flush on my cheeks. Her eyes narrowed, and she began to coax more sensation from me, trying to see how high I could get without breaking away. My breath was coming in fits and starts. But it was she who suddenly uttered a short cry of surprise and ecstasy. I was startled—flattered. She took my chin in her cupped hand and brought me to her mouth. Teeth, clean and sharp, cut my lips. Her tongue rippled against my inner cheeks and palate. I moaned inside her mouth, safe, where no one could hear me. My vagina was a fountain, little spurts of lubrication welling up out of me.

"I'm kissing you too hard," she whispered, and released me.

"I can take rougher treatment than that," I murmured in reply, and laid my cheek on her shoulder.

She twisted her hand in my hair and forced me to look at her. There was something like pity in her eyes, then that was replaced by a predatory joy. "Can you really," she threatened.

"I can play any game you can come up with."

"But I'm not playing."

I considered carefully. "If anyone changes their mind, it will be you," I promised quietly.

She squeezed my ass. Hard. "Do you know, Maisie, I have never let a dare go by. Not once in my whole little life."

She danced me into a dark corner, kissing me and up and down between my ear lobe and shoulder. Her lips were soft. She took little nibbles of me, like a doe working on a sapling. Now she pressed me against the wall, standing between me and the crowd.

We kissed, and she slipped her hands under the thin fabric of my blouse to fondle my breasts. My nipples responded instantly to her touch, pointed and hard as little pine cones. She used her tongue in my mouth, and I couldn't stop my hips from responding. She stroked my back, belly, kissed me again and again, pinching my nipples and squeezing my breasts.

"How does that feel?" she whispered in my ear. "Did you know you're dancing all over the place? Ooh, let me do that again. No—take your hand away—I want to. You want me to. I can tell you like it. You're so turned on, I think I could make you come right now, in front of everybody." She began to call me names—slut, bitch, whore, cunt—and they were rich and resonant in my ear, like an incantation. "You're a very bad girl," she said. "I think I should take you home with me and teach you a lesson. Only I don't know if I can wait until I get you home."

It seemed to me that everyone in the room must be staring. I tried to protest without drawing attention to us, but when Jessie started working on the buttons of my levis, I shrieked.

She stopped what she was doing, her hand resting on my hip. "Apparently, I'm not the one who's going to change her mind," she drawled.

I winced. "Touché. I concede the point."

"Mmm." She wound her fingers in my hair. "What else are you willing to concede?"

"Whatever you can make me concede."

"You won't go along peacefully, huh? I have to use force?"

"Don't you want to?"

Jessie laughed. "Point for you." She put her hands up to her throat and untied her scarf. I stood perfectly still while she threaded one end through the ring on my collar. "This should insure your compliance," she said, tying the knot with loving care.

The stairs were only a few steps away. She led me out, holding onto the other end of the scarf. I may have imagined it, but I thought I heard someone say, "Did you see that?" and someone else say, "Oh, my God!" behind us.

I concentrated on the high heels of her boots as she led me out of the building to her car. "They know about you," I said jealously

162

as she unlocked the door.

"And now they know about you, too," she said harshly. "Get in the car. I didn't ask you to worry about my maiden reputation."

The car was so little and low, I had to hunch myself and duck, then almost fall into the bucket seat. Jessie was already seated, whistling through her teeth and drumming her fingers on the steering wheel.

We drove for awhile without talking. It was Jessie who broke the silence. "You know, you almost scared me off back there with your fancy jewelry. I wondered if we were in the same league. I mean, I don't wear my handcuffs on my belt."

So I wasn't the only one scared of being outclassed. That was reassuring. I smiled with satisfaction, and didn't say anything.

"So where did you get them?" she demanded, a little impatiently.

"It's a long story."

"This is a long ride. Tell me."

I shook my head. "You won't believe it."

"I won't, huh. Come on, quit being coy."

I rubbed my face, feeling a little sleepy. Where to start...

"Well," I sighed, "let's see. My first experience with S/M was with Sue. And she had to hound me for months to let her tie me up and try some light spanking, nothing heavy-duty. Okay. Well, I found out I really dug it, and I started suggesting we move into it a little further. She freaked out. We broke up, ostensibly over class differences, and there I was with all these new feelings and lots of curiosity, and nobody to talk to about it. I think I tried once to explain to this friend of mine, my best friend in fact. We came out at the same college during different semesters. So I was trying to describe this new component of myself I had begun to unearth, and *she* freaked out, too. She said something like, 'After the months I've worked at the Rape Crisis Center, I can't stand to listen to this,' and ran like a bunny. The next time I called up a few of my other old friends, they treated me with what I thought was distaste. So I gave up calling anybody I used to know."

"Sounds familiar," Jessie said. "Where did you go from there?"

"I spent about a month just going to my shop and coming straight home. Staring at TV. Then I got disgusted with myself

163

and fed myself a couple of drinks and drove myself down to one of the men's leather bars. I was lucky the first time—it was real crowded, the bartender didn't spot me, so I hung out all night, tucked behind the jukebox, taking everything in a mile a minute. The next time I went there, it wasn't so busy, and they kicked me out. So I went down the block to the next bar. It was real hard. But I kept thinking, there must be women like me somewhere, I can't be the only one, and sooner or later they'll show up here, too. Because there is no place else to go." I paused to take a deep breath, but Jessie didn't say a word. She was fascinated. I wondered how much of my story was her story.

"Well, one night I was having a terrible time. I had hit my three favorite places. None of the men I knew were there, and I got bounced out. So I checked out this tiny little place I usually never bothered with. I just wanted a drink and a place to sit. So I walked in, asked for a beer, and the guy behind the bar says, 'I don't want to be rude, honey, but this is a men's bar. I think you better leave.' I didn't even try to argue, I just slid off the stool and headed for the door.

"'Can she stay if I buy her a drink?' somebody asked. I thought I was hearing things. It was a crisp, very female voice. I did this slow motion turn and panned the room. She was standing in the doorway, with the darkness behind her. As she moved toward me, I saw that she was wearing a black satin dress and a diamond choker. When she was about ten feet from me, she stopped, and threw her long, black hair back over one shoulder. She tilted her head and looked at me. It was obvious she found me very amusing.

"I don't believe this," Jessie said.

"Shut up." She continued to grumble, but I ignored her. "She made a little motion with her hand. I followed her to a table. Everything became more and more unreal. The bartender brought us each a tequila sunrise. She took off her gloves—slowly—and tossed them to me. I folded them and laid them in my lap. I couldn't understand why I'd caught her eye. I was wearing all the leather I had—a beat-up pair of boots and a jacket. I looked like I got lost on my way to see the Ramones.

"I think her first words to me were, 'Do you come here often?' Some cornball line like that. Her voice was rich, so powerful it was a little threatening. Like holding a conversation with a jaguar. She had my whole story in five minutes. From out of nowhere, she produced a little white card. There was an address on it, nothing else. 'Come there tomorrow at ten,' she said, and held out her hand for her gloves. When she turned to go, a flash of white thigh was exposed. Her dress was slit up the sides. And I saw that she had a riding crop stuck in her boot."

The grumbling had subsided into silent skepticism. I continued smoothly on.

"I presented myself the next day as requested. I dressed to represent my status, a white dress with a high neck and long, tight sleeves.

"She was seated in her living room, wearing the same outfit I had first seen her in. She had a lot of Victorian furniture—a large velveteen couch, stuff like that. The first thing she did was tell me to bring a tray with coffee and little cakes in from the kitchen. I think some of the coffee slopped over the edge of the cups onto the silver tray. The cups had been filled awfully high. And that wouldn't do. That wouldn't do at all. I didn't think the punishment was proportioned to the crime, but it was gratifying none the less.

"When it was finished, as we nibbled on pastries and drank the cold coffee, she made me an offer. She told me that if I would stay with her for about a month, she would give me a taste of every technique she knew, at the end of which time, if I had performed satisfactorily, she would reward me with permanent cuffs and collar. She also told me that when my training was complete, she would put me out, and I would never see her again.

"It was crazy, and I loved it. I agreed at once. Most days, I went to work at my shop just the way I always had, but at night I went back to her house and entered this fantasy world where I was her slave and slept on a cot at the foot of her bed. I helped her dress and undress, did typing and cooking for her, brought her things she needed. When it struck her fancy, she would find fault with something I had done and use that to build another lesson on. She was very careful, very knowledgeable, and she made sure I always got off. Sometimes she stopped just short of pushing things to the point where she found her pleasure because I couldn't handle it. But that was only necessary in the beginning.

"One night, she woke me out of a sound sleep and told me to follow her. We went into the room. She undressed me, oiled my skin, put me in standing bondage, then she braided the cuffs around my wrists and the collar around my throat. She had already packed my suitcase. Without saying a word, she brought it in and set it by the door. Then we played our last scene. It was all for her. That was the only time she ever gave me amyl, and she gave me quite a lot of it. Between beatings, she would use my mouth. When I was finally too exhausted to take any more, she left me standing on the platform and sat on the table in front of me and pleasured herself—first with her hands, then with a vibrator. I was angry, humiliated, frustrated and terribly turned on. I went crazy trying to get to her. And I needed to come so badly myself, I couldn't see straight. She started to laugh. She was still laughing when she lowered my hands, unchained me, and walked out. I could still hear her chuckling as she shut and locked her bedroom door. I dressed myself and left."

Jessie was hooting and pounding on the steering wheel. "I can't stand it, I can't stand it! Are you bullshitting me? Did that really happen? Hot damn! And I think I'm wicked and perverse."

All I could do was grin and swear that yes, it really had happened.

"Well," she yawned, reaching for another cigarette, "this is a challenge to my professional reputation. With competition like that, I better bring out the heavy artillery. Woman, I can't wait to get my hands on you. I can still feel those nice, soft tits of yours." She chuckled. "I really thought you were going to wiggle right out of your skin back there in that nice, dark corner. Do you do that for everybody who puts the make on you?"

"No."

"Just for me?"

"Just for you."

"Liar. Unbutton your jeans. Put one hand inside your pants. Can you feel your pubic hair?"

"Yes. It's crisp and curly."

"What color is it?"

"Black."

"You must not be a real blonde, then. Cigarette—but don't

move that hand."

I managed to light the cigarette with my left hand. She watched me, amused by my fumbling.

"Slide your hand down and just cup it over your cunt. But don't try to beat off. Just leave that hand quiet on your cunt, like a good girl."

"I can feel the heat—Jessie—"

"I think I'd like to listen to the radio," she said to no one in particular, and turned it on. She sang along with the music, her harsh, vibrant voice reminding me (if I needed reminding) who I was sitting next to.

She switched off the radio in the middle of a song. "You can put your finger between the inner lips, down by your hole. Are you wet?"

"Yes," I gasped. "I'm wet enough to drown someone."

"Put your finger just barely inside the opening. Move in little, light circles."

"I'm burning!"

"Burn."

There was no sound in the car save the purring of the engine and my own labored breathing.

"Can you get two fingers inside your cunt?"

"Easy."

"Do it. Fuck yourself. I want to hear it."

I buried fingers inside myself and pumped. The juices made sucking noises as my hand moved up and down.

"How do you get off? Do you put your finger on your clit?"

"No, I do it just like this."

"Do you want to come?"

"Yes. I can't stand this. I need—"

"I don't care what you need. You'll wait until I want to hear you come. Run your finger up and down between your inner and outer lips. Spread the wetness up and cover your clit with it."

"It's slippery and smooth. Feels like being stroked all over."

"Jostle your clit a little bit."

"I can't find it. It's gone up under the hood."

Her knuckles on the steering wheel had gone white. She was staring intently at the road, but her breathing had quickened.

"I need to come. Please, let me come. I'll be good for you later, I promise. I'll do anything you want. Anything. Just. . . let me. Come. Now, please, please." I was babbling, I was begging so hard.

God, she was pleased with herself. "You can start," she told me.

I cupped my hand over my mound and dabbled a finger in the molten hole of my vagina.

"Make more noise."

I let myself moan. I couldn't believe the things I was saying, the sounds I was making. My hand moved faster, harder, higher. But my climax hung off, waiting—

"Go on, come. Come now."

That was all it took. I had waited so long, my orgasm was unbelievably intense. My vagina tightened like a fist, then convulsed and shuddered. I counted contractions as I continued to hold and squeeze my vulva. Waves of pleasure ran down my thighs, melted away, and filled me with a warm, sleepy glow.

Jessie pulled into a driveway and turned off the engine. She reached for me and searched my body with her hands, feeling the film of perspiration that covered me from head to toe. She explored my cunt, running her fingers up and down the inner lips and probing inside me briefly. "You weren't kidding," she said. "You really are wet! Are you going to sing that pretty for me?" She nuzzled my neck. "That was quite a performance."

I didn't respond. My eyes were half-closed. I felt limp and langorous. She tapped my cheek lightly. "Wake up. We haven't even started yet." The blows began to sting, and I put my hand up to ward them off. She grabbed my wrist. "What happened to all that sweet submission, huh? You promised to do anything for me, remember? I do. You owe me, honey."

She got out, came around to my door, and dragged me out of the car. Tugging on the scarf, she said, "Heel," and headed for her door. I almost stumbled, then recovered my footing and followed her.

I couldn't guess where we were going. All I could see were storefronts. But she stopped in front of an iron grating and took out her keys. "No neighbors," she told me with a grin. "It took me three months to find this place. I couldn't afford to sound-proof my last apartment, and I got kicked out for making too much noise. The rent is cheap, too."

Nobody could hear us? I felt a twinge of alarm. I hardly knew her. Anything could happen. How could I trust her? Because she never once showed a sign of doubting herself, something in me responded. There are plenty of people you've known for years that you'd never consider allowing to tie you up. Who knows why I trusted her? It was an arbitrary decision, after all, and one perhaps not totally in my control.

She held the grating open behind her. We climbed the stairs, our heels clicking on the stone steps. Her key rattled the lock. She pushed me in ahead of her, locking the door behind us. It was absolutely dark. I could not tell if I stood in a room or a hallway. She moved closer to me until her breasts kissed my shoulders and stood, not quite touching me, for several seconds. Then she sighed. Her expelled breath contained such weariness and resignation—I was overcome by an irrational desire to hug her knees and weep.

She seized my wrists, brought the scarf back through my crotch, and tied my hands together. The deftness of her movements provoked my lust again. Being tied makes me feel safe and somehow confident and very, very sexy.

She moved away from me, returning with a lit candle. "We'll go that way to the bathroom," she said, pointing down the hall. I took a step in that direction. She slapped me, hard. I rocked back on my heels, and she hit me again. My face burning, I stared at the floor and tried to control my tears. "Not so goddam fast," she hissed. "Who gives the orders here? You?"

"No, no," I stuttered.

She struck out again. "Get down on your knees, damn you. Get down."

I almost fell in my hurry to avoid any more blows. I could not balance with my hands, which were tied behind me. Once on my knees, her hips were inches from my nose. "I'm sorry," I choked.

"Sorry," she sneered. "Do you think that's all it takes to get yourself off the hook? 'I'm sorry,'" she mimicked. "You're not sorry, you're stupid. You don't do anything until I tell you to do it. Have you got that? Or are you too stupid to take orders?"

I couldn't answer. I must have leaned toward her, for she took

169

me by my hair and pulled my head back. "Why are you in such a hurry?" she murmured, stroking my hot cheek. "Did you think I was going to fuck you in the bathtub?" I saw her hand go back —flinched—the grip on my hair tightened, and she held my head while she slapped me.

"You don't realize just how helpless you are," she crooned into my upturned face. "I could leave you tied up all night and never even touch you. I could open the front door and push you downstairs. Where would you be then? Hmm? Or I could go out myself, for a drive. Maybe back to the dance to pick up another piece of ass. There are plenty more where you came from. Don't you think you'd better behave yourself? You better think about someone else's pussy for a change. Keep me happy, babe, or I won't get you off. After all, that's what you came here for, isn't it? A little fancy sex? Someone who would tickle your slit?"

I was blushing furiously. Tears were starting to wet my cheeks.

"Oh, look, she's going to cry. Are you trying to turn me on? Hmm, damsel in distress? Quit looking at the ceiling. Get your head down where it belongs. Look at me, here."

Her hips were tantalizingly close. "I was going to let you eat my cunt," she whispered, "but now, I don't know." She unzipped her jeans. Her pubic hair sprang from the zipper like a handful of soft, dark feathers.

"Please," I moaned.

"Beg me. You don't really deserve it."

I exerted every ounce of my persuasive powers. I started with a simple offer to lick her clit, and went on to describe the incredible and probably impossible things I wanted to do to her.

"Whimper for it, bitch."

"Let me kiss your cunt. Let me suck on your lips, rub my nose and my chin against your clit and blow hot air over your vulva. I'll do it good for you. I'll lick you so lightly, so carefully, as long as you like. Please, Jessie."

She teased me, calling me a pussy-kisser, a cunt-lapper. Yes, something inside me said. I am all those things. And right now, that's all I want to be. I ached to redeem myself. My mouth heated, watered, hurt with the need to service her.

She shucked her pants. I kept my place. "Better," she said

approvingly. "You're learning." She moved forward. "Tilt your head back a little," she told me. She shoved her pussy into my face, enveloping my eyes and nose and mouth in her cunt. "Remember me," she said, rubbing her perfume into my skin. "That is my smell, the essence of me. Now open your mouth a little and give me your tongue. Suck me. Go ahead. Eat me out. Flick that little pink tongue on my clit. Come on, you wanted it. Do it."

I put my face between her thighs and devoured her, whimpering with greed. My mouth was full of her soft folds and thick honey and stray little curly hairs. She jumped when I hit a spot just above her clit, so I lavished every caress my lips and tongue could devise on it. It didn't take long. She clamped my head to her, shook and bucked, crying my name.

When she pushed me away, my cheeks were smeared with her juices. She cupped my head in both hands and wiped my face with her thumbs. Our eyes met. "Now you have a taste of what I want," she whispered. "I am going to possess you utterly, for my own pleasure, make you completely and totally mine. Are you willing?"

"I've never wanted anything more."

"That's the last time I'll ask for your permission or consent. Follow me." I struggled to my feet.

She took me into the bathroom, tossed two pearls of bath oil into the tub and emptied a packet of bubble bath in after them. While hot water rushed from the faucet, she untied my hands and commanded me to strip. Perched on top of the john, she watched me undress, keeping a firm hold on the scarf, which was still knotted to my collar. Once I was naked, she tied the end of the scarf to a hook set high on the back of the door. She handled and examined me, squeezing my breasts and buttocks, slapping me lightly a couple of times on the ass. When the tub was full, she retied the scarf to a handhold set in the wall above a large soap dish so I could get into the water. Then she settled back to watch me bathe.

Jessie obviously spent a lot of leisure time in her bathtub. There were several different brushes, cloths, soaps, scrubbers and sponges arranged on a bath wheel. And there were enough towels around for four people. I lathered myself thoroughly and slowly, rinsing with equal care. She made me stand up and face her to wash my cunt, smiled, and told me to wash it again.

When I got out, she dried me, using a very soft towel. All she had to do was pat me gently all over, and the moisture vanished from my skin. She would not let me dress again, but she did let me pee before wrapping me in another towel and leading me into another room.

She didn't turn on the lights, so I couldn't see clearly, but I picked out the vague shape of a piano in the corner, some rock 'n roll posters on the walls, and sliding doors to a large closet on my left. It was a long room, and she kept going, toward the back. There was a balcony on my right. The glass doors let in some light from the street, and I could see potted plants sitting outside. A tape deck and stereo sat in front of the balcony. The floor was covered with a deep, soft Oriental rug. To my left was her bed. It had four posters of even height, hand-carved statuettes of naked women. And there was a large wardrobe sitting against the back wall. It was here that she led me. She opened its doors. A light came on inside it.

Mirrors had been hung on the doors and back panel of the wardrobe. I was startled by the picture we made. We were a study in contrasts. I was small in front of her, very naked, my skin rosy from the heat of my bath. My full curves were juxtaposed with her height and angularity; the black velvet suit. She looked the part of a perfect gentleman-dyke who just happened to have a lady on a leash.

We spent some time looking at ourselves. Our reflection fell behind the whips and restraints she had hung inside the cupboard. She touched each one, setting them all to swaying. There was a Victorian walking cane, a riding whip, a cat, a bullwhip, and some others I didn't know any name for. Most of them looked too menacing to be applied to human flesh. I hoped they were there for effect only.

While my attention was engaged by the instruments of flagellation and various other toys in her closet, she reached for a long rope that dangled from the ceiling. She clipped the end of it through both bracelet rings, and removed her scarf from around my neck. I was sorry to see it go, it being the first thing that had bound me to her. She tickled my nose with the fringes, trying to make me laugh. I wouldn't. "Well, if you insist on getting sentimental about it," she shrugged, and tied it around my eyes.

I could hear her moving around, humming, picking things up, opening drawers. She turned on a little electric heater—I could hear its fan. She pushed a tape into the stereo, and Santana throbbed softly in the background, gathering power.

The hairs on my skin stirred slightly, announcing that she had returned and was standing quite close to me. "I'm going to touch you," she said, and left me time to wonder how and when. I anticipated a slap, a whip, a caress, a scratch—but not what actually happened.

She stroked me with oil. Warm oil. Her touch was firm and possessive, and left me feeling both valued and valuable. She rubbed the lubricant into my skin from the neck down, kneeling and placing my feet one by one on her thigh to massage them.

Then I felt cold metal swing against my belly. She passed a chain through the ring of my collar, through my legs, up my back, and padlocked it at the back of the collar. "Nice," I heard her murmur. "It gleams against your skin. You make a fetching slave."

I moved a little to feel the pull of the chain against my vulva. It was snug, providing just the right amount of friction. The oil made my thighs slip unexpectedly past each other, giving me a feeling of sensuous insecurity.

"You like?" she asked me, using a sleazy, Tijuana postcard salesman accent.

I did not respond.

"I like. Too bad you can't see yourself. You'll just have to use your imagination. In fact, that's all you're going to have for the next little while—your imagination. Because I'm leaving."

I was dismayed. I twisted my head, but the blindfold prevented me from catching any glimpse of her. And my ears were not reliable—I could not tell if her voice came from behind me, to my side, or in front of me.

"Think about all those nice play things you saw hanging in my closet. And imagine how alluring you are in chains, blindfolded, with your arms above your head." The palm of her hand barely brushed my nipples. "You have beautiful breasts anyway, but now—well. . ." I heard footsteps. "Try not to dwell on all the dreadful things I'm going to do to you when I get back," she called. "If I get back," she added thoughtfully, as she closed the door.

The minute she left, I lost all track of time. I seemed to be there, alone, for hours. The music was still going, but I wasn't familiar with how tape decks worked or with that album. Maybe it had played through several times.

My arms were not stretched so tight as to be uncomfortable, and the rug and electric heater kept me from getting chilled. But still, I fidgeted. Where was she? Was she taking a bath? Watching TV? I couldn't hear anything from the rest of the house. I squirmed impatiently. What if she had decided to leave and go back to the dance? Maybe she was asleep on the couch.

My frustration was invaded by an overwhelming sensory memory. I could hear her say, "Tilt your head back." And I was overcome by the perfume of her sex, felt her rub her pussy into my face. "Remember me," she had said. "This is me, my essence."

I no longer cared how much time had passed. I waited patiently, even blissfully, only shifting position to make myself more comfortable.

I did not hear the door knob turn, or her footsteps falling on the carpet. Once again, it was some imperceptible heating of my skin, an oh-so-slight stirring of the hairs on the back of my neck, that warned me I was again in her presence.

She removed the chain that bisected my body, lowered my hands and unclipped the rope that held my wrists together. Hooking her finger through both my bracelets, she led me—still blind-folded—in the direction of her bed. She positioned me so I could feel the edge of the mattress on the back of my calves.

"On your back and spread your legs," she ordered. "Get your hands up and out." She used a flat, silky rope to tie my hands to the corner posts of her bed, and secured my ankles the same way. "I'm going to take your blindfold off," she said, slipping a pillow under my head. "I want you to see how fuckable you look." The cool silk trailed across my face.

She had drawn a folding screen across the foot of the bed. On the back of the screen was a beautiful, delicate painting of a partially clothed Japanese geisha. She was seated in her bedroom, and between her feet she held a large mirror, tilted to reflect her genitals. Only the mirror was real, so I was the one who was caught in the mirror, not her.

My thighs were soft and round. They looked very white and vulnerable, spread open against the black satin bedspread. And my ass swelled invitingly, a little crease of it showing. My inner lips and clitoris nestled, rosy and wanton, in a full nest of dark curls.

"Look up," she said.

There was a mirror on the ceiling as well. I realized that if I was not looking at my own genitals, I would be viewing my whole body, stretched taut and helpless. There was no avoiding these mirrors. They confronted me continuously with my open, exposed crotch; my securely restrained limbs.

As I tested my bonds (my breasts quivered every time I moved), a peculiar, flickering light sprang onto the walls. Jessie was lighting candles. She slipped a new tape into the deck. I recognized the music—Paul Horn playing his flute in the Taj Mahal.

She appeared at the foot of the bed. My mouth went dry.

The candle she carried put half her face in shadow, giving her a cruel and hooded look. She wore a long, silk kimono about her slim shoulders, belted loosely to show a hint of her breasts. The sheer silk draped well on her angular frame, whispering like a shy woman every time she moved. She stared down at me, one hand trailing cigarette smoke.

My body sang with anticipation.

She found a place for the candle on a table by the bed. Then she drew closer, stood between my legs. "How do you like them?" she asked, referring to the mirrors. "Does it excite you? Shame you? It's meant to do both. I want you to be able to see everything that's done to you, so you can't close your eyes and say later it never happened." She drew her fingernail down the inside of my thigh. "Such delicate skin. Even the gentlest lover would leave her mark on you. And now I have my chance."

She moved again outside the range of my vision, back toward the wardrobe. I heard her speaking behind me. "Did you see anything over here to tickle your fancy?" She returned with a handful

175

of whips, and made a mock presentation of them to me. "A masochist's bouquet," she jeered, bowing. "How about this one?" She
held up the most grisly looking one of the lot. It had several tails
that ended in sharp bits of metal.

My courage failed me. "Actually, it's only good for quickies,"
she said, "and making hamburger." I slumped with relief, then
saw she was only teasing me. The monologue continued. "Now,
this one was given to me as a name day present by a little old nun
who only used it on Sundays—and then only on herself." That
one, which had three metal hooks on short cotton cords, she also
tossed away. "Actually," she said discarding the rest, "I want to
use something a little more personal." She stuck her cigarette in
her mouth and talked around it as she shrugged out of the kimono.
"Something you can remember me by."

Under the kimono, she was wearing blue jeans with a broad
leather belt and no t-shirt. I stared at her small, brown breasts,
seeing something I couldn't believe. She smiled at me and traced
the criss-cross scars with a forefinger, then turned so I could
follow them onto her back. "I wanted you to see these," she said,
"so you'll know that whatever I do to you has been done to me. I
know what you feel, lying there bound, awaiting punishment at
my hand. I know."

She unbuckled her belt and drew it slowly through the loops of
her levis. I tried to relax, to stop the tension building in my body,
but instead my muscles began to quiver and jerk.

She doubled the belt in her hand and drew her arm back, held
it poised above me. I cringed, trying to flatten myself against the
bed, as it came singing down—to hit the mattress.

"Ah—surprised you."

She trailed it down my body, brought it up again, struck suddenly—and the belt smacked the bed between my legs. I was
breathing hard. "Scared?" she said sympathetically. And did it
again.

"Do your nipples always pucker when you're frightened?" Her
fingers brushed the edges of my labia, her touch insulting me.
"You little whore, you're wet already, and I haven't even touched
you." She pushed two fingers slowly inside of me, turning her
hand from side to side. "Either you're not really scared, or you

have your wires crossed, honey." She thrust deeper inside of me and gently moved my cervix. "Little mushroom," she whispered, "hidden away, so spongy-soft and secret. No—don't wiggle away. Hold still." The friction warmed my vagina until I thought I would burst into flame. To lie passive was impossible. I struggled wildly—to escape or increase my pleasure, I hardly knew which.

"Stop that!" Her fingers were motionless within me. I rested, panting, and she began again. I moaned, and my hips rocked in response to the repeated, slow penetration.

"Lie still."

I tried to clamp my ass to the mattress. For a minute or two, I succeeded. But she was so skillful, fucked me so carefully, I could not restrain myself. A groan emerged from the pit of my stomach, and I writhed on the brink of orgasm.

She slapped the inside of my thigh with her free hand. "You'll make me angry," she warned. "I thought you'd learned your lesson." Her gaze wandered around the room. Without taking her hand out of me, she plucked a candle from the bedside table.

I could see thin trails of wax running down its side. Her pupils reflected two tiny flames. "Oh! no, no, no!" I cried.

"Then—don't—move." And her fingers worked in me again until my juices welled up in rings around her knuckles. She watched me with clinical detachment, knowing I must break sooner or later.

My thighs turned to water. I almost sobbed, and thrust my cunt against her hand. She tilted the candle. Hot wax spattered my thigh. I screamed a little—and came. She quickly pressed the heel of her hand against my clitoris and massaged it lightly until the jolt of pleasure had passed.

"You're a very slow learner," she said when I was through. Her tone was sinister. "You just came without my permission. Spread your legs wider."

I could not. She made adjustments to my bonds, and my legs were held further apart.

She brought the candle close again. "You can scream if you like," she said generously.

The first rain of fire fell upon my skin. I struggled and cried for mercy. "I can't stand this," I wept. "You have to," she replied.

Again and again, she let the molten liquid sear me. She watched my face carefully, spacing each incident so as to give me time to catch my breath, doling out the pain with absolute precision. She moved from thigh to belly to breast and back down to my thighs. I could no longer tell whether the burning wax hurt or not. I forgot what was producing these intolerable sensations. I gasped, cried out, beat the mattress—and moved up a notch on some emotional ladder.

When the candle had burned down to four inches, she blew it out. "Look at this," she told me. I swam out of chaos to raise my head and focus on Jessie's hand. She had long, slender fingers. Blue veins pulsed just beneath the brown skin. "Do you know what I'm going to do with it? Can you guess?" Her hand reached for the smaller of my orifices, began to titillate it. Her finger sneaked into my ass, nudging it open. I held my breath—as if that would do me any good. "Relax, or you'll just make it harder on yourself." She held the candle against the ring of muscle, twisted it, and pushed it in.

She bent her dark head and took my clitoris between her lips while she tormented my anus with the candle. I no longer thought about orgasm, pain, time, no longer itched or saw colors. I moved in response to her touch. There was nothing else, no other reality, and no whim of my own will moved me.

She must have left me long enough to take off her pants, because now she was kneeling over my face, encouraging me to suck her off, but snatching her clit out of my mouth when she got too close to coming.

She retreated and busied herself with my restraints. My wrists and then my ankles were released. "I'm not through with you yet," she panted, removing the candle from my ass. "Get up on your hands and knees. Put your ass up in the air."

This position was more humiliating than any bondage could be. I had no knotted cords to excuse me. I knelt here, offering myself to her of my own free well.

"Yes," she hissed. I felt the doubled-up belt caress my buttocks and the inside of my thighs. I waited, crying inside for her to begin. "Beat me," I finally begged. She did not need a second invitation.

The first light blow slapped my buttocks, stinging. Second. Third. I counted, my teeth clenched, my whole body shuddering in response to the belt. Gradually, I became aware that we were breathing in time with each other. She was moaning and gasping as loudly as I, and the blows were increasing in strength. I held myself there for her as long as I could, taking the weight of her arm on my quivering buttocks, but she finally beat me down onto the bed. I could not have endured that in silence, and she did not ask me to. I grabbed the mattress with my outstretched hands as she marked my shoulders and ass and the backs of my legs. There were a few seconds when we hung in perfect balance —she was beating me with every ounce of her strength, and I was at the outermost limits of my tolerance, almost out of my mind.

The blows ceased. She took me by the shoulders and threw me onto my back. The silk wings of her kimono fell on either side of us, a fragile shelter. With one of her hands, she pinioned both my wrists. She used her other hand to open and fill my cunt, then threw her hips against her hand and my pelvis, creating a burning rhythm of pressure against my urethra and clitoris and cervix until I was beside myself. Then her hands were on my shoulders. She rode hard on my hip bone, rocking sure and swift toward her own pleasure. I gripped her thigh with an immediate, bruising strength. We were slippery as two fish, skidding on the salt in our perspiration, our bellies clinging and making obscene noises when we pulled away from each other. There was a point I passed with my eyes closed, going so fast I didn't realize it was the point of no return.

The bubble of my self, the prison of my mind, exploded, expanded—I was twisting in her arms, and she in mine—I was hurtling forward on deep, sobbing currents of my breath, waves unleashed from the bottom of the sea. Then long throbbing seconds of liberation and silence and obliteration.

EPILOGUE

I woke the next day to find her hand still clasping my wrist. Not wishing to be released, I lay quiet beside her until she also emerged from sleep. Our eyes met and acknowledged each other—yes, I

179

know what we did to each other, it has passed and become part of us both. Then she yawned.

I laughed and snuggled down between her breasts. She radiated heat like an electric eel. She tousled my hair, gently tweaked my ear lobes, touched a bruise above my collarbone. "Do you have to be somewhere today?" she asked me. I was darting my tongue in and out as fast as it would go, ringing her nipple with tiny wet dots.

"What time is it?"

She squinted at the clock. "One thirty."

"Not now, I don't."

"Oh, did you miss an appointment?"

"Nothing special." I had promised to pick up some friends at the airport. Oh, well, they were grown men. Maybe the landlady would let them in.

"Then let's have some breakfast."

I demurred. "I'm a lousy cook."

"So go get a Sunday paper and I'll cook. There's a store about a block and a half from here."

She gave me her keys and sent me out the door. When I returned, the house smelled like bacon and eggs. We ate in near-silence, trading sections of the paper and passing each other the toast and butter. When we finished, I began to stack the dishes, but she stopped me. "No, leave them," she said. "I have to empty the dishwasher."

I stood in the middle of the kitchen with a dirty plate in my hand, not sure where to go or what to do. "I feel awkward," I said, so softly I wasn't sure she would hear me, and put the dish gently on the edge of the table.

"Dammit, I'm out of cigarettes," she complained, hunting through a drawer. "I'll have to go out and get some."

I tried to picture myself doing these things with her—emptying a dishwasher, walking down to the store for cigarettes—and decided it was easier to pour myself another cup of coffee. When I turned around from the counter, she was sitting at the table again, so I sat beside her. She took my hand, turned it over, and slipped her finger under the leather bracelet.

"I—uh, yes, I feel a little strained myself. Everything I want to say sounds like the understatement of the year. How shall I put it? I had a great time last night?" Did you? said her eyes.

I paused a little, not wanting to sound too glib. "It was the best," I shrugged. My voice was high and unconvincing. "It was the best ever," I repeated firmly. "I guess that's what makes today so difficult."

"Yeah. I hardly know you—I don't know if you play piano, I don't know what kind of shop it is you run, I don't know your shoe size—but I know you better than anyone else in the world."

I nodded. "Instant intimacy," I said flippantly. I was shaking cold inside, getting ready to run scared.

"So what do we do?" she asked me. "My temptation is to either lock you in my closet or bounce you down the front steps. I hate to let go of something that was so good, but I'm afraid I'll spoil it if I try to hang on. I'm afraid to try again, for fear it won't be the same."

"Shit, Jessie, I don't know what I want from you." Anger had crept into my voice. She shouldn't be asking me what I wanted. It was out of character. Then I got pissed at myself. I had a lot of nerve, expecting her to play master at the breakfast table. It would be stupid to think she hadn't asked me what I wanted every step of the way. Okay, so she didn't tip her hat and say, "Miss Sally, would you keep company with me?" But she was checking me out. I could have said no any time. She was asking me an honest question, and I'd better get my act together. "I know I don't want a 24-hour-a-day S/M relationship," I said quietly. "I'm not a social masochist. I run my own little graphics business and enjoy taking care of number one like a reasonably sane adult woman."

She grinned with relief. "Hey, that's not what I want, either. I can't top somebody full-time. I cop a famous quote, kicking ass is hard work."

I shook my head, smiled, drank coffee.

She picked up my hand again, toying with my wristlet. "I know there's one thing I want to do," she said.

"Name it."

"Come into my bedroom."

Despite the unmade bed and the toys strewn on the floor, magic still hung in the air. We had enacted a vital ritual here, a ceremony essential to us both. She asked me to kneel in the center of the rug. I complied, blinking in the hot sun that streamed in through the balcony.

Jessie stood between me and the glass doors, shading me. She fished a pocket knife out of her levis, and unfolded its longest blade. I don't know what I expected. The crazy thought flashed through my head that she was going to carve her initials on me, like a tree. I didn't dream of protesting.

She ran her thumb along the edge of the blade. "You are wearing the tokens of another woman," she said. Her words were carefully measured out. "I find that. . .distracting. May I?"

She lifted one wrist and cut the band of leather.

"I don't need anything as crude and obvious as this to set my mark on you. Do I?"

She cut my other wrist free.

She paused before severing my collar, her thumb holding it to the knife, to look into my face. "If I call you, you'll come to me, won't you?" she demanded.

"Yes," I whispered.

A loop of leather fell onto my thighs. When she brought me to my feet, it fell to the floor. I rubbed my wrists. They felt curiously light without the bracelets. And my neck—I was more acutely aware of where my collar *had* been than I ever was of its actual presence.

I shook my head in amazement. Her boldness was more appealing than iron chains. Her confidence created an intangible bond between us. A determination was kindled in me to justify that confidence she had in her own power.

"You—" I began. And could not finish.

She nodded, well-satisfied. "Come on, then. I have to get some cigarettes anyway. I'll show you where the bus stops."

This is an excerpt from a longer work, to be published as part of a collection of the author's pornographic short stories.

The Art of Discipline:
Creating Erotic Dramas of Play and Power

SUSAN FARR

I would like this preamble to serve as a short statement of where I think "sadomasochistic" expressions of sexuality fit into the women's movement. The body of my piece is intensely personal. This introduction makes explicit some political implications.

What I here choose to call "discipline"—physical pain inflicted on one adult by another with mutual consent—is "the most proscribed of all our sexual proclivities."[1] Our society tolerates and advocates both indiscriminate and systematic violence where consent is absent (woman-battering, rape, war), but issues stringent taboos against consenting adults exploring the complexities of power and sexuality within highly controlled situations. I believe that apparent paradox is due to our society's wishing to withhold experience with and knowledge about power from most people so that abuses of power by elites can be protected.

Some voices within the women's movement similarly wish to proscribe not only s/m behavior, but s/m thoughts. Since any data one would wish to cite show that s/m fantasies and/or behavior *are* a part of women's/lesbian sexuality in our society, such attitudes presumably encourage those of us who share this interest to remain underground or to change our sexuality to conform to acceptable patterns. This clearly constitutes the oppression of a sexual minority and is politically repugnant to me.

I believe those with the inclination and the courage to explore realms of pain, power, and sexuality should be free to do so. Power is not an invention of men, to be wished out of existence in a new women's society. Power is the capacity to make things happen—power is energy—and we would do well to know as much as we can about it.

*   *   *

I am a person who trusts her body and its sensations more than her mind and its thoughts. This is a difficult discovery after years of formal schooling designed, presumably, to make my mind a well-trained, highly reliable tool. Still, my body serves me better, for I have learned that my body is more sensitive by far to my feelings than my mind is. I can reach feelings through touching that are inaccessible to my thoughts.

For one thing, thoughts are censored: some things are simply unthinkable. But a body that is freed to do whatever feels right will do the undoable. Some of my deepest feelings lie clearly in the realm of the unthinkable. I want to feel these feelings in, I suppose, an ultimate attempt to know myself.

For the past three years I've been exploring my feelings through physically hurting my lover and through submitting to her physically hurting me. We spank each other with our hands, tie each other up and deliver a beating with a belt or paddle, discipline each other with a switch or whip. The punishment is always by mutual consent, and the severity, though most often mild, is sometimes sufficient to leave an occasional bruise or a faint welt the next day. It does hurt, and it feels very good to me, whether I'm on the giving or receiving end.

Giving or getting a spanking is a sexual turn-on for me. Or, more accurately I should say, *imagining* giving or getting a spanking is a turn-on. (As it is, the Kinsey researchers report, for 20 percent of American men and 12 per cent of American women who, "report some degree of sexual arousal by sadomasochistic stories."[2]) Such fantasies have been with me as a stimulant to masturbation and as an accompaniment to sex for as long as I can remember. Doing something to express the fantasies had never seemed possible until my relationship with Rae. Her excitement at the prospect, her lack of a long history of guilt over bad thoughts, her reassuring, fun-loving, and innocent manner all conspired to give the two of us permission to hit each other, not in anger but

184

in love.

My feelings about the actual physical sensation, the blow as opposed to the fantasy, are ambivalent. When I'm to receive a spanking, I both love it and dread it, seek it and fear it, feel the pleasure and feel the pain. Afterwards I feel very open, very dependent, very clear, and very satisfied. When I'm to deliver a spanking, my feelings are more single-minded. I feel powerful, responsible, and in control, both of myself and of the situation. Afterwards I feel very strong and very loving. Rae and I always hold each other close after a spanking. The person who's been spanked feels vulnerable and in need of warmth and comfort; the person who's delivered the spanking needs to offer strength and love. Also, the person who's done the spanking needs to be re-assured that she's done a good thing even though she's hurt her lover. Often one will say. "Thank you for the good spanking," and the other will say, "I enjoyed it myself."

So far I can identify two analytically distinct but emotionally and physically interconnected functions of discipline for us. One function has to do with play—with play-acting, with sexual fore-play, with imaginative rituals, with scary dramas of threat and pleading and relief. The other is something about power—about dominance and submission, about anger and its expression, about distance and intimacy, about aggression. These two expressions, the playful and the powerful, come concretely together each time one of us feels the need to administer or submit to a spanking. The working out of play and power between our bodies has served to keep clean and fresh and comprehensible the working out of play and power between ourselves.

It is the play part of discipline rituals that most attracts me.[3] The whole experience is erotically charged. The desire to be sexual and the desire to be combative are complexly intertwined. Sometimes the sex play evolves gradually from a beginning struggle, like bear cubs wrestling and pawing and cuffing each other, to a more focused expression in genital love-making. Other times the punishment is clearly demarcated from the love-making. although the love-making will follow very soon after the mutual comforting that completes a spanking episode. Rae and my love-making is intense but gentle, not violent. The desire for a violent

185

component in the sexual experience has been fulfilled through the more explicit medium of aggressive play. And sometimes we want to make love, but we're too tired or there isn't enough time, or some other constraint prevents us. Then a few playful slaps can substitute; the physical impact is achieved, the adrenalin flows, but the loving contact is made in only a very short time.

Having the slap in my repertoire of sensual/loving behaviors means that I do not always have to rely on the kiss to express affection. I like to express affection openly, but always kissing and saying "I love you" is certainly repetitive, often lacking in imagination, and can become cloying. A cuff says "I love you" too, but in a sharper, less sweet way. Often our terms of endearment reflect the same recognition of the importance of contrast. We don't always call each other "darling," sometimes it's "noodle face."

Another playful use of discipline in our relationship is as a motivator. It can convert drudgery into cheerful slavery: "You wash the kitchen floor today or else...." What was simply onerous is now erotic. And it can highlight the importance of doing some task long postponed: "I want you to renew your driver's license by the end of the week or you'll face a licking." What was a lonely burden is now shared. The expression of dominance is also an assumption of responsibility. The acceptance of submission is also an agreement to act. The threats need never be carried out—although if they were, that would, of course, be fun—because the task always gets done. The threat acts simply as that extra stimulant to get things moving.

Neither Rae nor I has an unusual tolerance for physical pain. The pain experienced in whipping is converted into pleasure in several ways. The anticipation of the whip is pleasurable because the threatened experience is exciting, dangerous, fearful. The exact flavor is expressed in *The Image* where the "victim" is "summoned by her friend [also a woman] in a voice full of menaces, or perhaps promises."[4] The pain itself is tolerable because, when a person is sexually aroused, her pain threshold rises. It simply doesn't hurt as the same blows would in a non-erotic situation. Further, one's tolerance for pain rises with exposure. The security which comes from having weathered one spanking insulates one against the next.

While the essence of punishment play is eroticism, the structure of it is pure theater. After all, the one partner is not a master, the other a slave; the one is not pure command, the other pure obedience; the one is not really so fearsome and the other is not truly fearful. What is going on is a drama where the two principals, where Rae and I, act at being master and slave, play at being fearsome and fearful.

One clue to how much of drama and how little of reality is involved is that the roles change. The vulnerable submissive of today is the firm and strict dominant of tomorrow. The other clue is that the whole episode can be called off with a word. In fact, people who engage in aggression rituals[5] usually agree on some code word (not a word that might be used as part of the dialogue, like "Oh, please stop") by which the curtain can be dropped on the whole show should either party want to go home.

Thus, part of the fun of discipline is constructing the mini-drama that you are both playing out. Although the scenario could be conceived of in advance, Rae and I simply ad-lib it, creating the scene extemporaneously. There are some stage directions issued as orders, "When I get home tonight I want to find you face down on the bed," but most of the dialogue and action is pure improvisation.

While it is true that the art of discipline is playful, it is sometimes a very serious form of play. For what is being dramatized is the exercise of power, and power is surely one of the most sensitive areas of an intimate relationship.

Because Rae and I are both women, the power discrepancies that society structures between men and women are not present. Perhaps that is one reason—although we each have a preference for one of the roles, I the submissive, Rae the dominant—we in fact exchange roles frequently. We are not trying through punishment rituals to redress a basic structural imbalance in the relationship. Instead we are using physical expressions of aggression to work out in overt ways temporary dislocations and hostilities.

Inflicting pain on another is surely an exercise of power, though it may not be an assertion of power over the other. Let me give an extended example. Rae and I wish for ourselves and for each other the opportunity sometimes to have sexual relationships with women outside our relationship. Though this represents an admirable degree of flexibility in theory, it is always hard to sustain in practice. The person having the affair feels attractive, desired, powerful, but in my experience the person not having the affair feels, to one degree or another, scared, angry, trapped, and powerless. That person can escape her feelings of being blocked, can do something, can reassert her power by giving the other a beating. It is an exercise of power in the neutral sense of power as the capacity to get things done, to unblock energy, to make things happen. The "faithful" one (this time around) can regain some initiative in the relationship by demonstrating her strength.

If I give Rae a whipping after she has had sex with someone else, it also expresses directly how angry and jealous I feel. It is an exertion of power over, no question about it. It gives me an outlet for the "negative" and very natural feelings that exist regardless of my commitment to the principle of non-monogamy. The punishment also functions to relieve the guilt of the person having the affair, another "negative" and natural feeling that exists regardless of sincere beliefs that the upsets of occasional non-monogamy are preferable to the suffocation of unrelieved monogamy. The truth of it is that one of us feels angry, and the other feels guilty, and the spanking relieves both of our emotional burdens, leaving the relationship clear again.

I cannot accomplish the same catharsis by talking ("I think I feel kind of hurt by all this.") or shouting ("Goddamn it, I'm angry!") A sensible talk leaves me still feeling strangled, and a shouting match leaves me simply stirred up. When I am ready really to let go of my anger or jealousy, and when Rae is ready really to let go of her guilt (or vice versa), then a physical encounter can accomplish the expiatory ritual that both parties need.

Perhaps this is the place to talk about restraint. Discipline means not only that a drama is being enacted where a person is being disciplined—in the sense of a child being spanked—but that great discipline—in the sense of self control—is being exercised in the enactment of the drama. I have used the title "The Art of Discipline" because it conveys the sense of imaginative creation and control of one's medium that I believe such rituals demand.

Before I give Rae a whipping for "being unfaithful" I have already come down from whatever extremes of jealousy I may have felt. The anger I feel is not fresh and immediate, but has been tempered by time and reason. I am ready to give it up entirely, and that is the function of inflicting pain. Through inflicting suffering I am acting out my capacity to let go of my anger. Through enduring suffering she is acting out her capacity to let go of her guilt. We are saying together that our relationship has survived the disruption of infidelity.

If the situation were so threatening that I could not accept Rae's affair, that I could not give up my anger and jealousy, discipline rituals would not play a part at all. I would ask her to stop the affair. The drama of expiation allows one to recognize and tolerate the affair. When something is intolerable in a relationship, it must be stopped, not dramatized.

This discussion of punishment rituals used as a response to non-monogamy is one example of how physical aggression can function to keep a relationship clean. I would much prefer that Rae come after me with a whip for some infraction than that she punish me emotionally. The former has rules, the most important being my consent, while the latter is a potentially damaging free-for-all. To obtain my consent she must explain the justice of the punishment. Psychological torments require no explanation. The spanking has an end, while mental punishments seem to go on forever. In short, I would much prefer a licking to being mindfucked.

The apparent power relationship being enacted in a punishment ritual is that the dominant person is in control, the submissive person completely vulnerable. This is indeed the scenario being followed, but the reality behind the scene is more complex. The first rule of discipline games is that they are played by mutual consent and end immediately when either party wishes them to. It is the "victim's" consent that is crucial because she must endure the pain. It is the victim's tolerance for pain that sets limits to the severity of the punishment. And it is the victim's delinquency that constitutes the justification for the proceedings. Thus the behind-the-scenes senior author of the production that features an imposing punisher is the victim herself. The illusion, however, is the opposite. The victim, by accepting her submissive role, is allowed to play out the illusion of complete powerlessness. She can no longer do as she wishes, and is thus completely free. The punisher, in accepting responsibility for the direction of the scene, is allowed the illusion of complete powerfulness. She can do as she wishes, and is thus completely free. Through different paths both parties have arrived at a feeling of complete freedom. It is only temporary, and it is an illusion, but it is very compelling.

*   *   *

For lovers to safely stage such erotic power dramas, it is essential that they trust one another. For trust to develop, it is crucial that the lovers be honest with each other. Being open, vulnerable, expressive—which in this case would include sharing one's erotic power fantasies—encourages intimacy, which generates trust, which provides the safety within which lovers can act out sexual fantasies. The acting out of the fantasies becomes the self-revealing expression of intimate truths which contributes to new depths of trust and love. In the process, lovers become real to each other. It's like the process of becoming Real described in the children's book, *The Velveteen Rabbit*.[6] The Skin Horse is explaining,

"Real isn't how you are made," said the Skin Horse. "It's a thing that happens to you."

"Does it hurt?" asked the Rabbit.

"Sometimes," said the Skin Horse, for he was always truthful. "When you are Real, you don't mind being hurt."

"Does it happen all at once, like being wound up," he asked, "or bit by bit?"

"It doesn't happen all at once," said the Skin Horse. "You become. It takes a long time. That's why it doesn't often happen to people who break easily, or have sharp edges, or who have to be carefully kept. Generally, by the time you are Real, most of your hair has been loved off, and your eyes drop out and you get loose in the joints and very shabby. But these things don't matter at all, because once you are Real you can't be ugly, except to people who don't understand."

1. *S-M: The Last Taboo,* Gerald and Caroline Greene (New York: Grove Press, 1974), p. 136.
2. *S-M: The Last Taboo,* p.5.
3. For perspective I feel I should say that Rae and I make love far more often without discipline play being involved than with it. But this piece is intended to share with you the role physical punishment plays in our relationship, not the role it doesn't play. Suffice to say it is only one aspect of a complex relationship.
4. *The Image,* Jean de Berg (New York: Grove Press, 1975), p. 75.
5. The phrase is from *Creative Aggression,* Dr. George R. Bach and Dr. Herb Goldberg (New York: Doubleday & Co., 1974).
6. *The Velveteen Rabbit,* Margery Williams (New York: Doubleday, 1958), p. 17.

Impromptu S/M

JAYE

Feeling down and depressed, I went to the SAMOIS meeting hoping that the company of my friends might comfort me. And, indeed, my sadness was met with hugs and words of support, though no one knew what troubled me.

I curled up on a pillow throughout the meeting, participating minimally, but feeling good about being there.

The meeting ended, and those few people who had not yet left stood around chatting. Three or four women examined a riding crop that was someone's new acquisition, and, as I looked their way, it was handed to me, handle first.

As my friends know, I take greatest pleasure in the masochist role in S/M, and vehemently resist most attempts to get me to switch. So, feeling rebellious at that moment, I did not take the proffered whip but responded brusquely, "Aren't you handing me the wrong end of that?"

Everyone laughed and I turned away thinking the matter ended. Not so, for a second later I felt the light tap of the crop's tip on my breast. Looking up, it was the woman who had offered the crop to me a minute ago with its handle firmly in hand.

She continued to strike my breasts with strokes that became harder, sharper. As my nipples responded to the stimulus, so did my clit and my cunt, there seeming to be a rope of nerves that joined these parts of my body in an inseparable intimacy that my other body parts must surely envy.

She showed skill, this woman. She did not simply beat me, something I would not have liked, but, fitting the intensity of her strokes to my response, seduced me into taking more, pushing farther and farther away the boundary of that place where these sensations would be experienced as pain and then taking me to the very edge of that border.

I felt safe. My friends stood watching, their silent participation adding to my security and pleasure. I let go. With immense relief, abandoning all dignity, care, and responsibility, I submitted fully to the whip. And like a bird in flight, freed of the earth's pull, I soared.

My body began to move eagerly to meet each stroke of the crop as each one took me and held me for long, delicious seconds right at the edge of orgasm, on the ridge of the cliff at the instant before the earth gives way beneath one's feet and one falls to the depths of sweet release.

All too soon she stopped and lay the crop down. She hugged me, shaking, and I trembled with her, tears in my eyes. I smiled and was hugged by each of my smiling friends, all of us struggling to once again breathe normal air after leaving the rare air of the heights to which the act had taken us.

I left the house and walked to my car feeling warmed, comforted, loved, satisfied; my heavy heart lightened.

The Leather Menace:
Comments on Politics and S/M

GAYLE RUBIN

I.

> Since Christianity upped the
> ante and concentrated on sexual
> behavior as the root of virtue,
> everything pertaining to sex
> has been a "special case" in
> our culture, evoking peculiarly
> inconsistent attitudes.
>
> Susan Sontag[1]

It is difficult to simply discuss the politics of sadomasochism
when the politics of sex in general are so depressingly muddled.
In part, this is due to the residue of at least a century of social
conflict over sex during which conservative positions have
dominated the terms of discussion as well as the outcome of many
discrete struggles. It is important to know and to remember that
in the United States and Britain, there were extensive and
successful morality campaigns in the late nineteenth and early
twentieth centuries. Social movements against prostitution,
obscenity, contraception, abortion, and masturbation were able
to establish state policies, social practices, and deeply entrenched
ideologies which still affect the shape of our sexual experience
and our ability to think about it. In the United States, the long
term agenda of the conservative right has helped to maintain

deep reservoirs of ignorance and sexual bigotry by its unrelenting opposition to sex research and sex education. More recently, the right has been spectacularly successful in tapping these pools of erotophobia in its accession to state power. The right will now use its hegemony over the state apparatus to renew and deepen its hold over erotic behavior.

Even the elementary bourgeois freedoms have never been secured in the realm of sexuality. There is, for instance, no freedom of sexual speech. Explicit talk about sex has been a glaring exception to first amendment protection since the Comstock Act was passed in 1871. Although there have been many skirmishes to establish exactly where the line will be drawn or how strongly it will be enforced, it remains true that it is still illegal in this country to produce (or show or sell) images, objects, or writing which have no other purpose than sexual arousal. One may embroider for relaxation, play baseball for the thrill, or collect stamps merely for their beauty. But sex itself is not a legitimate activity or goal. It must have some "higher" purpose. If possible, this purpose should be reproductive. Failing that, an artistic, scientific, or literary aim will do. Minimally, sex should at least be the expression of a close personal relationship.

In contrast to the politics of class, race, ethnicity, and gender, the politics of sex are relatively underdeveloped. Sexual liberals are defensive, and sexual radicals almost non-existent. Sex politics are kept far to the right by many forces, among them a frequent recourse to terror. Our sexual system contains a vast vague pool of nameless horror. Like Lovecraft's pits where unmentionable creatures perform unspeakable acts, this place of fear is rarely specified but always avoided. This reservoir of terror has several effects on our ability to deal with sex politically. It makes the whole subject touchy and volatile. It makes sex-baiting painfully easy. It provides a constant supply of demons and boogiemen with which otherwise rational people can be stampeded.

In the United States throughout the twentieth century, there have been periodic sex scares. In the late 1940's and early 1950's, the Cold War was inaugurated with a wave of domestic repression. Along with anti-communism, loyalty oaths, and the

195

post-war reconstruction of gender roles and the family, there was a paroxysm of sex terrorism whose most overt symptom was a savage repression against homosexuals. Gay people were purged from government positions, expelled from schools, and fired from jobs (including academic jobs with tenure). Newspapers carried screaming headlines as police rounded up suspected perverts and gay bars were raided. Government agencies, legislative bodies, and grand juries held hearings and investigated the "sex deviate problem." The FBI conducted surveillance of gay people. All of these activities were both justified by, and contributed to, the construct of the homosexual as a social menace.

The repression of gay people during the Cold War has been absent from histories of the period, and the abuses suffered by homosexuals during the 1950's have never been questioned. The anti-gay repression was seen as a hygenic measure since gay life was depicted as seedy, dangerous, degraded, and scary. The impact of the repression was in fact to degrade the quality of gay life and raise the costs of being sexually different. During the 1950's, the Communist Party was just as apt to purge homosexuals as the state department. The ACLU refused to defend homosexuals who were being persecuted. The entire political spectrum, from protestant republicans to godless communists, accepted more or less the same analysis of homosexuals as scum. This period is an object lesson in the mechanics of sexual witch hunting and needs to be better known.[2]

It should be fairly obvious that the late 1970's and early 1980's are similar in many ways to the period in which the Cold War began. For whatever reason, military build-up, family reconstruction, anti-communism, and enforced sexual conformity all go together in the right wing program. But we are not simply repeating history. Among other important differences, the positions of target sexual populations have changed dramatically. The gay community is under attack and is vulnerable, but it is simply too large and too well-organized to be attacked with the impunity of the 1950's. Instead of a few tiny organizations whose names, like the Mattachine Society, gave no indications of their focus, there are now hundreds of explicitly gay political organizations. More importantly, there is an effective and extensive gay press which can document and publicize the war against homosexuals. Gay people enjoy some political legitimacy and support in the non-gay population. This does not imply complacency. The Jewish community in pre-WW II Poland was large, literate, and possessed a thriving press and was nevertheless wiped out by the Nazis. But it does mean that people know what is going on and can mount some resistance. It means that it is more difficult and politically expensive to conduct anti-gay persecution.

It is the erotic communities which are smaller, more stigmatized, and less organized which are subject to virtually unrestrained attack. Just as the political mobilization of black people has been emulated by other racial and ethnic groups, the mobilization of homosexuals has provided a repertoire of ideology and organizational technology to other erotic populations. It is these smaller, more underground groups who enjoy even fewer legal rights and less social acceptance who are bearing the brunt of current sexual repression. Moreover, these communities, particularly boy-lovers and sadomasochists, are being used as wedges against the larger gay community.

It lies well outside the scope of this essay to fully analyze the issues of cross-generational sex. But thus far, it has been the most strategically located, so a few comments are in order. In the United States, gay lovers of youth have been *the* front line of the right's battle against the gay community which has been picking up steam since the spring of 1977.[3] Lovers of youth enjoy virtually no legal protection, because any sexual contact between an adult and a minor is illegal. This means that a fully consensual love affair is, in the eyes of the law, indistinguishable from a rape. Moreover, sentences for consensual sex with a minor are usually longer and harsher than sentences for violent rape of adult women, assault and battery, or even murder. Secondly, lovers of youth are the cheapest targets for inflammatory rhetoric. Very little public education has occurred to dislodge the stereotypes which depict adult-youth relationships in the ugliest possible terms. These images of drooling old sickies corrupting or harming sweet innocent children can be relied upon to drum up public hysteria. Such stereotypes have also been used to quash any discussion of the way in which statutory rape laws function, not so much to protect young people from abuse, as to prevent them from acquiring sexual knowledge and experience.

Sex between people of different ages is not an exclusively gay phenomenon. On the contrary, all statistics on cross-generational sex indicate that the majority of instances, and the vast majority of non-consensual incidents, are heterosexual (older male, younger female). Nevertheless, most of the media coverage and legal attention has been directed at gay men. Each time another gay person is arrested for an age offense, the ensuing headlines serve to reinforce the stereotype that it is primarily a gay practice.

This claustrophobic and demonic discourse, the illegality of the sexual practices, and the ease with which the issue can be used to smear other gay people have made boy-lovers the favored target of state repression. The community of men engaged in cross-generational sex has been under seige for over four years and has been subjected to the kinds of police activity and media propaganda that were directed at homosexuals in the 1950's. Recently, NAMBLA, the North American Man/Boy Love Association, has had the dubious honor of becoming the first gay civil rights organization directly attacked by the government in the current wave of repression against dissenting sexuality. Sadly, this community has been treated by the left and the women's movement in much the same way that homosexuals were treated by so-called progressives in the 1950's. The gay movement has been repeatedly baited on this issue. When homosexuals are all accused of being "child molesters," it is legitimate to deny that all, or even a large percentage of, gay people engage in cross-generational sex. But it is crucial to add that not all adults who do have sex with minors are molesting or harming them. All too often, homosexuals have defended themselves against the accusation of child stealing by joining with the general condemnation of all adult-youth sex and by perpetuating the myths about it. Many lesbians have been doubly baited, dissassociating themselves from the practice but accepting stereotypes not only that all lovers of youth are rapists, but also that gay men tend to be lovers of youth.

Sadomasochism is the other sexual practice which to date has been used with great success to attack the gay community, and at greatest cost to those who actually practice it. Unlike sex between adults and minors, S/M is not, per se, illegal. Nevertheless there are a variety of laws which have been interpreted to apply to S/M sexual encounters and social events. It is easy to bend the applicability of existing laws because S/M is so stereotyped and stigmatized, and thus shocking and frightening. The shock value of S/M has been mercilessly exploited by both media and police.

In 1976, Los Angeles police used an obscure nineteenth century anti-slavery statute to raid a slave auction held in a gay bathhouse. The next morning, four-inch headlines screamed, "POLICE FREE GAY SLAVES." The slaves were, of course, volunteers, and proceeds from the auction were to benefit gay charities. The event was about as sinister as a Lions Club rummage sale. But sixty-five uniformed officers, two helicopters, a dozen vehicles, at least two phone taps, several weeks of surveillance of the staff of a local gay magazine, and over $100,000 were expended to bust the party and arrest some forty people. Once arrested, they were detained for many hours in handcuffs, not allowed to go to the bathroom, and subjected to full strip searches. It is only the moral stupidity induced by anti-S/M attitudes that could make anyone think that the volunteer slaves had been rescued, or that the tender mercies of the L.A.P.D. were preferable to those of their intended Masters. The statute used was actually an anti-prostitution law aimed at forcible prostitution. All charges under that statute were dropped, but four of the principals were charged with felony pandering and eventually bargained guilty pleas to misdemeanors.

S/M sex has occasionally been prosecuted under assault laws. Since assault is a felony, the state can press charges without a complaint from or even over the objections of the "victim." Once a sexual activity is construed as assault, the involvement of the partner is irrelevant, since one cannot legally consent to an assault. Since few judges or jurors can imagine why anyone would do S/M, it is easy to obtain convictions and brutal sentences. In a recent case in

Massachusetts, Kenneth Appleby was sentenced to ten years in prison for hitting his lover lightly with a riding crop in the context of a consensual S/M relationship.⁴ The Appleby case has some murky elements, but it sets a frightening precedent. It could happen that an S/M couple is making love. Police, perhaps called by neighbors alarmed by the noise, or perhaps looking for an excuse to arrest one of the parties, break in on the scene. They arrest the top and charge her (or him) with assault. The bottom could protest that they were only making love as her or his lover is hauled off to jail. If the couple is gay or otherwise unmarried, the submissive could even be subpoenaed and forced to testify against her or his partner in court. While the protests of the bottom might not save the top from prison, they might be used as evidence to declare the bottom mentally incompetent. Again, only the distortions of anti-S/M bigotry could locate the abuse of power in this scenario within the S/M relationship rather than with outsiders who interfere with it.

The legal vulnerability of S/M is best demonstrated by a string of police actions in Canada. In December, 1978, Toronto police raided a local leather oriented gay bath, the Barracks. They charged several men under the bawdy house laws and confiscated lots of sex toys, including dildos, butt plugs, leather harnesses, whips, etc. The bawdy house laws were originally passed as anti-prostitution measures. No prostitution was alleged to have occurred at the Barracks. But the law contains a vague phrase referring to a "place where indecent acts take place." The police were arguing that S/M sex is indecent and that any place where it occurs is a bawdy house. While this interpretation has not been clearly upheld in court, the arrests and trials have continued and generated much havoc in the interim.

Press coverage of the Barracks raid was sensationalistic. The news media jumped at the opportunity to show, in loving detail, the confiscated equipment. The Toronto gay community protested the nature of the charges, the raid, and the press coverage. A defense committee was formed.

In June of 1979, one of the members of the defense committee was arrested for "keeping a common bawdy house" in his own home. Again, no prostitution was alleged. Their redefinition of a bawdy house as a place where indecent acts took place, and of S/M sex as indecent, enabled police to bring the charges based on the man's S/M playroom. His toys, equipment, even his leather jacket and hat were confiscated as evidence, along with membership lists of the Barracks defense committee and the gay caucus of a political party.

In February, 1981, the four major gay baths in Toronto were hit with a massive raid. Over three hundred men were charged under the same bawdy house laws and hauled out into the winter snow in their towels. The Barracks was raided a second time, but the other three baths catered to a mainstream gay clientele. Having first redefined the bawdy house laws with regard to gay S/M, the police were now expanding their application to cover ordinary gay sex. This neatly circumvented Canada's consenting adults law and provoked a gay riot.

On April 14 of this year, the scope of the crackdown expanded again. Robert Montgomery, who runs a small business making custom leather gear and sex toys, was charged with fifteen separate offenses. In addition to the now obligatory bawdy house laws, relating to his apartment, several charges were brought having to do with making, selling, distributing, and possessing to distribute obscene material. The obscene material in question included the leather items and sex toys. In effect, the Canadian police have now reclassified sex toys and leather gear as pornography, and therefore prosecutable under the porn laws.

The reason behind Montgomery's arrest became clear a week later. Six men who own or have interests in gay baths in Toronto were charged with an array of offenses including keeping a common bawdy house, distribution and sale of obscene matter, and conspiracy to live off the proceeds of crime. The men charged were prominent gay businessmen, lawyers, and gay political activists, including George Hislop, a gay political official. The charges against them relied upon the whole carefully constructed edifice of redefined sex laws which the police had been building for three years. Any gay bath can be prosecuted as a bawdy house. Sex toys, leather items, enema bags, dildos, and even lubricants can be treated as contraband. In this case, the obscenity charges were related to the sale of sex equipment (including some items made by Montgomery) in shops at the baths. If these charges stick, anyone who owns or has an interest in a gay bath or sex related business can be prosecuted for conspiracy to live off the proceeds of crime.

On May 30, the gay baths were raided in Edmonton. On June 12, two men were convicted in the original Barracks case, and on June 16, the last two gay baths in Toronto were raided. What has happened very clearly in Canada is that S/M has been used to set several legal precedents which are now being used to decimate mainstream gay institutions and the bastions of mainstream gay political and economic power. Police have used the media, and manipulated sexual prejudice and ignorance, to criminalize whole categories of erotic behavior without a single new law being passed.

Nothing quite so blatant has happened yet in the United States, but we already have similar laws on the books. In California, for instance, a bawdy house is defined as a place resorted to for "purposes of prostitution *or lewdness*" (my emphasis). There is also a clause which prohibits keeping a house "for purposes of assignation." Given the current sexual climate in the U.S., whose congress has just allocated some twenty million dollars to promote teenage chastity, it does not seem farfetched to imagine people getting arrested for having assignations in their own living rooms. It takes even less foresight to predict that the next few years will see a rash of morality campaigns to exterminate vulnerable sexual populations. There are many signs that S/M is on the verge of becoming a direct target of such a campaign.

Police already harass the institutions of the leather community with a great deal of impunity. In San Francisco, the vice squad and the ABC (Alcoholic Beverage Commission) have either warned, raided, brought suspension proceedings against, or revoked the licenses of virtually every leather bar within the last five years. No other group of gay bars, let alone heterosexual drinking establishments, has faced anything like this kind of concerted enforcement of the liquor laws since 1970. This unrelenting harassment of the leather bars has not raised a peep of protest from the rest of the city's gay community. In fact, from reading the local gay press, it would be difficult to even know that it was taking place. By contrast, when mainstream gay institutions like the Jaguar bookstore have been hassled, both press coverage and gay community support have been extensive.[5]

Meanwhile, the straight media have discovered that they can bait homosexuals, smear sadomasochists, and increase their circulation or ratings all at once. The infamous CBS "documentary" *Gay Power, Gay Politics,* used S/M to question the credibility of gay political aspirations. The program implied that if gay people are allowed to acquire significant political power, S/M will be rampant, and people will be killed doing it. This analysis rested on three completely phony connections.

The program gave the false impression that S/M is especially prevalent in San Francisco, and that this high level of S/M activity results from gay political clout. The New York based reporters failed to mention that almost every major city has an S/M population, that San Francisco's is not particularly large, and that S/M institutions are more numerous and developed in New York, a city that has failed to pass a gay rights ordinance, than in San Francisco, one which has.

Secondly, the program gave the false impression that S/M is a specifically gay (male) practice. The reporters failed to mention that most sadomasochists are heterosexual and that most gay men do not practice S/M. In fact, most of the S/M section of the program was filmed at the Chateau, a heterosexually oriented establishment.

Thirdly, S/M was presented as a dangerous and often lethal activity. Most of the evidence for this assertion consisted of the reporter, George Crile, asking leading questions in order to get his interviewees to confirm his prejudices.[6] At one point, Crile told a story about a place "where they have a gynecological table. . .with a doctor and a nurse on hand to sew people up."[7] There is no such place in San Francisco, although there are certainly people who do have sex on surplus hospital equipment, and some establishments have physicians on call. This is a rather responsible attitude, since health problems can occur during sexual activities, just as they can during sports events, academic lectures, or at the opera. Yet it was presented in a completely sinister light.

Crile interviewed Dr. Boyd Stephens, the San Francisco coroner, who estimated that ten percent of the homicides in San Francisco were gay related and that some were S/M related. Dr. Stephens later told reporter Randy Alfred that the ten percent figure included the killing of homosexuals by heterosexuals. Alfred points out that this percentage is about the same, or less than, the percentage of homosexuals in the population of San Francisco.[8] On another occasion, Dr. Stephens estimated that about ten percent of the city's homicides were *sex* related (given the amount of sex which takes place, it would appear to have a remarkable safety record). Yet the coroner has been widely misquoted (*Time Magazine, Peoria Journal Star,* and several different times in the *San Francisco Chronicle*) as the source of a completely fabricated statistic that ten percent of San Francisco's homicides are related to S/M.

After *Gay Power, Gay Politics* was aired, KPIX, the local CBS affiliate, presented a panel of local gay figures to respond. Most of them were successfully baited on the issue of S/M, hastening to disassociate themselves from it without challenging the distorted picture of S/M itself. Harry Britt, gay member of the board of supervisors, was the only panelist who criticized the coverage of S/M as well as the coverage of homosexuality. The CBS special has been widely rapped for its reporting on homosexuality. But its coverage of S/M has escaped scrutiny and has set a new low standard for the treatment of S/M in the media.

In March, 1981, KPIX ran a four part series on S/M on the 11 o'clock news. Called *Love and Pain,* the series used sensationalized facts, unsubstantiated claims, and a half-digested version of the anti-porn movement's analysis to present S/M as a public menace. The program repeatedly equated S/M with violence, called sex toys dangerous weapons, and made a wild claim that the city's emergency rooms were inundated with injuries caused by S/M activity.

Injuries and accidents do occur in the course of sexual activity, and S/M is not exempt. But by and large, S/M, particularly when practiced by people in touch with S/M communities, has a safety record most sports teams would envy. Among the people I know, there are more health problems caused by softball or long distance running than by whipping, bondage, or fist-fucking. The S/M community is obsessed with safety and has an elaborate folk technology of methods to maximize sensation and minimize danger. These techniques are transmitted largely by older or more experienced members to neophytes. S/M oppression renders this transmission difficult. Scaring people away from the community puts people in some real danger of trying things they do not know how to do.

A point of competition among tops, sadists, dominants, Mistresses, and Masters is over who is the safest (as well as the hottest, the most imaginative, and the most proficient). People who do not play safely—tops who get too drunk, bottoms who are too reckless—are identified and others are warned of them. Reputations in a small, gossip-ridden community are always fragile, so there is in fact a good deal of social control over patterns of play. People who are scared into viewing this community as dangerous are outside the protection it actually affords.

No community can completely protect its members from accidents or from people who are, for whatever reason, actually violent or dangerous. The S/M community has its criminals, just like any other. It is just as concerned that they be apprehended and put out of commission. But far more people end up in the hospital as a result of playing sports, driving cars, or being pregnant than from having S/M sex. One of the biggest sources of injury in San Francisco right now is queer-bashing, fed in part by anti-S/M hysteria. One of the worst things that I have heard of happening to an S/M person occurred when a gay man who was leaving a leather bar was assaulted by a gang of bashers. He suffered serious head injuries and the loss of an eye.

The idea that S/M is dangerous is self-perpetuating. A friend of mine died recently. He had a heart attack while he was having sex in his lovingly built playroom. When the police saw the S/M equipment they threatened to charge his lover with manslaughter. They notified the press, which aired lurid stories of "ritual sado-masochistic death." When the death was ruled accidental, the stories were quietly pulled, but no retraction or followup appeared to correct the lingering impression that S/M had caused the death. When men have coronaries while fucking their wives, the papers do not print stories implying that intercourse leads to death. Nor are their widows threatened with criminal charges. The only reason to link my friend's death to his sexual orientation was the preconception that S/M leads to death. That preconception generated the news stories. The news stories reinforce the preconception. Many people will have their prejudices about S/M corroborated by these ill-conceived "news" reports.

Besides promulgating the idea that S/M is dangerous to its practitioners, the KPIX program also alleged that S/M is harmful to those who do not do it. The program argued that S/M imagery in the media is a kind of miasma from which no one can escape. Therefore, S/M was "corroding the fabric of society," it was affecting everyone, and something ought to be done about it. Historically, crackdowns on activities which primarily affect those who are involved in them are rationalized on the basis of some similarly flimsy connection with social decay. Notions that marijuana, prostitution, or homosexuality by some vague mechanism lead to violent crime, disease, or creeping communism are used to rationalize punitive social or legal action against otherwise innocuous activities.

Love and Pain did not call for new laws to make S/M activity criminal. But the reporter, Gregg Risch, did propose that parents who do S/M be relieved of the custody of their children. The program did a whole segment on a woman who is living with her lover and her two-year-old child in a rural S/M community in Mendocino County. The reporter interviewed the child's grandmother, who was horrified and wanted to take the child. He also interviewed a shrink who pontificated that the child might be damaged by exposure to its mother's sexual orientation. He called for the Mendocino County authorities to come in and take the kid away from its mother.

Custody law is one of the places where sex dissenters of all sorts are viciously punished for being different. Lesbians and gay men are not the only groups whose rights to keep or raise offspring are drastically limited. The state may come in and snatch the children of prostitutes, swingers, or even "promiscuous" women. Society has a great deal of power to insure that sex dissenters are separated from young people, their own children as well as the next generation of sex perverts. A rough rule of sexual sociology is that the more stigmatized the sexuality, the higher the barriers are to finding one's way into that community, and the older people are when they finally get over them.

Risch expressed a great deal of dismay that so many S/M people were of child rearing age. All that this means is that the S/M community is full of adults—hardly cause for alarm. He did concede that S/M people might be allowed to keep their children if they were careful to hide their sexuality from them. But he felt that out of the closet sadomasochists should relinquish their offspring. One of the functions of custody law and practice is to reproduce conventional values. When lesbian mothers are granted custody on the condition that they do not live with their lovers, when swingers are forbidden to swing, when S/M people are required to hide, it is clear that sex dissenters are being denied the right to raise their children according to their value system. This insures that even if perverts have and keep their children, those kids will be inculcated with the dominant social mythology about sex.

In the wake of both *Gay Power, Gay Politics,* and *Love and Pain,* local news coverage of S/M has gotten worse. Less than two weeks after the KPIX series, the *San Francisco Chronicle* reported that the coroner had been conducting workshops on S/M safety, and that there was an "alarming increase in injuries and deaths from sado-masochistic sex."[9] Again, the phony statistic was quoted that ten percent of the city's homicides were S/M related. Dr. Stephens, the coroner, is currently suing the paper for libel. Aside from the inaccuracies of the article, it is true that the coroner has displayed a remarkable professionalism in dealing with the minority sexual populations of San Francisco. He has taken the trouble to learn about these communities, has displayed good judgment in dealing with them, and has earned their respect. For his trouble and his professionalism, he was given harsh treatment in the press and was chastized by Mayor Feinstein, who was quoted as saying, "It is my belief that S&M is dangerous to society and I'm not eager to have it attracted to San Francisco."[10]

In July of 1981, a large area burned south of Market Street, and press coverage was entirely sensational. The fire started on the site of a former gay and leather oriented bathhouse, the Barracks. The Barracks has been closed for years and the building was being remodeled as a hotel. But the press reported that the fire started in a "gay bathhouse." The area which burned is in the midst of the leather bars, so many gay men and S/M people lived on the street. But the neighborhood is mixed. There were old people, artists, Filipinos, and a good assortment of low income families living there as well. The largest single group of fire victims consisted of over twenty displaced children. Yet the media portrayed the fire as a gay and S/M event, as if the sexual orientation of some of the victims had somehow caused it.

One of the buildings that burned belonged to a man who manufactures Rush, a brand of poppers. The fire department suspected that Rush had caused or fed the fire and was searching for large quantities of it. No Rush was ever found. The fire department also hypothesized that since S/M people were known to live on the alley, that there might be bodies of slaves chained to their beds in the rubble. No bodies were ever found.

Media coverage of the fire promulgated the image that masochists are completely helpless, that they spend their time chained in their quarters, and that in the event of an emergency, they are simply abandoned by their callous keepers. Buried far back in the news reports on the third day were comments by neighborhood residents who pointed out that if anyone had been in bondage when the fire broke out, their lover or trick or friend would have done everything to save them. If a parent fails to save a child caught in a fire, no one assumes that families cause death. Had anyone been accidentally burned anywhere in proximity to S/M equipment or space, the tragedy would have been interpreted as sinister evidence that S/M people are inhuman monsters. Coverage of the fire was premised on the idea that S/M people do not care about one another. The straight media simply did not report on the human dimensions of a great community crisis.[11]

The papers did not mention, for instance, that the initial relief effort was run out of the Folsom Street Hotel, a fuck palace catering to the gay male leather community. They did not report that the Hothouse, a leather oriented bathhouse, immediately held a benefit for the victims. No whisper hit the papers that every South of Market bar and bath contributed some kind of aid and that all the leather bars became dropoff points for donations of food, clothing, and equipment for the fire victims, gay and straight. The *Chronicle* ran a picture of a burned out S/M playroom next to the story about how there might be dead slaves lying in the ruins. It did not report that an auction of used jockstraps was held at the Gold Coast, a leather bar, to raise money for the homeless.

All of this slanted media coverage is constructing a new demonization of S/M and probably heralds a campaign to clean it up. It is very similar to what happened to homosexuals in the 1950's. There were already plenty of antigay ideas, structures, and practices. But during a decade of headlines, arrests, investigations, and legislation, those pre-existing elements of homophobia were reconstituted into a new and more virulent ideology that homosexuality was an active menace which needed to be actively combated. Currently, there are already plenty of anti-S/M ideas, structures, and practices. But these are being drawn into the creation of a new ideological construct that will call for a more active extermination campaign against S/M. It is likely that many sadomasochists will be arrested and incarcerated for such heinous thought crimes as wanting to be tied up when they come.

The form such campaigns often take is that police use old laws, as they have done in Canada, to make a few spectacular arrests. The media cover the arrests the way they covered the fire, or my friend's death, and turn tragedy into an excuse to further harass the victims and their community. At some point, there will be an outcry for new laws to give police more power to deal with and control the "menace." These new laws will give police more summary powers against the target population and will lead to more arrests, more headlines, and more laws, until either the S/M community finds a way to stop the onslaught or until the repression runs out of steam.

Already, in the wake of the fire, a San Francisco supervisor considered introducing legislation to ban the sale of S/M equipment in the city. Many "feminist" anti-porn groups would support legislation against S/M material on other grounds. If our reading material and sexual technology were contraband, our community could be decimated by the police. And this kind of campaign, like those against homosexuals thirty years ago, will be seen as a hygenic measure, supported by conservatives and radicals alike. It will scapegoat a bunch of people whose only crime is exotic sexual tastes. And while all of this has been taking shape, what has the women's movement been doing? Why, it has been conducting a purge against its own rather tiny S/M population. The rhetoric of this purge is what most feminists think of as the "politics of S/M".

II.

Homosexuality is a response—consciously or not—to a male supremacist society. Because it is a response to oppressive institutions and oppressive relationships it is not necessarily a progressive response or one that challenges the power of the monopoly capitalist. We see that the pressures that capitalist society puts on each individual are tremendous... Today people are grasping at all kinds of straws, at exotic religious sects, mysticism, sex orgies, Trotskyism, etc.

Revolutionary Union[12]

While gay people can be anti-imperialists we feel that they cannot be Communists. To be a Communist, we must accept and welcome struggle in all facets of our lives, personal as well as political. We cannot

I see sadomasochism as resulting in part from the internalization of heterosexual dominant-submissive role playing. I see sadomasochism among lesbians as involving in addition an internalization of the homophobic heterosexual view of lesbians. Defending such behavior as healthy and compatible with feminism, even proselytizing in favor of it is about the most contra-feminist anti-political and bourgeois stance that I can imagine.

Diana Russell[13]

Sadomasochistic activity between/among lesbians is an outcome and perpetuation of patriarchal sadistic and masochistic culture.

ry[14]

struggle with male supremacy in the factory and not struggle at home. We feel that the best way to struggle out such contradictions in our personal lives is in stable monogamous relation between men and women...Because homosexuals do not carry the struggle between men and women into their most personal relationships, they are not prepared, in principle, for the arduous task of class transformation.

Revolutionary Union,
continued

The fact is, the whole culture is S/M, we're all sadomasochists. The people in SAMOIS, or gay people who wear leather, have a more severe form of the disease.

Susan Griffin[15]

SAMOIS is entitled to exist as a group devoted to S/M, but why should we let them get away with calling themselves lesbian-feminist?

tacie dejanikus[16]

The first time I came out was over a decade ago, when I realized, at the age of twenty, that I was a lesbian. I had to come out again, several years later, as a sadomasochist. The similarities and differences between these two experiences have been most instructive. On both occasions, I spent several months thinking that I must be the only one on earth, and was pleasantly surprised to discover there were large numbers of women who shared my predilections. Both debuts were fraught with tension and excitement. But the second coming out was considerably more difficult than the first.

I came out as a lesbian just when a bad discourse on homosexuality, the product of the anti-gay wars of the 1950's, was coming apart. I did not experience the full force of homophobia. On the contrary, to be a baby dyke in 1970 was to feel great moral self-confidence. One could luxuriate in the knowledge that not only was one not a slimy pervert, but one's sexuality was especially blessed on political grounds. As a result, I never quite understood the experience of being gay in the face of unrelenting contempt.

When I came out as an S/M person, I got an unexpected lesson in how my gay ancestors must have felt. My youth as a sadomasochist has been spent at a time when, as part of a more general reconsolidation of anti-sex and anti-gay ideology, a new demonization of S/M is taking shape. This is happening in the society at large and in the women's movement. It is a long way from 1970 to watch the images of your love turning uglier by the day, to fear being arrested, and to wonder how bad it will get. It is especially depressing if a once progressive movement in which you have spent your entire adult life is leading the assault. The experience of being a feminist sadomasochist in 1980 is similar to that of being a communist homosexual in 1950. When left ideology condemned homosexuality as bourgeois decadence, many homosexuals were forced out of progressive political organizations. A few of them founded the Mattachine Society. Now that large parts of the feminist movement have similarly defined S/M as an evil product of patriarchy, it has become increasingly difficult for those of us who are feminists to maintain our membership in the women's community.

Some feminist bookstores have refused to carry SAMOIS publications or books having a positive attitude toward S/M. Some stores which do carry such material have it shelved obscurely, or have put up cards warning customers against the contents. One store has even prepared a packet of anti-S/M readings which are included with any purchase of pro-S/M books. "Sadomasochistic" is routinely used as an epithet. A group is putting out a book called *Against Sadomasochism,* the advertising for which has promised a response to the "threat" posed by the existence of SAMOIS. The flyer for the book expresses horror that some of us have actually been "invited speakers at university classes" and that there has been an effort to "normalize sadomasochism."

I used to read the feminist press with enthusiasm. Now I dread each new issue of my favorite periodicals wondering what vile picture of my sexuality will appear this month. Papers and journals are reluctant to print pro-S/M articles, and usually only do so if accompanied by reams of disclaimer and at least one anti-S/M essay. However, essays that trash S/M are not held until the magazine can solicit a positive viewpoint.

Recently the Women's Building in San Francisco decided that SAMOIS cannot rent space in the building. Among the stated purposes of the building are a commitment to end oppression based on sexual orientation and a promise to respect the diversity of individual women. The Women's Building has a very open policy. Mixed groups, men's groups, community groups, non-feminist groups, and private parties regularly rent space. The building has frequently rented space for weddings. It is a sad commentary on the state of feminism that heterosexual weddings, sanctioned by religion and enforced by the state, are less controversial than the activities of a bunch of lesbian sex perverts.[17]

In 1980, the National Organization of Women passed a misleadingly labeled resolution on "lesbian and gay rights." What this resolution actually did was condemn S/M, cross-generational sex, pornography, and public sex. The resolution denied that these were issues of sexual or affectional preference and declared NOW's intention to disassociate itself from any gay or lesbian group that did not accept these definitions of sexual preference. When there was an attempt ten years ago to purge NOW of lesbian members, NOW was not stampeded into denying the legitimacy of gay rights. The campaign against the leather menace has succeeded where the attack on the lavender menace failed. It has put NOW on record as opposing sexual freedom and the civil rights of erotic minorities.

There are many reasons why S/M has become such a *bête noire* in the women's movement, and most originate outside of feminism. With the glaring exception of monogamous lesbianism, the women's movement usually reflects the sexual prejudices prevailing in society. Feminists have no monopoly on anti-S/M attitudes. The medical and psychiatric establishments have moved somewhat on homosexuality, but on virtually every other sexual variation they hold barely modified 19th century views. The psychiatric theories of sex in turn reflect the sexual hierarchies which exist in society. Another general rule of sexual sociology is that the more persecuted a sexuality, the worse its reputation.

A second force for which the women's movement is not responsible is the state of sex research and sex education. While the movement has a lamentable tendency to adopt some of the worst elements of sex research, the field as a whole is underdeveloped. Sex is so loaded and controversial in western culture that research on it is loaded and controversial. Sex research is inscribed within the power relations that organize sexual behavior.

Challenging those power relations with new data or original hypotheses brings one into conflict with deeply held folk theories of sex.

The sex field also reflects its marginality. Whereas almost every institution of higher learning has a department of psychology, there are virtually no departments of sexology. There are fewer than a dozen academic sites in the United States where sex research is conducted. There are few courses taught on sex at the college level, and pre-college sex education is still tenuous. Knowledge of sex is restricted. Getting into the Institute for Sex Research is like getting into Fort Knox. Almost every library has its sexual materials in a locked case, or a special collection, or oddly catalogued. The younger one is, the harder it is to have access to information about sex. The systematic restraints on curiosity about sex maintain sexual ignorance, and where people are ignorant, they are manipulable.

There are other reasons for the controversy over S/M which are more intrinsic to the women's movement and its history. One of these is the confusion between sexual orientation and political belief which originated in the idea that feminism is the theory, lesbianism is the practice. There are elements of truth in the idea that being a lesbian brings one into conflict with some basic elements of gender hierarchy. But like many good ideas, this insight has been overused and over-applied. It has made it difficult to accept that there are heterosexuals who are feminists, and that there are lesbians who are not. It has actually inhibited the development of lesbian politics and consciousness. It has led to the belief that lesbianism is only justified politically insofar as it is feminist. This in turn has encouraged feminist lesbians to look down on non-movement dykes. It has led feminist lesbians to identify more with the feminist movement than with the lesbian community. It has encouraged many women who are not sexually attracted to women to consider themselves lesbians. It has prevented the lesbian movement from asserting that our lust for women is justified whether or not it derives from feminist political ideology. It has generated a lesbian politic that seems ashamed of lesbian desire. It has made feminism into a closet in which lesbian sexuality is unacknowledged.[18]

If feminist politics entail or require particular sexual positions or forms of erotic behavior, then it follows that other kinds of sexual activity are specifically anti-feminist. Given prevailing ideas of appropriate feminist sexual behavior, S/M appears to be the mirror opposite. It is dark and polarized, extreme and ritualized, and above all, it celebrates difference and power. If S/M is understood as the dark opposite of happy and healthy lesbianism, accepting that happy and healthy lesbians also do S/M would threaten the logic of the belief system out of which this opposition was generated. But this analysis is not based on the realities of sexual behavior. It is predicated on a limited notion of the symbolic valences of both lesbianism and S/M. Torn from real social context, sexual differences can symbolize all kinds of other differences, including political ones. Thus, to some people, homosexuality is fascist, and to others it is communist. Lesbianism has been understood as narcissism and self worship, or as an inevitably unfulfilled yearning. To many right wingers, gayness in any form symbolizes the decline and fall of empires.

There is nothing inherently feminist or non-feminist about S/M. Sadomasochists, like lesbians, gay men, heterosexuals, etc., may be anarchists, fascists, democrats, republicans, communists, feminists, gay liberationists, or sexual reactionaries. The idea that there is an automatic correspondence between sexual preference and political belief is long overdue to be jettisoned.

This does not mean that sexual behavior should not be evaluated. How people treat each other in sexual contexts is important. But this is not the same issue as passing judgment on what are essentially cultural differences in sexual behavior. There are plenty of lesbian relationships which are long term and monogamous, in which both partners switch roles or do the same thing, in which all touching is gentle, but in which the partners are mean and nasty to each other. The idea that lesbianism, especially when practiced by feminists, is a superior form of sex often leads people to ignore the actual interpersonal dynamics. Conversely, the idea that S/M is warped leads to an inability to perceive love, friendship, and affection among S/M people. S/M partners may occupy polarized roles, the touching may be rough, and yet they may treat each other with respect and affection. In all sexualities, there is a range of how people act toward one another. Ranking different sexualities from best to worst simply substitutes for exercising judgment about specific situations.

The ease with which S/M has come to symbolize the feminist equivalent of the Anti-Christ has been exacerbated by some long term changes in feminist ideology. Few women in the movement seem to realize that what currently passes for radical feminism has a tangential relationship with the initial premises of the women's movement. Assumptions which now pass as dogma would have horrified activists in 1970. In many respects, the women's movement, like the society at large, has quietly shifted to the right.

Feminists in 1970 were angry because women, the things women did, and female personality traits were devalued. But we were also enraged at the restrictions placed on female behavior. Women were not supposed to engage in a range of activities considered masculine. A woman who wanted to fix cars, get laid, ride a motorcycle, play sports, or get a Ph.D. could expect criticism from the society and support from the women's movement. The term "male identified" meant that a woman lacked consciousness of female oppression.

By 1980, the term "male identified" had lost that meaning (lack of political consciousness) and has become synonymous with "masculine." Now, women who do masculine things are accused of imitating men not only by family, church, and the media, but by the feminist movement.[19] Much contemporary feminist ideology is that everything female—persons, activities, values, personality characteristics—is good, whereas anything pertaining to males is bad. By this analysis, the task of feminism is to replace male values with female ones, to substitute female culture for male culture. This line of thinking does not encourage women to try to gain access to male activities, privileges, and territories. Instead, it implies that a good feminist wants nothing to do with "male" activities. All of this celebration of femininity tends to reinforce traditional gender roles and values of appropriate female behavior. It is not all that different from the sex role segregation against which early feminists revolted. I, for one, did not join the women's movement to be told how to be a good girl. There are many labels for this brand of feminism, but my preferred term is "femininism."[20]

Femininism has become especially powerful with regard to issues of sexuality and issues of violence, which it not surprisingly links together. Sexuality is seen as a male value and activity. The femininist view of sex is that it is something that good/nice women do not especially like. In this view, sex is not a motivating force in female behavior. Women have sex as an expression of intimacy, but orgasm is seen as a male goal. The idea that sexuality is most often something men impose upon women leads to the equation of sex with violence, and the conflation of sex with rape. These were the sexual theories I was taught growing up. I never expected to have them rammed down my throat by the women's movement. Man the Id and Woman the Chaste are Victorian ideas, not feminist ones.[21]

The re-emphasis on feminine values, especially sexual chastity, has led to a shift in the mode of argument for feminist goals. Instead of arguing for justice or social equality, much feminist polemic now claims a female moral superiority. It is argued that we should have more, or total, power in society because we are more equipped for it, mainly by virtue of our role in reproduction, than men. I did not join the women's movement to have my status depend on my ability to bear children.

I fear that the women's movement is repeating the worst errors of a century ago. The nineteenth century feminist movement began as a radical critique of women's role and status. But it became increasingly conservative and similarly shifted the burden of its argument onto a reconstituted femininity in the form of alleged female moral superiority. Much of the nineteenth century movement degenerated into a variety of morality crusades, with conservative feminists pursuing what they took to be women's agenda in anti-prostitution, anti-masturbation, anti-obscenity, and anti-vice campaigns. It will be an historical tragedy of almost unthinkable dimensions if the revived feminist movement dissipates into a series of campaigns against recreational sex, popular music, and sexually explicit materials. But this appears to be the direction in which feminism is moving.[22]

By a series of accidents, and through the mediating issue of pornography, S/M has become a challenge to this entire political tendency, which has ridden to power by manipulating women's fears around sex and around violence. Therefore, when feminists argue about S/M, there is much more at stake than sexual practice. Some women are arguing for the logical coherence of their political beliefs. Others of us are arguing that political theory about sex is due for a major overhaul based on a more sophisticated sociology of sex. But what often seems most at stake is the shape of feminist ideology and the future direction of the movement. There are ways of understanding S/M which are compatible with "femininism" and its attendant political programs. When these become more articulated (and they will, in the not too distant future), S/M will seem to be less of a threat to the hegemonic ideology of the women's movement. But for now, the fight over S/M has been the locus of a struggle over deep political differences in the women's movement.

Given the immense symbolic load that S/M has acquired, it is not surprising that it is difficult for participants in this debate to absorb information about S/M that would make these arguments difficult to sustain. Nevertheless, the picture of S/M which is assumed in the current diatribes has almost no relationship to the actual experience of anyone involved in it.

III.

...for "consent" to be a meaningful criteria all the parties involved must have some measure of real choices. Women, for instance, have been "consenting" to marriage for centuries. Women in China had "consented" to the footbinding of their own daughters. This is coerced-consent, and it hardly constitutes freedom. The most "heavy" masochist, who gives his hands and feet to be shackled to some rack, who offers his body to be gang-banged, fist-fucked, and pissed upon—he "consents," but if he has so internalized society's hatred of him as to offer his own body for a beating, then his "consent" is merely a conditioned reflex.

letter to Gay Community News[23]

Coming out has several meanings. Sometimes it refers to the point at which a person realizes that they are gay or have some other variant sexuality. Coming out in this sense is a form of self recognition. Another meaning of coming out is that of public declaration, of being willing to let other people know about it. In yet another sense, coming out is a kind of journey people take from the straight world where they start into the gay or other variant world they want to occupy. Most of us are born into and raised by straight families, educated in straight schools, and socialized by straight peer groups. Our upbringing does not provide us with the social skills, information, or routes of access into non-conventional sexual lifestyles. We must find our way into those social spaces where we can meet partners, find friends, get validation, and participate in a community life which does not presuppose that we are straight. Sometimes this journey is fairly short, from the suburbs of large cities to the gay bars downtown. In small towns, it usually means finding an underground network or building a more public community. Often it means migrating from middle America to a bigger city, such as New York, Los Angeles, Chicago, or San Francisco. A classic account of this kind of coming out is the fifties pulp novel, *I am a Woman*.[24] Laura, the heroine, suffers vague malaise in the midwest, so she takes a bus to New York City. Eventually, she stumbles into a lesbian bar in Greenwich Village. She instantly realizes who she is, that there are others like her, and that this is home. She finds a lover, develops a gay identity, and becomes an adult, functioning lesbian.

This kind of migratory behavior is characteristic of sexual minorities. There are many barriers to the process. These include the marginality of dissenting sexual communities, the amount of legal apparatus built to control them, the social penalties to which their members are subject, and the unrelenting propaganda that portrays them as dangerous, sleazy, horrid places full of dreadful people and unspecified pitfalls. It is extraordinary that young perverts, like salmon swimming upstream, continually and in great numbers make this journey. Much of the politics of sex consists of battles to determine the costs of belonging to such communities and how difficult it will be to get into them.

I came out as a lesbian in a small college town that had no visible lesbian community. A group of us formed a radical lesbian feminist group which eventually grew into a fairly large, albeit young, public lesbian community. The nearest pre-movement lesbian community was thirty miles away, where there were actually a couple of lesbian bars. There was one mostly male gay bar called the Flame. I had heard for years that it was the kind of place you wanted to stay away from. There were vague implications that if you went there, something bad would happen. But it was the only gay bar in town, and I was drawn to it. I finally screwed up my courage and walked in. The minute I got past the front door I relaxed. It was full of very innocuous looking gay men and a couple of lesbians. I instantly realized that these were my people, and that I was one of the people I had been warned against.

Before I walked into the Flame, I still thought that gay people were rare and scarce. Going through that door was like going through the looking glass. On the other side of that taboo entrance is not a place of terror, but a huge, populous, prosperous, bustling world of homosexuals. What is most incredible about the whole experience is that so large a part of reality could have been kept so invisible to my entire generation. It is as if one grew up under the impression that there were no Italians, or Jews, or Chinese in the United States.

Seven years later, I was again sweating in front of another tabooed threshold. This time it was the door to the Pleasure Chest in New York City. I must have walked up and down Seventh Avenue twenty times before I finally got a friend to go in with me. It took a little longer to get used to the S/M world than to the gay world. But by now I feel as at home in leather bars and sex toy shops as I do in lesbian bars and gay restaurants. Instead of the monsters and slimy perverts I had been led to expect, I found another hidden community. The S/M community is not as large as the gay community, but it is complex, populated, and quite civilized. Most parts of the S/M community take a responsible attitude to newcomers, teaching them how to do S/M safely, S/M etiquette, and acquired wisdom. Preconceived chimeras disappear in the face of actual social practice. I had been worried that my eroticism would require that I give up control over my life or become some kind of mindless nebbish. One of the first lessons I learned was that you can do S/M by agreement *and* it can still be a turn-on. There is a lot of separation between the straight, gay, and lesbian S/M communities. But there is also pan-

S/M consciousness. As one wise woman who has been doing this for many years has said, "Leather is thicker than blood."

The largest sub-population of sadomasochists is probably the heterosexuals. Of these, most appear to be male submissive/ female dominant. Much of the straight S/M world revolves around professional female dominants and their submissive clients. There are also some straight or predominantly straight social clubs and political organizations through which heterosexual sadomasochists can meet one another. In the last few years, the straight S/M community in New York City began to have regular nights at a bar. And even more recently, an S/M sex club opened which has a predominantly heterosexual clientele.

I should point out that contrary to much of what is said about straight S/M in the feminist press, heterosexual S/M is *not* standard heterosexuality. Straight S/M is stigmatized and persecuted. Whatever the metaphoric similarities between standard sex and S/M, once someone starts to use whips, ropes, and all the theatre, they are considered to be perverts, not normal. The relationship between heterosexual S/M and "normal" heterosexuality is at most like the relationship between high school faggots and the high school football team. There is some overlap of personnel. But for the most part all that fanny-patting and even an occasional blow-job does not make the jocks into fags. And the former would rather beat up the latter than accompany them to the nearest gay bar.

Gay male sadomasochists are less numerous than heterosexuals, but they are much better organized. Gay men have developed an elaborate technology for building public institutions for sexual outlaws. When the gay male leather community emerged, it followed the organizational patterns of the larger homosexual community. The first gay male leather bar opened in New York in 1955. The first one in San Francisco opened about five years later. There was a population explosion of leather bars along with gay bars in general (including lesbian bars) around 1970. In San Francisco today, there are five to ten leather bars and about five baths or sex clubs that cater to the gay male leather community. There are also several social or charitable organizations, motorcycle clubs, a performance space, assorted shops, and a couple of restaurants for the South of Market crowd. Although leather styles were faddish in the larger gay community for a couple of years, and leather/macho has replaced drag queen fluff as the dominant gay stereotype, the leather community is a distinct subgroup. The average gay man is not into leather or S/M. But the average gay man is probably more aware of sexual diversity and erotic possibilities than most heterosexuals or lesbians.

Lesbian social organization is smaller scale but similar to gay male. Bars have been for many years the most important public community space. Since 1970, feminist political organizations and cultural institutions have provided another major context for lesbian social life. Unlike gay men, lesbians have not yet developed more specialized sexual sub-groups. There are lesbians who do everything that gay men and heterosexuals do. There are girl-lovers, sadomasochists, and fetishists (probably for flannel shirts, hiking boots, cats, softball uniforms, alfalfa sprouts, and feminist tracts). There are many transvestites and transsexuals (especially female to male). But lesbian sexual diversity is relatively unnoticed, unconscious, and unorganized.

When I came out as a lesbian sadomasochist, there was no place to go. A notice I put up in my local feminist bookstore was torn down. It took months of painstaking detective work to track down other women who were into S/M. There was no public lesbian S/M community to find, so I had to help build one. At least in San Francisco, there is now a visible, accessible avenue for lesbians to find their way into an S/M context. SAMOIS is a motley collection. We have lots of refugees from Lesbian Nation, a good number of bar dykes, and many women who work in the sex industry. It is clear in retrospect that what has happened in the last three years or so is another mass coming out. There are now about as many sadomasochists in most lesbian communities as there were radical feminist lesbians in 1970. There would be groups like SAMOIS in virtually every lesbian community in the U.S. if the costs of coming out were not so excruciating. It takes someone being willing to put out the word and serve as a focus for other dyke perverts to start coming out of the woodwork. But most women have watched SAMOIS get trashed and are afraid to be treated the same way.

My second coming out has been much more difficult than the first. The S/M community is even more underground and harder to find than the lesbian community. The routes of access to it are even more hidden. The aura of terror is more intense. The social penalties, the stigma, and the lack of legitimacy are even greater. I have rarely worked so hard or displayed such independence of mind as when I came out as an S/M person. I had to reject virtually everything I had been told about it. Having struggled this hard to assume a stigmatized identity (one "they taught me to despise"), I find the idea that I have been brainwashed infuriating and ludicrous. A sadist is likely to be regarded as a dangerous character. A top is vulnerable to legal prosecution. In the current debate on S/M, a top risks having their testimony dismissed. A masochist has more credibility in defending S/M. But a masochist risks being held in contempt. I am in much less danger of being treated badly by tops or sadists than by the people who want to protect me from them.

It is an unfortunate habit of sexual thought that people so readily assume that something they would not like would be equally unpleasant to someone else. I hate to run. I might someday change my mind, but at this point it would take a lot of coercion to get me to run around the block, let alone for five miles. This does not mean that my friends who run in marathons are sick, brainwashed, or at gunpoint.

People who are not into anal sex find it incomprehensible that anyone else could enjoy it. People who gag at oral sex are baffled that anyone else would actually enjoy sucking cock or eating pussy. But the fact remains that there are uncountable hordes for whom oral sex or anal sex are exquisitely delightful. Sexual diversity exists, not everyone likes to do the same things, and people who have different sexual preferences are not sick, stupid, warped, brainwashed, under duress, dupes of the patriarchy, products of bourgeois decadence, or refugees from bad child-rearing practices. The habit of explaining away sexual variation by putting it down needs to be broken.

The idea that masochists are victims of sadists underlies much of the debate on S/M. But tops and bottoms are not two discrete populations. Some individuals have strong and consistent preferences for one role or the other. Most S/M people have done both, and many change with different partners, at different times, or according to situation or whim.

Nor are the social relations between tops and bottoms similar to the social relations between men and women, blacks and whites, straights and queers. Sadists do not systematically oppress masochists. Of course, class privilege, race, and gender do not disappear when people enter the S/M world. The social power individuals bring to the S/M community affects their ability to negotiate within it, whether as tops or bottoms. But class, race, and gender neither determine nor correspond to the roles adopted for S/M play. The oppression which is connected to S/M comes from a society bent on keeping people from engaging in non-conventional sex and which punishes them when they do.

The silliest arguments about S/M have been those which claim that it is impossible that people really consent to do it. The issue of consent has been clouded by an overly hasty application of Marxian critiques of bourgeois contract theory to sex law and practice. Marxists argue that just because someone voluntarily enters into an agreement to do something, does not mean that they have not been coerced by forces impinging on the decision. This is a useful distinction since social relations of class, gender, race, and so forth in fact do limit the scope of possible decisions which can be made. So do the social relations of sexuality, but not by forcing people to be perverts.

In sex law, consent is what distinguishes sex from rape. But consent is a privilege which is not enjoyed equally by all sexualities. Although it varies according to state, most sexual activity is illegal. The fewest restrictions apply to adult heterosexuality. But adult incest is illegal in most states, and adultery in many. In some states, sodomy laws even apply to heterosexuals, who may be prosecuted for oral or anal sex. Homosexuality is much more restricted than heterosexuality. Except for the states which have passed consenting adult statutes decriminalizing homosexuality, it is still illegal to have gay sex. Before 1976, a gay person in California did not have the legal right to have oral sex with their lover, and could be prosecuted for doing it. Minors have no right at all to consent to sex, although it is usually only adult partners who are prosecuted. But sexually active youth can be sent to juvenile homes and are subject to other penalties.

In addition to clearly defined legal restrictions, sex laws are unequally enforced. And in addition to the activities of police, forces like religion, medicine, media, education, family, and the state all function to pressure people to be married, heterosexual, monogamous, and conventional. One may more reasonably ask if anyone truly "consents" to be straight in any way. Coercion does occur among perverts, as it does in all sexual contexts. One still needs to distinguish rape and abuse from consensual situations. But the overwhelming coercion with regard to S/M is the way in which people are prevented from doing it. We are fighting for the freedom to consent to our sexuality without interference, and without penalty.

IV.

We are sworn that no boy or
girl, approaching the maelstrom
of deviation, need make that
crossing alone, afraid, or in the
dark ever again.
The Mattachine Society, 1951[25]

Current radical (mostly feminist) writing on S/M is a hopeless muddle of bad assumptions, inaccurate information, and a thick-headed refusal to accept evidence which contravenes preconceptions. It needs to be taken apart point by point. But prejudice is like a hydra. As soon as one avenue of sexual bigotry is blocked, alternative channels are developed. Ultimately, acceptance is gained by political power as much as by rational argument. Bigotry against S/M will flourish until it is more expensive to maintain than to abandon. Like the social discourse on homosexuality, this discourse on S/M sets up phony issues and poses phony questions. At some point, we need to step out of this framework and develop an alternative way to think about sexuality and understand its politics.

Minority sexual communities are like religious heretics. We are persecuted by the state, the mental health establishment, social welfare agencies, and the media. When you are a sex pervert, the institutions of society do not work for you, and often work against you. Sexual dissenters face an endless stream of propaganda which rationalizes abuses against them, attempts to impair their self esteem, and exhorts them to recant.

In addition to social hierarchies of class, race, gender, and ethnicity, there is a heirarchy based on sexual behavior. The most blessed form of sexual contact is heterosexual, married, monogamous, and reproductive. Unions that are unmarried, non-monagamous, non-reproductive, involve more than two partners, are homosexual, or which involve kink or fetish, are judged as inferior and punished accordingly. This hierarchy has rarely been challenged since its emergence, except by the gay movement. But it is a domain of social life in which great power is exercised. The "lower" sexual orders are human fodder for the prisons and the mental institutions.

It is time that radicals and progressives, feminists and leftists, recognize this hierarchy for the oppressive structure that it is instead of reproducing it within their own ideologies. Sex is one of the few areas in which cultural imperialism is taken as a radical stance. Neither the therapeutic professions, the women's movement, nor the left have been able to digest the concept of benign sexual variation. The idea that there is one best way to do sex afflicts radical as well as conservative thought on the subject. Cultural relativism is not the same thing as liberalism.

One of the sad things about the current debates on sex in the women's movement is that they are so stupid and regressive. Once the impulse to purge all sex freaks from feminist organizations passes, we will still have to face more intelligent arguments. Among them will be a kind of neo-Reichian position which is pro-sex but which understands the more stigmatized sexualities and practices (pornography, S/M, fetishism) as symptoms of sexual repression. Unlike Reich, the neo-Reichian position may accept homosexuality as a healthy or natural eroticism.

What is exciting is that sex—not just gender, not just homosexuality—has finally been posed as a political question. Rethinking sexual politics has generated some of the most creative political discourse since 1970. The sexual outlaws—boy-lovers, sadomasochists, prostitutes, and transpeople, among others—have an especially rich knowledge of the prevailing system of sexual hierarchy and of how sexual controls are exercised. These populations of erotic dissidents have a great deal to contribute to the reviving radical debate on sexuality.

The real danger is not that S/M lesbians will be made uncomfortable in the women's movement. The real danger is that the right, the religious fanatics, and the right-controlled state will eat us all alive. It is sad to be having to fight to maintain one's membership in the women's movement when it is so imperative to create broad based coalitions against fascism. The level of internal strife around S/M should be reserved for more genuine threats to feminist goals. If we survive long enough, feminists and other progressives will eventually stop fearing sexual diversity and begin to learn from it.

Author's Note

I have benefited immensely from innumerable conversations about sex, politics, and S/M with Pat Califia. The work that Allan Berube, John D'Emilio, and Daniel Tsang have done to exhume the story of gay persecution in the fifties has taught me how sex repression works. My sense of the politics of sex in the nineteenth century evolved during conversations with Ellen Dubois, Mary Ryan, and Martha Vicinus. My sense of the context for the politics of sex during the Cold War is largely due to input from Lynn Eden. Conversations with Jeff Escoffier and Amber Hollibaugh have sparked many lines of thought about the social relations of sexuality. I have been taught much of the recent history and many of the fine points of S/M by I.B., Camilla Decarnin, Jim Kane, Jason Klein, Terry Kolb, the Illustrious Mistress LaLash, Steve McEachern, Bob Milne, Cynthia Slater, Sam Steward, Louis Weingarden, and Doric Wilson. While responsibility for the opinions expressed in this essay is mine, I want to express my thanks to all these individuals for their insights, their information, and their generosity.

This essay has been revised somewhat for the second edition of *Coming To Power.*

1. *Styles of Radical Will,* 1969, New York, Farrar, Straus, and Giroux, page 46.
2. I am indebted to Allan Berube, John D'Emilio, and Daniel Tsang for much of what I know about it. Each of them has generously shared their research in progress. For published sources, see the following: John D'Emilio, "Dreams Deferred," three parts, *The Body Politic,* November 1978, December/January 1978/1979, and February 1979; John D'Emilio, "Gay Politics, Gay Community: The San Francisco Experience," *Socialist Review,* January/February 1981; Allan Berube, "Behind the Spectre of San Francisco," *The Body Politic,* April 1981; Jonathan Katz, *Gay American History,* 1976, New York, Thomas Crowell, pages 91–119, and 406–420. See also John Gerassi, *The Boys of Boise,* 1966, New York, Collier.
3. For further details, see Pat Califia, "The Age of Consent," two parts, *The Advocate,* October 16 and October 30, 1980; Mitzel, *The Boston Sex Scandal,* 1980, Boston, Glad Day Books; Roger Moody, *Indecent Assault,* 1980, London, Word Is Out.
4. Meanwhile, Dan White got seven years for the coldblooded murder of two public officials, one of them gay, and Ronald Crumpley was acquitted of the murder of two gay men (and the wounding of several others) by reason of insanity.
5. Lest I be misunderstood, the point is not that the Jaguar should not be supported. It should. But the contrast in community response to the troubles of the Jaguar and the troubles of the Bootcamp was stunning.
6. Randy Alfred, text of complaint against *Gay Power, Gay Politics,* lodged with the National News Council, July 10, 1980, page 4.
7. Alfred, page 5.
8. Alfred, page 5.
9. Pearl Stewart, "Safety Workshops for S.F. Masochists," *San Francisco Chronicle,* March 12, 1981.
10. Marshall Kilduff, "Angry Mayor Cuts Off Coroner's S&M Classes," *San Francisco Chronicle,* March 14, 1981.
11. *San Francisco Chronicle,* July 11–July 14, 1981.
12. Revolutionary Union, statement *On Homosexuality,* 1976. Note that the statement was referring to both lesbians and gay men.
13. "Sadomasochism as a Contra-feminist Activity," *Plexus,* November 1980.
14. ry, "S/M Keeps Lesbians Bound to the Patriarchy," *Lesbian Insider/Insighter/Inciter,* July 1981.
15. M.A. Karr, "Susan Griffin," *The Advocate,* Marcy 20, 1980.
16. tacie dejanikus, "Our Legacy," *Off Our Backs,* November 1980.
17. Correspondence and other documentation of the interactions between SAMOIS and various feminist institutions (including the Women's Building and *Off Our Backs*) are on file at the Lesbian Herstory Archives in New York City.
18. The phenomenon of feminism as a closet for lesbianism is discussed by Chris Bearchell in "The Cloak of Feminism," *The Body Politic,* June 1979, p. 20.
19. I should add that the term has also simply become an all purpose insult whose meaning is simply that the speaker does not approve of the person or activity to which it is applied.
20. An excellent historical study of some of these shifts in feminist ideology can be found in Alice Echols, "Cultural Feminism: Feminist Capitalism and the Anti-Pornography Movement," unpublished manuscript, June 1981, Women's Studies Program, University of Michigan.
21. There is a certain amount of bad faith around sex in all this. There is plenty of sex in the women's movement, and most feminists are just as obsessed with it as anyone else. But it has gotten hard to call things by their real names, or acknowledge lust as an end in itself. There is rampant euphemism, and a self-centered notion that "feminist sex" is a higher form of erotic expression. And the boundaries of what can be "feminist sex" shrink by the day.

22. Among the histories which shed light on the relationship between nineteenth century feminism and various sexual populations and issues are these: Linda Gordon, *Woman's Body, Woman's Right,* 1976, New York, Penguin; Judith Walkowitz, *Prostitution and Victorian Society,* 1980, New York, Cambridge; Judith Walkowitz, "The Politics of Prostitution," *Signs,* Autumn, 1980; and Jeffrey Weeks, *Coming Out: Homosexual Politics in Britain, from the Nineteenth Century to the Present,* 1977, New York, Quartet.
23. Neil Glickman, "Letter to the Editor," *Gay Community News,* August 22, 1981.
24. Ann Bannon, 1959, Greenwich, Connecticut, Fawcett Publications.
25. Cited in John D'Emilio, "Radical Beginnings, 1950–51," *The Body Politic,* November, 1978, p. 24.

Passion Play

MARTHA ALEXANDER

It was 3:15 and Meg would be arriving soon. She had just gotten into town after a long week of exercising her political finesse at the National Women's Studies Association Conference, and delivering a paper on "The Redefinition of Community as a Trend Toward Exclusion." Carole was eager to hear all the stories. Who was sleeping with who and how that modified, solidified or reversed political alliances. Who stabbed who in the back. Who got trashed outright. What the updates were on the current ideological drift. And then they'd play that ongoing game of figuring out who were the main power players, who were the rising stars.

Carole had been looking forward to Meg's visit for months. Although it would be fun guessing who was who in the political monopoly, she was really more interested in the personal. Because of the distance, it wasn't often that they could spend time with each other. It had been years since Bloomington where Meg and Carole had lived together and though career and a variety of relationships had moved them in separate geographic directions, the two women maintained a close, loving and, when possible, sexual relationship.

The doorbell rang. Carole ran to the window and looked down to see the top of Meg's head, her jet-black curly hair blowing in the spring breeze. Carole pressed the buzzer to release the lock on the street door downstairs. As she walked to the door of the large studio apartment, she checked herself in the mirror. Very short sandy hair with enough gray to be noticeable now without needing a close inspection. Paint-spattered, though freshly washed, jeans and a red t-shirt which tightly stretched across her almost flat chest. Looking pretty good, she thought. She unfastened the deadbolt and the chain, opened the door to the landing and leaned over the railing.

"Hey, Meg!" she shouted down the stairwell.

Meg paused in the middle of the second flight and looked up, grinning and somewhat exasperated, "God, how come you always find these bird perches to live in? Huh?"

Meg shook her head and resumed trudging up to the fourth floor. As soon as she reached the top she dropped the heavy satchell she was carrying and set her bursting briefcase against the railing. The two women hugged, a long close embrace. After Meg caught her breath, they kissed. As Carole moved from lips to cheek to neck, the fragrant smell of Meg's jacket filled her nostrils. She touched her lips to the slick/soft black leather, and then slowly pulled back. For a few moments the two women just stood there quietly smiling and looking at each other.

"I'm so glad to be here," Meg said breaking the silence. "God you look great."

Carole laughed, "Come on in," and the two of them gathered up Meg's paraphernalia, took it into the apartment and closed the door.

That night they went to Greek Town for dinner and stuffed themselves on gyros with lemon, an appetizer made from fish roe which had a name neither of them could remember, lemon-rice soup, and spanakopita, topping it all off by sharing a very large and syrupy piece of baklava and two small cups of thick, spiced Greek coffee. They talked politics all the way home and on into the night until they hardly had the strength to climb up into Carol's loft bed.

Waking up in mid-morning, they took an elevated train into the Loop and bought coffee and donuts for breakfast on their way over to the Art Institute. Carole had been wanting to show Meg her latest work and they decided to do that first thing, so that they'd have the rest of the day open to play. The lake sparkled in the morning sun as they walked down Monroe Drive before turning right onto Columbus. Carole watched Meg's reflection in the windows of the Institute's new wing as they went up the steps.

She could feel the aura of Meg's strength, confidence and power radiating around her. Few people in her professional circle knew that besides Meg's academic degrees, she also held a black belt in Akido. Carole looked at Meg, saw the jacket which hid the muscular shoulders. Her gaze drifted to Meg's ass, large, round and firm and right out there in sight. What a great fanny, Carole thought. She'd always loved Meg's bottom. Very substantial, but yielding.

They returned to the apartment in the early afternoon before the city exhaustion set in, and quickly climbed into the shower to wash away the grime. Meg got out first and dried herself off, while Carole luxuriated in the last moments of super-hot water before the tank ran out. Carole turned off the tap and pulled back the curtain. Meg was combing her towel-dried hair, trying to see her reflection in the steamed up mirror.

"Meg, will you dry me off?"

Meg smiled. "Sure, dear," she said, getting a clean towel from the cabinet under the sink. She rubbed and pat-dried Carole, beginning with her face and neck, then to shoulders, arms and hands to the fingertips. As Meg moved down Carole's body, she kneeled on the floor to better reach her legs, knees and feet. As each foot was dried, Carole stepped out of the tub. She looked down at Meg, who looked up, waiting.

"Get up and help me get dressed," Carole said as she turned and walked into the other room. Meg stood up and followed. Carole flopped down in an old easy chair near the long windows which filled her apartment with soft golden light in the late afternoon.

She liked this place better than any other she'd lived in. It was one of the first of a series of warehouses to be converted into living quarters back in the late '50's. For Carole, there was something soothing about the open brickwork, exposed ducts and heavy wood crossbeams. There were no illusions that the building was something other than what it was. No whitewashed, plastered-over walls or indirect lighting to mask the ruggedness of the original structure. It was a basic, functional living space. A solid place to begin her days from, and return to in the night. And, of course, there were the windows. Carole often thought she liked them most of all. Big, industrial, many-paned windows. There weren't any buildings across the street and since she lived on the top floor, the windows didn't need to be curtained. She looked at Meg quietly standing in the wide ribbon of sunlight that splashed across the floor.

"Oh Meg, you're so beautiful."

Meg smiled and scrunched up her strong shoulders in that little girl kind of shrug that she didn't often let out. Thirty-eight-year-old professional feminists had their survival roles to conform to just like anyone else. Meg was no exception. Except here. Except with Carole. With Carole she was always able to let down her defenses, relax and play.

"What can I do for you?" Meg asked.

"What can you do for *who?*" Carole said.

"Pardon *me,*" Meg said, embarassed at her obvious mistake. She corrected herself, "What can I do for you, Mistress?"

"Better. Much better. Forgetting yourself these days?"

"I'm sorry, Mistress. I . . ."

"Never mind," Carole said with a slight edge in her voice. "I don't want to hear your whining excuses. Get me my pants. They're in the top drawer. My boots, too. In the closet."

Meg walked out of the sun and over to the dresser. She opened the drawer and found Carole's leather pants laid out on top of the other clothes. Meg picked the pants up and draped them carefully over her arm, closed the drawer and went to the closet for the boots. She brought them to Carole, knelt down in front of her and set the boots to one side. After she guided Carole's right foot and then the left into each pant leg, Carole stood up. Meg worked the skin-tight pants up Carole's legs and fit the supple leather around her ass and thighs. Pulling the two sides together across her stomach, she smoothed the wide front flap down over Carole's tangled pubic hair and laced the pants together. Carole sat on the wide arm of the chair as Meg picked up the boots and began to put them on Carole's feet. When she finished, Meg sat back on her heels and looked up at her lover.

Carole looked superb. The soft leather almost a part of the rest of her soft skin, the small breasts with the firm upturned nipples, the wisps of silvery brown hair peeking out from her armpits. Meg welcomed the feelings rising in her of contentment, praise, and willing obedience, mixed with pleasure and excitement.

Carole reached toward Meg and began to caress her face, rubbing her cheeks and chin, pushing at her full lips and probing her mouth when Meg began to suck at and lick Carole's fingers. With her other hand, Carole massaged Meg's head until she saw the tension start to fade from her body. Then digging her hands into Meg's curly hair, Carole pulled her up to kneeling again and pushed Meg's face into her crotch. Meg breathed the aroma of leather, mingled with the smell of saddle soap and oil. Meg's shoulders rose and fell with her deep inhales and exhales. She began to moan and lick the seam of Carole's pants. Abruptly, Carole pushed Meg away, got up from the chair and walked to the other side of the room.

"So now what am I going to do with you?" Carole said in mock irritation. "Just looking at that bland skin of your is monotonous, and I really don't want to be bored."

"No, Mam," Meg said sheepishly. "What would please you?"

"If you put some proper clothes on that naked body of yours, that would be a decent start. Come here."

Meg hesitated.

"Get *up* and come over here, I said."

Meg went and stood in front of Carole, eyes downcast. Carole picked up a large round container from the dresser, opened it and pulled out a big powder puff. She began to pat talcum all over Meg's body. She stroked Meg's skin with the velvety pad and used it to nudge and tease her nipples.

"No," Meg whispered.

"Did I hear you say something?" Carole asked.

"I don't want to do this," Meg said under her breath.

"What do you mean you don't *want* to do this. You *love* to do this. Or have you changed since your last letter?"

"No. Uh, I mean, yes. Uh . . ."

"Well, what is it?" Carole said sternly. "Yes or no? Answer me."

"No, I haven't changed, Mistress. Yes, I like doing what you ask and pleasing you, but . . ." Meg hesitated again.

"But, what?"

234

"But I don't like *this*," Meg said anxiously, "I...don't like what you're doing right now."

"All I'm doing is putting talcum powder on you after your shower," Carole said as she took Meg's jaw firmly in her hand and drew Meg's head up to look her in the eye. "Are you going to act like a baby about it? Going to throw a temper tantrum?"

"Carole, you *know* how much I hate being a 'girl'. It's embarrassing, humiliating..."

"I know," Carole said wisely.

"I have my dignity!" Meg said in a determined and flustered way.

"I know that, too, and I'd hoped you had left it with those tight-assed ladies back at NWSA," Carole said, stepping back to appraise Meg's body which was quivering with indignation. "Now look in the bottom drawer and put on everything you can find that's pink."

"Pink?" Meg was horrified. "You bitch!"

"My, my, feisty aren't you? Do I have to punish you before we even get started?" Carole said as she began to touch and rub Meg's breasts.

"Carole, no," she said, resisting. "How long have you been plotting this?"

"Long enough to get *very* irritated at you if you start acting like a spoiled brat."

Carole ignored the rest of Meg's squirming protests and pulled at and squeezed her right nipple until she stopped talking and started reacting to the pressure of the touch. When she began to groan and make some noise, Carole said, "Good, I like to hear you appreciate me."

Carole loved threatening Meg with lace or anything on that order. Meg worked so damned hard at being noble and unflappable. Carole knew that frills would almost always break Meg's tight composure and get to her in a way that explicit pain would not. Over the years they had played all sorts of sex games together, but after four days of tough political maneuvering, she knew the last thing Meg needed was a torture scene.

With Meg, more than anyone else, Carole felt a strong and deep emotional connection. It was partly the length of time they had known one another, partly a love and respect for each other's creativity and intellect, and partly the way their sexuality had evolved. There was something special, remarkable, in the way they played together. Meg gave herself like a gift to Carole, a powerful statement from a powerful woman; and with the responsibility Carole took on, Carole always felt she was being honored. Meg became a field, an emotional canvas onto which Carole received great freedom to expand her imagination.

"I said, put them on," Carole repeated.

"Uh uh, no. Don't make me do it, hon. I'll feel like a fool."

"You seem to be forgetting yourself again," Carole said as she began to trace a line with her fingertips on Meg's jaw from ear to chin.

"But Car . . ."

Carole slapped her sharply on the full, fleshy part of her cheek. Meg let out a gasp, as much from the shock as from the sting.

"Now you have a nice pink cheek to match your nice pink panties," Carole said sweetly, then with a little edge in her voice, "I suggest you put them on before I get angry."

"Yes, Mistress," Meg said, looking soberly at Carole. She turned and knelt on the floor to open the bottom drawer. In it she found a skimpy hot pink G-string, little more than a small triangle of lace in the front and back with narrow ribbons on either side to fasten it together. There was a silky camisole, also hot pink, with rasberry-colored sheer lace panels which would reveal her breasts, and two very frilly garters in rasberry lace with pink ribbons running through the openwork and tied in dainty little bows. Meg took it all out and set each item on the floor and turned to close the drawer.

"That's *not* all," Carole said.

Still feeling the tingle of the slap, Meg looked back and saw them. Gold lame, strapless, high-heeled slippers with wispy, puffy pink feathers over the toe. After that, the pink, patterned stockings were hardly a shock. Carole had really outdone herself this time, Meg thought. She started to protest all over again, but before she could get a word out, Carole reprimanded her.

"Either put them on or don't waste my time. That's all there is to it."

Meg took a deep breath, sat back and slowly put on the G-string, tying the front and back together with the ribbons. She slipped the camisole over her head and pulled it down over her large full breasts and wide midriff. Her breasts strained at the lace. Slowly she took the first stocking, slipped her thumbs in and worked them down to the end. She drew up her leg until her knee almost met her chin, poked her toe into the gathered hose and slowly worked it up her leg. She picked up one of the garters, slipped it over her foot, pulled it along her calf to the middle of her thigh.

"The little bows go in front," Carole told her. "And make sure the pattern isn't crooked."

"Yes, Mam," Meg said as her familiar crimson blush rose up and blended in with the pink outline of Carole's hand where it had landed on her cheek. She put on the second stocking and garter.

"Would the good Mistress allow me to stand up to do my stockings and put on my shoes?" Meg said, almost teasingly.

Carole gave her a hard look. Meg was testing her resolve. "Of course," she answered, "but do it over there in the sunlight where I can get a better look at you."

Meg got up, picked up the slippers, went over to the patch of sun, set them down in the middle of it, stepped into each slipper and began to adjust her stockings. Carole walked a circle around Meg, inspecting her from head to toe. Meg finished and stood quietly. It looked as if her blushing was trying to match what she was wearing. So far, Carole was quite pleased with her handiwork; it was driving Meg nuts to be dressed up like that. Carole could tell Meg was turned on. Her own wetness inside the tight leather pants was growing and she thought she was even beginning to smell her own scent, her dampness further softening the warm leather.

"Not bad. Not bad," Carole said, "but you're not finished yet."

She looked closely at that special place near the base of Meg's neck, near the soft hollow of skin framed by the two rounded points of her collarbone. Ah, there it is, Carole thought. That old muscle twitch which Carole knew was an indicator that she was on the right track. For a while, Carole had been afraid of being too rusty, afraid she couldn't pull the scene off without laughing, but no—she still had the touch. As good as ever.

Meg realized Carole had something hidden in her hand. Whatever it was that Carole had in mind, Meg knew it would be insidious. Once Meg had wondered out loud why she always hung around with artists. Carole had calmly looked at her and said, "It's because we've got such great imaginations." They were in mixed company at the time, but they both knew what Carole had meant and Meg blushed.

Carole set the hidden object down on a small table just behind Meg. Meg knew she was forbidden to turn around and look. The tension of the waiting was agonizing.

"You look fine, so far," Carole said. "but you need a few things to jazz up that outfit of yours."

Carole could almost see Meg's mind racing, trying to figure it all out. Carole reached around her and picked up something and moved her open palm to just under and in front of Meg's chin.

"Like them, sweetheart?"

Carole held two gaudy, pink and white dime store fake rhinestone clip-on earrings. Meg nodded, slowly and seriously.

"I'm so glad," Carole said, "I got them just for you." She quickly fastened them to Meg's earlobes. The tight pressure of the spring-clips made Meg wince, but she didn't complain. "Kiss me," Carole told her.

They kissed for a long time, Carole using her tongue to search around Meg's mouth and along the tender insides of her lips and gums. Carole massaged Meg's breasts and began biting her lips as they kissed, gradually increasing the pressure until Meg began moaning again and relaxing into Carole's body.

"Stand up!" Carole said, pulling back from the kiss. "No sloppy posture, hear me?"

"Yes, Mam," Meg responded, straightening up, taking a deep breath and pushing her chest out.

"Hummm. I'm not quite satisfied with you yet."

Carole opened the drawer of the table and rummaged around. Eventually she held up a tube of lipstick. She took the cap off and with one hand, held Meg firmly by her hair, and with the other, she applied the color, electric pink. Meg's lips were soft and wide and the lipstick made her mouth look especially full and noticeable.

Carole leaned against the table and folded her arms across her bare chest. With one hand she began to touch and squeeze her own nipple.

"Make a little circle," Carole gestured, "and show me how well you can walk in your lovely shoes...And no stumbling," she added.

Meg swayed a little from time to time as she tried not to make any mistakes. Carole moved up behind her, quickly putting something around Meg's neck and fastening it. Meg saw a glint of light and thought for a moment that it was a necklace, but by the way it felt and the sound of a small lock snapping into place, she knew it was a collar. Carole immediately slipped two fingers under it and pulled Meg over to the mirror. Meg looked at herself. The lipstick, the gaudy earrings, the obnoxious pink and raspberry costume clashed with her sense of propriety and conservative style. She looked like a fingerpaint nightmare, but it was the collar that really did it. The collar was a narrow band of pink leather, encrusted with hundreds of tiny fake white rhinestones, and along with the little padlock, there was a small metal tag hanging from the D-ring.

"You make a great little poodle, don't you, Meggie?" Carole said, pleased with herself, "...with that curly hair of yours, and all powdered and pampered and made up. And such a nice, pretty collar, too. It's just right, don't you think?"

Meg stared at her reflection.

"What was that, Meggie?" Carole asked. "I didn't hear you."

It was hard for her to answer. To answer was a confirmation that she was really part of what was happening and not simply a detached observer. Carole yanked her by the collar right up to the mirror so that her breath steamed hazy spots on the glass.

"Tell me," Carole said firmly, "don't you think you're pretty this way?"

"Yes, ...Mistress," she stammered. "I'm...very...pretty."

It was a complex image for Meg to face. It was her and it wasn't her. In her way of thinking, she almost considered wearing women's clothing as a form of cross-dressing, it was so against her character. To confront this image, this real and unreal image looking back at her—that *was* her, for the moment at least—was shocking.

Carole almost always managed to get through Meg's inhibitions. She was good at it, and solid. If she lost her grip on the tension and movement of the scene, Meg could be left in a kind of limbo. She needed all of Carole's toughness, confidence, strong will and determination to push against if she was to really let go of her own rigid resistances and the constant churning of her mind, to float free. This, beyond the simple physical sensation, was what she wanted. Carole would guide her. Carole knew Meg's weaknesses and used them for Meg's pleasure and her own. It was exhilarating beyond words to be out there on the boundaries, on the keen edge of emotion. Carole was skilled and devious, and when she allowed her intuition to take over, her timing was perfect.

"See, Meggie," Carole said, fingering the small metal oval attached to the collar. "This is a very special present. It says:

'My name is Meggie, and I am lost.

Please return me to my owner,

Carole Schwartz. Reward.

Phone: 675-8923.'

Now you won't have to worry any more when I let you outside," Carole said as she stroked and petted Meg's head. "Everyone will know where you belong." Carole saw Meg's blushing renew at the escalated humiliation.

"Now get on the floor," Carole said, "and show me what a good doggie you can be." Carole glanced around the room as Meg, in her raspberry and pink lace, got down on her hands and knees. "Go fetch me that paper over there."

Meg crawled across the floor and barely hesitated when she reached the folded and unread day-old newspaper.

"That'sa good doggie," Carole said in a sing-song voice usually reserved for kittens, puppies and very small babies. "Bring me the paper."

Meg paused to take a breath and then picked up the Sun-Times in her mouth and crawled back to Carole, setting it down at her feet. Carole picked the paper up and rolled the first section into a tight tube. Meg was still on her hands and knees as Carole bent down to touch her. She scratched Meg behind the ears, ran her hands along Meg's body and underneath to her stomach, pubic hair, then back up to her lowhanging breasts. There she kneaded Meg's large, erect nipples between thumb and fingers. Meg's posture slumped as she gave in to the stimulation.

Whack! Carole hit Meg on the ass with the rolled newspaper. "This is a dog show, Meggie." *Whack!* "You have rotten form for a show dog." *Whack!* "Back straight." Carole hit her again. "Head up."

Meg groaned as wide red marks spread out from the lace triangle which barely covered her ass. Carole lightly ran her hand over Meg's bottom and then pulled at the ribbons to undo them. The panties dropped away. She stroked her fingers down Meg's crease, pausing to tickle her anus before continuing down to feel her labia. Meg was sopping wet. Carole was sopping wet. Carole slid her fingers along the soft folds of Meg's cunt, in and out, circling around her large and swollen clitoris. Eventually it became irresistible and Meg began to rock her ass back and forth to meet Carole's touch.

Whack! "Bad dog. Stand still," Carole said, as she retightened the rolled paper. "I didn't say you could wag your tail." She slowly began to walk away, "Now heel." Meg crawled along inches behind Carole as she walked once to the far side of the room and then back again.

"Good dog, good dog. I'll give you a yummy later," Carole promised, "but first you have to perform for the judge."

Carole pulled a leash from another drawer of the dresser, but it wasn't a regular leash. Besides being pink to match the collar, the last 18 inches had been split into two leads. Attached to the end of each was a clothespin.

"Sit, Meggie."

Meg sat back on her heels and Carole knelt down and clipped a clothespin to each of Meg's nipples. Meg flinched, her eyes closed, her mouth opened with a gasp.

"Bad dog. Sit up!" Meg resumed her more erect sitting position and slowly opened her eyes. "Let's see how well you walk on the leash," Carole said, standing. She started to walk away, pulling lightly on the lead. The tension of the clothespins pulling at her tender nipples made Meg instantly get back on her hands and knees and closely follow Carole as she walked around the room.

"Stay," Carole said, dropping the leash. She walked over to the easy chair, turned around and unlaced her leather pants and pulled the front flap wide open. "Come, Meggie, come to Carole."

Meg crawled toward her, scuffing the toes of the slippers and tearing runs in her stockings.

"Show Mommy how much fun this is," Carole said. "Be a good, friendly doggie and kiss my boots." Meg bent lower and started to kiss Carole's feet. Some of the lipstick smeared on the leather.

Whack! Carole hit her with the paper again. "Lick that stuff off this minute or I'll take you back to your kennel where you belong."

Meg licked at her boot in earnest, her self-consciousness melting. She let go, feeling and acting according to Carole's commands. Carole reached down and pulled Meg up sharply by her hair.

"Lick Mommy nicely now, and I'll give you a nice reward."

Meg obeyed quickly, burying her face into Carole's pubic hair, licking and sucking at Carole's clitoris in all the ways she knew that Carole liked. Carole took the end of the leash and tugged on it. She could see Meg's breasts move in whatever direction she pulled, up or sideways. The increased pressure and strain caused Meg's whole body to move with it and undulate. And every time Carole pulled, there would be a new surge of energy from Meg who would automatically suck harder on her clit. Carole knew, too, that Meg would feel each surge in her own cunt.

Carole's orgasm was quick and full, but she purposefully held back many of the outward signs of pleasure and release. Instead, she pushed Meg away, changing her tone to one of harsh disgust. The twist in the scene would be a jolt to Meg, but she felt confident that Meg could take it, she needed to catch Meg off guard.

"What the fuck are you doing crawling around on the goddamn floor like a piece of trash?"

"Carole??" Meg said, sounding confused and a little scared.

"I want to know what you're doing, all primped up like some two-bit floosey."

"Car..." she said, confused, "...you wanted me..."

"But you hate it, don't you?"

"You know I..." Meg stammered. Carole cut her off again.

"You look like some lousy, cheap, disgusting slut."

Meg cringed. The edge in Carole's voice and the derision clawed at her.

"You really amaze me," Carole continued. "You act so fuckin' cool all the time and then you come half way across the country just so you can sleaze at my feet."

Meg shuddered, her skin blotchy red. Carole didn't let up with the scorn.

"How many of your friends know about you, anyway? How many, Meggie? You go to your conferences and work yourself crazy and do they listen to you? Not many, I bet. And if they knew what a cunt you were, even fewer would pay attention. You're a pig, sweetheart. That's what I think."

Meg was close to tears. Carole rode on Meg's reactions, but didn't let up. She tugged on the leash and Meg shuddered again.

"On your hands and knees, dog. The show isn't over." Carole stood over her and slid three fingers easily in Meg's very wet and open cunt. "I'm gonna fuck you just the way you deserve. Just like a goddamn dog." Meg was quivering and panting.

Carole pressed into Meg with force and pulled out, exerting pressure against the walls of her vagina. She swirled her thumb in Meg's wetness and then pushed it into Meg's ass. Meg groaned. Carole brushed her little finger back and forth across Meg's erect clit and shook and pushed and pulled her thumb and fingers in and out of Meg. Meg's breathing quickened in a familiar way. Carole slapped and spanked Meg hard on the ass with her other hand, saying, "You're a bad, bad dog."

Meg came, howling loud and strong.

The two women collapsed in a heap on the floor. Meg kicked off the shoes, and was still breathing heavily as Carole quickly unfastened one clothespin and then the other. They laid there for a long time without needing to talk, holding and stroking one another as the patch of sunlight narrowed to a line, then disappeared.

"It's been a long time," Meg finally said in a soft voice.

"I know, honey," Carole answered, brushing the hair from Meg's forehead.

"You were so hard," Meg whispered.

Carole lightly kissed Meg's cheeks, the soft corners of her eyes and licked at the tears that were glistening there. "I know."

Meg nestled into Carole's shoulder, feeling safe and more secure than she had in months. "Carole?"

"Mmm?"

"I'm *so* glad to be here."

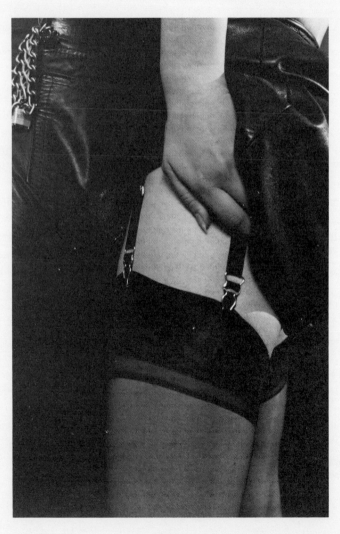

A Personal View of the History of the Lesbian S/M Community and Movement in San Francisco

PAT CALIFIA

It is difficult to write a history of events which involved so many people with very different needs and points of view. Statements of fact are as accurate as I can make them. However, I alone am responsible for interpretations of the meanings of those facts. This article reflects my politics and my view of the emergence of the lesbian S/M community of San Francisco. It does not reflect the politics of Samois, nor is it endorsed by Samois.

The women's movement of the sixties and early seventies was a hostile environment for sadomasochistic women. There was practically no discussion of female sadism, and not much more talk about female masochism. The most liberal feminists admitted that some women had masochistic fantasies, but this admission was only the introduction to a discussion about how such fantasies could be cured by rooting out internalized oppression, self-destruction and misogyny through intense consciousness-raising and carefully selected reading. Within feminist rhetoric, S/M existed only as a metaphor for sexual inequality in a male-dominated society. As a sexual minority, women who practiced S/M (instead of just fantasizing about it) were ignored.

This self-deception and silence couldn't last. Women are just too stubborn and intelligent for that. Besides, feminist ideology was spreading to women in every walk of life, including S/M brothels, leather bars and private friendship networks of dykes who did S/M. Barbara Ruth's article "Cathexis" is the earliest publication I have been able to locate that challenged the dichotomy between feminism and S/M. Ruth has suffered a high personal cost for having the guts to say she was a masochist and a lesbian feminist, but her courageous words permanently changed the pat, smug assumptions feminists had been making about S/M and challenged other S/M dykes to begin taking the women's movement's repression of their sexuality a little more seriously. Joan Bridi Miller ("Sado-Masochism—Another Point of View," *Gay Community News,* 1976) was another woman who was brave enough to expose this stigmatized part of her life before there was any kind of organized support.

For the first time, women in the movement were not confronting sadomasochists as literary figures or psychiatric case histories. We were real women—sisters—who were being vulnerable, describing our sexuality to a skeptical and hostile audience. It was inevitable that the emergence of this issue in print would be followed by face-to-face confrontations.

On October 10, 1976, a conference was held on Women's Health and Healing at Los Angeles City College. The conference included a workshop called "Healthy Questions About S/M." It was led by two women who had been doing S/M for years. They led it anonymously since they both worked for feminist institutions and were afraid of losing their jobs.

Women were supposed to sign up for workshops in a public information center. When I wrote my name on the signup sheet for "Healthy Questions About S/M," a group of women who were apparently waiting around just to see who would go to this perverted event ran up to the bulletin board, read my name, and began pointing me out to other women in the information center.

When I got to the workshop, about 12 other women were there. Most of them had little experience with S/M and a lot of fantasies. They were understandably afraid of being prematurely labeled and harassed, so most of them had signed up for the workshop being held next door, taken seats in the back, then crept out and attempted to sneak into the S/M workshop. However, this didn't do them much good, since there was a line of women outside, keeping track of who went in and out of the room.

We huddled in there, feeling threatened and scared. One woman who hated S/M had come to the workshop, and she began to make an angry statement about the connections she saw between the patriarchy, rape, and S/M. I don't know how the workshop leaders got us to start talking about sex in such a strained context, but they did. I still remember an older dyke talking about cruising gay men's leather bars with her lover in the early sixties, looking for other women who shared their sexual interests.

As a terrified and titillated neophyte, this information fell on me like rain on the desert. Despite my vigorous participation in the women's movement, my S/M fantasies had not been "cured," and in my attempt to renounce by "sick" sexuality, I had boxed myself into a monogamous relationship with a woman who had sex with me only a few times a year. I was desperate for change, for relief, for a sex life without self-hatred. I began to realize that I had been lied to. S/M *was* a part of women's sexuality. It was possible to do it and survive. After all, that fifty-year-old dyke had survived isolation and the contempt of her peers and remained whole and happy. And if a dozen women were so interested in this subject that they would put up with this much shit to come talk about it, surely I could find partners and friends. I wouldn't be alone. That had been my greatest fear.

When I got back to San Francisco, I began to tell everyone I knew that I was into S/M and looking for partners and support. I figured if I made myself visible enough, if there were other S/M lesbians in San Francisco, they would be able to find me. I began to extricate myself from my self-destructive relationship, and I began to write about my sexual fantasies. This new honesty in my work broke a long dry spell that had made me very unhappy.

A friend of mine saw an ad in the *Berkeley Barb* for an S/M support group for women. I answered the ad, and it turned out that this group (which later became Cardea) was part of The Society of Janus, a support group for S/M people which was founded in San Francisco in 1975. I joined Cardea, and occasionally met other dykes that way. Cardea was also a valuable source of information about how to do S/M safely. However, most of the members were bisexual or straight, and many lesbians would not join a group whose members related to men.

Nevertheless, there had never been a women's group like Cardea before, and gossip about the group made lesbians more aware of S/M. Then the *Lesbian Tide* published part one of an inaccurate transcript of the Los Angeles workshop, and this created so much controversy that the *Tide* never published the second part of the transcript. Private discussions became public during November, when the Bacchanal, then a lesbian bar in Albany, held "Sex Month." The bar hosted talks on disability and sexuality, bisexuality, prostitution, a slide show of images of female genitals, a presentation on lesbian sexuality, and a talk on Sexual Magic (the speaker's term for S/M).

The woman who gave this talk was Cynthia S., the founder of the Society of Janus. The bar was very crowded the night she spoke, and the audience was tense, but generally quite supportive. They even helped the speaker silence a few hecklers. She spoke with dignity and clarity about the real (as opposed to mythological) content of S/M sex, the nature of S/M relationships and some of the reasons why people find it so difficult to accept this sexuality. It was the most explicit information about S/M eroticism the community had heard so far, and more than a few women who would later join Samois began "coming out" that night.

Anita Bryant began her campaign to Save Our Children in 1977. The emergence of an anti-gay backlash, coupled with fundamentalist Christianity, had the mainstream lesbian and gay community up in arms. The impact of the backlash on other sexual minorities is less well documented. Because Bryant's hate campaign involved painting the ugliest, most sensationalistic picture of the gay community possible, she naturally focused on fringe and minority elements of the community. This created a mean-spirited and frightened attitude in the mainstream gay movement. Pedophiles, transsexuals and transvestites, tearoom cruisers, hustlers, young gays and S/M people were disavowed and urged to keep quiet and become invisible. This was not the best possible climate for organizing S/M lesbians. Those of us who were not political were afraid to go to a meeting and those of us who were political were often involved in "larger" political causes and had no energy left over for founding our own community.

Nevertheless, Cardea continued to meet, and an attempt was made to begin a support group for S/M dykes. In August, one of the women who had led the Los Angeles workshop put an ad in *Plexus* about starting a lesbian S/M group. She held the first meeting at the Tenderloin Clinic, then a gay mental health organization, on September 15. Women attended who had met each other through Cardea, through the Los Angeles workshop, through friendship networks and a lesbian sexuality discussion group. About 20 women attended. They met one more time, but there was not enough sustained interest to create an organization with ongoing meetings.

By the end of 1977, the lesbians who would eventually start Samois were hanging out in the Society of Janus, a mixed group that was mostly gay men; in Cardea, which had many women members who did S/M professionally; at the Catacombs, a gay male fist-fucking club which allowed women to come to their parties; and at gay men's leather bars, especially the Balcony and the Ambush. None of these places were ideal for us, but it is historically important to remember that the first people who supported lesbian sadomasochists were gay leathermen and professional (usually bisexual) dominatrixes. Although there were two lesbian bars that did not hassle women who wore leather or S/M regalia (Scott's in San Francisco and the Bacchanal in Albany), there was no lesbian leather bar or any public, easy accessible place where a dyke could just drop in and assume she would find other sadomasochists.

The climate within and outside of the women's movement became more and more hostile. By 1978, the feminist anti-pornography movement was very powerful in San Francisco. Women Against Violence in Pornography and the Media (WAVPM) had hundreds of members, many of them lesbians, and they frequently attacked S/M and S/M imagery in their literature. They even reprinted an old article by Ti-Grace Atkinson called "Why I'm Against S/M Liberation." This rhetoric made it very hard for us to come out to our non-S/M friends and lovers and made us feel very unwelcome in lesbian bars and organizations. Bryant had won in Florida, and the Briggs Initiative, a measure that would have required school boards to fire gay teachers and any teacher who discussed homosexuality in the classroom, was put on the ballot. The San Francisco gay community reacted by pressuring the Board of Supervisors to pass a comprehensive gay rights law in March, but it also reacted by condemning its own minority and outlaw elements.

By now, my network of friends had grown large enough to make a support group seem feasible. And it was clear that we urgently needed one. I didn't feel welcome or safe anywhere—on the streets or in lesbian bars; on public transit or in the Women's Building. Three of us decided to make another effort to form a group. Invitations were mailed out to everybody on the Cardea mailing list, a poster was designed and put up in the bars (where most of them were defaced or ripped down), and we tried to call everybody we knew who might be interested. We thought six or seven women would come.

Our first meeting was on June 13, 1978. Seventeen women were there. The first meeting was very tense and not much fun for me. It seemed to me we were wary of each other, afraid to hope the group would turn into something that could make our lives better, and so horny we hurt. We mostly discussed business —what to call the group, whether or not we were a feminist group, what would we do (consciousness raising, learning S/M technique, education in the lesbian community, write letters to the editor), and tried to define the term "lesbian" (i.e., could bisexual women come to our meetings?).

That same month, one of the bisexual women whose status was being debated loaned her house for the first formally planned, all-women, S/M group sex party. These private sex parties have been hosted by various women every since, and they are a vital part of the lesbian S/M community. Without our own bars or baths to cruise in, we need a way to find sex partners. It is difficult for many lesbians to do S/M in their own homes, especially if they have disapproving vanilla roommates. Orgies were a sensible solution to this dilemma. Of course, not all of us liked or participated in sex parties.

Looking back, I think that some of our community's biggest problems and biggest successes have revolved around S/M lesbians' need to find women to play with. If you are a member of an erotic minority, already-existing institutions do not work for you. They do not help you find lovers or friends, and often they actively try to prevent you from doing so. If people are so isolated that they can't find other folks to share their sexual preferences with, you don't have much of a community or an organized front to take on other political tasks. On the other hand, the things that people need to find partners (sexual technique and communication skills, dances, orgies, parties) are rather different from the activities necessary to fight political battles (stuffing envelopes, writing letters, calling the Mayor's office, meeting with the vice squad, picketing). There has always been tension in Samois over how much we will focus on being a social group where women can meet other S/M women, and how much we will focus on other political action.

Because our community is small, we have had incredible problems with incest, couples breaking up, jealousy, unrequited lust, and promiscuity. These problems have often spilled over into the group, and we've dealt with them as best we could. We found that when people could label these problems for what they were and get couple counseling or mediation, they did not disrupt the group. But when these problems were mislabeled as political differences, they carried a charge of sexual anger that made them impossible to solve.

The Gay Freedom Day Parade was held the last weekend in June. For the first time, an S/M organization (as opposed to leather bars or S/M baths) marched in the parade. The Society of Janus had a small contingent. I was one of the co-coordinators of Janus, so I marched with the group, and a few Samois members joined us. Although Janus had applied for and received a permit to be in the parade, our contingent was hassled by monitors who did not believe we had a right to be there. They tried to expel us from the parade on the grounds that we violated a parade regulation excluding images that were sexist or depicted violence against women.

I'll grant you, we must have looked weird to the monitors. We were definitely out of the leather ghetto, marching with other political and social groups. One of the members was driving a big red jeep, and one of the women members of Janus had chained

251

herself to the hood, to make it look more like a float. At the monitors' insistence, she eventually unchained herself. I could understand that their concerns about safety made this a reasonable request. But then the monitors became hysterical about a lesbian couple who were marching together. The bottom had a ripped-up shirt that showed her whip marks, and she was wearing a jewelry chain around her wrist and fingers. The top was holding the other end of the chain. "Take that chain off that woman!" one of the monitors kept screaming. "Unchain her!"

"I can't," replied the unruffled mistress. "I welded it on myself this morning."

The monitors disappeared, frothing at the mouth, and called the head of security, who turned out to be a lesbian who was just as rabid as they were. I argued with her about our right to be in the parade practically the entire way down Market Street. While we argued, photographers kept leaping in front of the contingent and taking pictures of us and journalists kept shoving microphones in my face. One of the reporters shouted at me, "How would you feel about someone who wanted you to cut their leg off?" The crowd was equally hostile. We were booed and hissed, there were shouts of "fascists" and "Nazis," and some people threatened us or spit at us.

There was a lot of confusion about who we were. Many of the spectators assumed we were the gay Nazis, despite the fact that not a single swastika was in evidence. This confusion was increased when Priscilla Alexander published "Masters and Slaves by Any Other Name" (*Bay Times,* July 1978) and compared us with Nazis.

After the parade, Janus set up a booth and distributed literature. A lot of people came up to talk to us (mostly gay leathermen), but even the S/M people thought it was weird that we were in the parade. They were ashamed of their sexuality, afraid to make it public, afraid it would attract more misunderstanding and harassment, and didn't understand why anybody would think S/M was a political issue. We also got a lot of shit from gays of all sexualities who thought in the Year of Briggs we should all come to the parade in pinstripe suits and polyester pantsuits. Of course, the San Francisco *Chronicle* ran a large picture of our contingent with their story of the parade, which confirmed these fears.

Nevertheless, I was proud to march with Janus, and I think it was long overdue for S/M people to make themselves more visible in the gay parade. Individual sadomasochists and the gay businesses South of Market have made a big contribution to the gay community, and we are entitled to recognition and respect. In times of repression, it is always tempting to police and censor your own community. But I don't believe gay people can make themselves conventional enough to escape persecution. We are hated because we have a different kind of sex, the wrong kind of sex. I have always wanted freedom to be as queer, as perverted, on the street and on the job as I am in my dungeon. I don't think radical perverts should obey gay or lesbian or feminist mind police any more than they should obey the vice squad.

This has been another ongoing conflict in Samois. Some of us want our sexuality to be a private matter, and want nothing more than to remain members in good standing of the lesbian feminist community. Those of us who identify primarily as S/M people, rather than lesbian feminist, tend to be more public about our sexuality, more identifiable on the street, and more friendly toward other sexual minorities.

Samois had its second meeting on July 10. We voted on a list of possible names, and picked "Samois." The name comes from *The Story of O*. Samois is the estate of Anne-Marie, a lesbian dominatrix who pierces O and brands her. We wanted a name that would suggest lesbian S/M without saying it in so many words. The comparison with "code" names for older gay organizations like the Mattachine Society and Daughters of Bilitis is obvious. We also wanted to use something from *The Story of O* since anti-porn groups were trying to ban the book from women's bookstores and were picketing the movie. However, if we had known our group would become known on a national scale, I doubt we would have picked that name. It's too obscure and too hard to pronounce.

We decided that we were bored with business and had to get some sex into our meetings, so we agreed to alternate meetings where we would discuss a set topic with meetings that would be programs on various S/M techniques. We formed a CR group as a subsidiary of Samois, and then we broke into small groups to try and get to know each other better.

The structure of the group was very loose, and remained so for about a year. We did not have a newsletter. We decided each time we met when and where the next meeting would be. And the meetings were open to anybody who heard about them. We didn't charge dues or have any officers.

Cardea held one of its last meetings in September, a tour of a professional dominatrix's playroom. By then, the women who started Cardea had turned it over to lesbian leadership. As lesbians left Cardea to join Samois, no one came forward to replace them, so Cardea folded. There remains a need for an S/M support group that can welcome all women.

In October, the month before elections, the vice squad began to harass Folsom Street, the area where most of the leather bars are located. The Alcoholic Beverage Commission managed to revoke or suspend many of the bars' licenses. Among the bars that had problems were the Ambush, the Black and Blue and the Bootcamp. Before this crackdown, there had been some open sex in the backrooms of some of these bars. After the crackdown, the bars cleaned up their acts and closed down the backrooms. They became more suspicious of outsiders, and thus less friendly to women. Some of them became private clubs so they could continue to have sex on premises, so women could no longer go there at all.

The *Bay Area Reporter (BAR)* and the *Sentinel,* San Francisco's two gay papers, did not cover this harassment. No gay organization protested it. Nor were most Samois members very upset. Most of them identified primarily with the lesbian community, which has a tradition of indifference toward police activity against gay men. However, I and a few other women who had been hanging out South of Market were upset by this anti-vice campaign, since it made the social space available to us even smaller.

Proposition 6, the Briggs Initiative, was defeated in November of 1978, and all of us were elated. However, our happiness was short-lived. Less than three weeks later, Mayor George Moscone and gay Supervisor Harvey Milk were murdered by ex-cop Dan White. The deaths of our liberal mayor and our first elected publicly gay official were followed by an ugly wave of anti-gay violence and police harassment of gay bars. Finally, the vice squad's activities hit gay print in the *BAR* and the *Sentinel.*

By November, in just six months, we had become a very controversial presence in the lesbian community. Women were urging Samois to talk with or debate WAVPM, since WAVPM was perceived as having the correct feminist position on S/M. This was the beginning of a long conflict with WAVPM that is pretty much the prototype of Samois' problems with other feminist institutions. We have rarely been treated with common courtesy by other feminist groups. Instead, we have been put down, put off, lied to, insulted, and generally treated shabbily. I think feminism has always dealt badly with dissent and new ideas, and it's important for feminists to do better with these issues if they want the women's movement to stay current, flexible and democratic. In particular, the treatment of Samois makes it clear that even *lesbian* feminists didn't learn a whole lot from the way the women's movement initially reacted to lesbianism, and we all know what happens to folks who won't learn from history. So I'm going to digress from the chronological order of my history so I can tell the whole story of WAVPM and Samois.

WAVPM was hosting Feminist Perspectives on Pornography, the first national conference of the anti-porn movement. Samois wrote to WAVPM requesting permission to do a workshop on lesbian S/M. Our letter was never answered. A few days before the conference began, we heard (unofficially) that the leaders of WAVPM wanted us to stay away from the conference. This shocked some of our members who were also members of WAVPM. They believed that WAVPM opposed heterosexual S/M pornography, and supported that position, but they also believed WAVPM could and should have a different, supportive position on lesbian S/M.

We decided to have our own workshop to respond to WAVPM anyway, so a few of us visited the conference and put up posters for it. I and Gayle Rubin attempted to attend the entire conference, but we were told by Laura Lederer that we were not welcome because there was no room for dissenters, only supporters of the anti-porn movement. When we expressed outrage over this, Lederer fetched Lynn Campbell, who informed us that the conference was overcrowded and we could not be admitted because there was no room. Nobody came to Samois' workshop, so we spent the time reading anti-porn literature and talking about the negative impact WAVPM had on our lives.

I should mention here that some Samois members remain supporters of the feminist anti-porn movement and members of WAVPM. Samois has never managed to come up with a consensus about pornography. The only thing most of us agree on is that the anti-porn movement puts out distorted information about lesbian S/M, and should stop doing so.

After the conference, we wrote to WAVPM again and asked them to present their slideshow on pornography to Samois. They advertised the availability of their slideshow to interested groups, and used it frequently as a recruitment tool. WAVPM responded by asking us why we wanted to see it. After an exchange of letters and phone calls, they finally refused to show it to us because our group "glamourized violence against women." They also said they were afraid we would find the slideshow erotic.

We were hurt and angry about this, so many of us attended the slideshow in other contexts. I was already suspicious of the WAVPM characterization of all porn as violence against women, since I had seen some porn that didn't seem sexist and definitely wasn't violent, and I knew women who had worked in the sex industry, and they didn't seem like victims to me. When I saw the slideshow, I was frightened by the sexual ignorance of the presenters and their willingness to exploit the audience's sexual prejudices to win converts.

The images were presented in a manipulative way. Bondage photos were followed by police photos of battered women. S/M porn was repeatedly taken out of context and labeled as "violent," even though it looked like consensual S/M to me. Record album covers and fashion advertisements were lumped in with the pornography. Nothing was dated and few sources were cited, so the audience had no idea how representative the material was of porn you could actually go see and buy. The presenters kept assuring us that much, much worse material was available. Their definition of porn was circular and sloppy. They defined any sexist or violent image as pornography, then turned around and used that assumption to "prove" that all pornography was violent and sexist.

Lesbian sexuality was not discussed. Some vague distinction was made between "erotica" and "porn," but no examples of "erotica" were shown. This made me especially uncomfortable since many heterosexuals were present, and one of the favorite images of "violent" pornography was soft-core, glossy images of women kissing or going down on each other.

The presenters' definition of violence was as tautological as their definition of pornography. There was no sense of context or scale. The lesbian porn was presented as being just as violent as a woman getting stabbed. Wearing high heels or being tied up was described with as much horror as getting raped. Corsets were condemned with as much vehemence as wife-beating. Anal sex was apparently a violent practice. Teenage girls apparently couldn't have sex without being violated. And women in the sex industry were apparently being raped by the camera, not by the vice squad.

Questions about the first amendment and censorship were evaded. Anybody who questioned WAVPM's definition of porn or violence was accused of having bad consciousness about violence against women. Anti-S/M remarks were made frequently.

As more and more members of Samois saw this slideshow, more and more anger accumulated. Some of us were angry because they did not like their sexuality as lesbians being equated with anything male or patriarchal. Others were angry because we liked some pornography and didn't want to see all of it wiped out. Those of us who wanted to produce erotic literature for other S/M lesbians were afraid that WAVPM would make it much more difficult for us to publish and circulate our own work. All of us felt that the picture presented of S/M was biased and distorted.

So we wrote to WAVPM again, requesting a meeting. By now, we didn't care about the slideshow, we just wanted to discuss common issues. In April, 1979, we received a reply from them, informing us that they were too busy to see us until after their yearly membership drive. Apparently, they could use bigoted images of our sexuality to recruit new members, but they couldn't be bothered to deal with real sadomasochists.

By July, we had still not received word from WAVPM, so we wrote to *Plexus*, describing how we had been treated and demanding a meeting. We also sent a copy of this letter to WAVPM and received no response. *Plexus* did not print our letter until October, and when it appeared, it was with a response from two individual members of WAVPM, Beth Goldberg and Bridget Wynne. While stating their organization did not have "a specific. . . policy on S/M," Goldberg and Wynne reiterated WAVPM's determination to put "an end to all portrayals of women being bound, raped, tortured, degraded, or killed for sexual gratification." They stated that WAVPM's priority was to end this imagery, not meet with us.

The general feeling in Samois was that this was hypocrisy. WAVPM obviously had a de facto position on S/M, since they lumped images of bondage and consensual S/M in with images of rape and murder. The fact that WAVPM had not had the courtesy to send us a copy of this letter was also annoying.

The conflict simmered until March of 1980, when we had a special meeting to talk about the antiporn movement and the assorted positions Samois members had on it. This discussion was fortuitous, because the shit hit the fan in April. Flyers appeared advertising a "forum on sadomasochism in the lesbian community." This event was to be a fund-raiser for WAVPM and was sponsored by them.

We were stunned. How could they hold a public forum about our sexuality when they had no "official" position on S/M and no time to meet with us? But it got even more outrageous. Julie Greenberg, the coordinator of WAVPM, called us and invited two Samois members to appear on the panel. Well, I asked her, was WAVPM going to split the proceeds of the benefit with Samois? Certainly not, she replied. Then we refuse to appear on your panel, I said. Why should we give you a token appearance of fairness when you've refused to meet with us, and why should we raise money for you after you have treated us so contemptuously?

WAVPM began to receive quite a bit of criticism for the way they had organized this "forum," and they finally agreed to have some of their members meet with us two days before the forum. However, the general membership of WAVPM was not allowed the dangerous experience of contaminating contact with us. Only a hand-picked group of 25 were informed of and invited to the meeting. It was held at the Women's Building, where WAVPM had their office, two days before the forum.

Those of us who went to talk with WAVPM were in a state of

shock. It was obvious that we could do little to educate women who felt so strongly that S/M was evil. After dealing with them for more than a year, we had little hope of appealing to their sense of fair play or justice. We had never faced a tougher audience, but we still went through with it, trying to get these women to see us as human beings, not monsters.

It was a partial success. A few of the WAVPM members began to think they had behaved badly by planning this event. They once again invited two of us to speak, and this time they offered to split the money with us. But this invitation was issued the day before the forum, and nobody had the time to prepare a speech. Also, by then, we knew who was going to be on the panel, and nobody wanted to appear with the cards stacked that heavily against them. We decided that this token invitation could not make up for more than a year of abuse and neglect, so we decided to picket the forum.

This was controversial within Samois. Some of us thought picketing was too radical, some of us did not want to "divide the women's movement" by publicly criticizing another feminist organization, some of us didn't think WAVPM was that important. But the majority vote was solidly behind protesting the forum.

The forum took place on April 18, 1980 at an auditorium on the University of California at Berkeley campus. When we arrived, we discovered that we were not the only picketers. A woman was handing out a leaflet criticizing the forum as anti-lesbian propaganda. She was angry that straight women were going to be on a panel attacking lesbian sexuality. We lined up outside the auditorium and waved our picket signs and handed out leaflets (headed "This Forum is a Lie About S/M") and hoped nobody would call the police. The crowd, the panel and we were tense and nervous. Nobody liked the animosity that was in the air.

After the audience was seated, we went inside and arranged ourselves in the back of the auditorium. The panel was introduced by Julie Greenberg and moderated by Valerie Miner. Panel members were Diana E.H. Russell, one of the founders of WAVPM; Susan Leigh Starr; Linda Scaparotti and Susan Griffin. Each of the panel members took about 30 minutes to deliver her diatribe.

Griffin's presentation was especially chilling. She said that everyone in our patriarchal society is sick with the disease of sado-masochism, but the members of Samois and other people who openly practiced S/M had an especially virulent form of the disease. She called upon the women's community to heal this disease. Other panel members associated S/M with battery in lesbian relationships, with rape and mutilation, with pornography, with white slavery. Individual members of Samois were named, misquoted and attacked for being pro-rape or fascistic.

After the panel finished telling us that we were human garbage, there was a question-and-answer period. The moderator called on as few Samois members as possible. However, many of the women in the audience had become extremely angry, listening to the psychiatric language and the inflammatory descriptions of violence against women, and they rose to criticize the way the forum had been organized and the remarks made by panel members. Lesbians were especially angry to hear other lesbians being described as sick. Of course, many present agreed with the panel and had their own upsetting stories to tell—stories of being beaten by their husbands, of being molested as children, stories that they were convinced revealed the true essence of S/M.

In the long run, this forum did much to discredit WAVPM as an authority on women's sexuality. The arrogance and hatred displayed by panel members probably did more to get women to listen to Samois than all of our most carefully reasoned articles put together. But at the time, all we could think about were our shattered friendships, the doors slammed in our faces, and our broken hearts.

After the forum, I heard rumors that there was a fight within WAVPM between members who wanted the organization to take an official position against S/M and members who wanted to refrain from doing so. WAVPM never developed a policy on S/M. However, they are still in business, leading "feminist tours of the porn district," taking tourists through North Beach and pointing out the bondage magazines in every adult bookstore. And they continue to show their slideshow, which puts out the same tired misinformation about S/M. The anti-porn position is not as popular as it once was, however, and I give Samois credit for opening up the debate on this issue and creating more room for feminists to take better positions on pornography.

Samois was doing more than fighting with WAVPM, however. We held our first public presentation at Old Wives Tales, a feminist bookstore in San Francisco, on January 18, 1979. We brought enough literature for 30 or 40 women, and were completely unprepared for the 140 who showed up. I don't know how everybody managed to squeeze into the bookstore. Those of us who had agreed to speak were freaked out. Some of us had never spoken in public before, certainly not to that large a crowd, and certainly not about something as controversial as S/M. Somehow, we got through it—holding hands, hugging, encouraging each other—and managed to talk about feminism and our sexuality, the history of Samois, how we felt about the confusion between S/M and violence, and what we did sexually (including a demonstration of S/M equipment and a talk on safety).

By February, we had our first officers and began to charge dues so we could send out a newsletter. We started holding orientations to screen new members. (We had learned by experience that it wasn't fair to new people to just let them walk into, say, a flagellation demonstration, with no preparation.) We rented a post office box and were talking about publishing a booklet.

In March, Samois voted to march in the 1979 Gay Freedom Day Parade. We turned in our application and almost immediately got embroiled in a conflict with the parade committee. One of the monitors who had harassed the Janus contingent wanted to prevent a repetition of that confrontation. She and some other members of a parade subcommittee were trying to pass a regulation that would ban leather and S/M regalia from the parade. This was supposed to be a natural extension of the ban on sexist imagery or imagery that promoted violence against women. Even when we were not dealing with the anti-porn movement, their ideology haunted us.

A few of us joined the subcommittee and protested the regulation. The arguments over it were ugly and emotionally draining. We had to sit and listen to people making bigoted remarks about us and then try to respond calmly and rationally. We told people over and over again that we were not fascists or rapists; that we

were not disruptive or violent; and that we had as much right to be in a gay parade as drag queens or lesbian mothers or bar owners. At one point, I asked the monitor, "How are you going to enforce this regulation anyway? Thousands of people turn up for this parade who have never heard of your rules, and some of them will be wearing leather." "Well, when people don't obey the monitors, we turn matters over to the police," she responded.

By leafleting Folsom Street and calling everybody we knew who was an S/M person or a supporter, we managed to get enough votes at the next meeting to pass a regulation supporting people's freedom to wear whatever they wanted to the parade.

In April, we designed our first t-shirts and ordered them from the Women's Press Project. We selected "The Leather Menace" as our slogan to remind people of NOW's attempt to purge "the lavender menace." They arrived in time for us to wear them to the parade. We also managed to get our first booklet, *What Color Is Your Handkerchief?*, printed for sale at the parade. Incidentally, the Ministry of Truth (MOT), a committee of Samois that wrote our official statements and publications, chose its name from *1984* as a joke. We had been called fascists so often that it was beginning to be predictable, so the MOT decided to rattle everybody's cage a little. Samois' propaganda arm didn't exactly self-select for reverence or circumspection. In conjunction with the book, the MOT designed and printed our first Hanky Color Code for lesbians.

Our contingent in the parade began with half a dozen people and gradually got larger as we moved up Market Street toward the Civic Center. After the parade, we opened a booth and sold t-shirts and books and talked to people about our group. Janus also marched in the parade, which made me feel less outnumbered, and the crowd was friendlier.

Publication of a booklet and our appearance in the parade made us a lot more visible. By August, we had so many requests for speakers that we set up a speaker's bureau and wrote some guidelines for speakers.

Old Wives Tales in San Francisco carried *What Color Is Your Handkerchief?*, but by September, A Woman's Place bookstore in Oakland was still refusing to carry it. We began to telephone and write, asking them to carry the pamphlet. Women began to visit the bookstore and request it. Two members of the collective argued for stocking *What Color,* and they were treated so badly around this and other issues that they eventually resigned from the collective. Independent of Samois, a petition signed by about 20 supporters was delivered to the bookstore, accusing the collective of censorship and demanding that they carry the Samois pamphlet. *A Woman's Place* finally gave in to community pressure, and *What Color* appeared on their shelves—along with disclaimer cards, written by collective members, telling prospective buyers that S/M was anti-feminist. Actually, without the disclaimer cards, I doubt anybody would have been able to find the pamphlet, since the collective only shelved two copies at a time, and turned them in so the title was not visible.

In October, S/M became a hot topic at the Michigan Women's Music Festival. A few Samois members and other S/M dykes were there, and they led a workshop that was attended by more than 40 women.

The Bacchanal held their second annual Sex Month in November, and we did another big public education program for more than 100 women. This time, we got a much more positive and supportive response. We added a new feature to our program— a slideshow of images of lesbian S/M. We did this specifically to counter the anti-porn movement's chilling effect on lesbian sexual imagery. We wanted to challenge the assumption that sexually explicit pictures or language were degrading or bad for women.

By the end of 1979, Samois had existed for almost two years, and the group had some severe growing pains. Internal conflict, vagueness about our goals, pressure from the outside, and burnout among the leadership forced us to set up some meetings to assess our group and try to set some new directions. Among the things we discussed was a policy that we have no sex or drugs at meetings. This policy had come into being when we decided Samois should not sponsor sex parties because of possible legal problems, and after we had some problems with people coming to meetings drunk or stoned. Some members wanted a chemical-free space and other members felt we should at least be able to have beer at a potluck. Also, some members felt that they were harassed for being affectionate with a lover or couldn't plan a really hot meeting because of the no-sex rule. We decided to retain the rule, but tried to emphasize that since one of Samois' major purposes was to do sex education for members, we couldn't interpret this rule so rigidly that we couldn't deal with our sexuality at meetings.

Another big controversy was over the issue of separatism and bisexual members of Samois. After intense discussion, it became clear that Samois was not a separatist group, and that most of us wanted Samois to be open to any woman who did S/M with other women. Our separatist members were disgruntled by this majority vote, and became much less active in Samois after that point.

We also decided to conduct a membership drive to bring new energy into the group. Some of us (myself included) would have preferred to limit the size of Samois, but the majority vote was for expansion. We had many, many requests from women who wanted to join Samois, so we decided to hold orientations more frequently.

During this period of reorganization, it became clear that someday Samois would split into special interest groups. Several divisions were possible—a split between more experienced and less experienced women; a split between separatists and non-separatists; a variety of geographical splits as people found more S/M dykes in their town; and a series of splits based on who was ex-lovers with who. Samois was the kind of organization that appears as the first stage of politicization and community formation. It was open to just about any woman who had an interest in lesbian S/M; it did basic consciousness raising and education; it had only the most basic politics since consensus was difficult to achieve with such a variety of members. However, until there were enough of us to make more specialized groups feasible, we would have to coexist and work together. The compromises, negotiations and diplomacy necessary to make that work took up much of the energy of the leadership of Samois.

It was during 1979 that Samois adopted our policy on confidentiality. We decided that each woman who joined Samois was entitled to come out as little or as much as she wanted, and that no one should divulge the identity of other members without their permission. Breaking this rule was (and is) the only offense serious enough to get somebody kicked out of the group.

Outside of Samois, the private sex parties took a giant leap forward and moved out of private homes and into the Catacombs. Enough women were interested in attending the parties to make renting a specialized play space possible. Since the Catacombs was equipped with leather slings, a cross, a cage, and other large bondage devices, we could expand our erotic horizons in ways that just weren't possible in a studio apartment with plywood walls. The owner of the Catacombs, Steve McEachern, was far-sighted and radical enough to support women's exploration of S/M even though he was a gay man with little experience of women's sexuality. The lesbian S/M community in San Francisco owes much to his outrageousness and independence.

The next year, 1980, was a year of heavy media coverage—both in the mainstream and the gay/feminist press—for Samois and S/M in general. Negative reviews of our pamphlet and attacks on lesbian S/M appeared in *Lesbian Connection, GPU News, The Body Politic, Gay Community News, Plexus, Sinister Wisdom, Off Our Backs,* and many other places. Individual S/M dykes and Samois as a group responded to many of these articles. However, these responses were often not printed. We encountered a pattern of censorship in feminist publications. For example, *Plexus* refused to print our letter responding to a series of articles (many of which have been reprinted in *Against Sadomasochism). Off Our Backs* took an entire year to decide they would not run an ad for *What Color Is Your Handkerchief?,* and returned our check in October 1980. They also refused to print our letter protesting this censorship. The editors of the *Sinister Wisdom* special issue on violence (Fall 1980) refused to print any of the pro-S/M material they received. Some feminist institutions apparently decided that S/M was so dangerous and alluring that they could not allow other women to hear about Samois and make up their own minds.

Censorship reared its ugly head again at A Woman's Place bookstore in March. Collective members removed our pamphlet from the shelves. When asked why they had taken this action, they said it was because Samois members were ripping down their disclaimer cards, and the cards were a necessary condition for *What Color* remaining in their store. Samois had not asked anyone to remove the cards, but we could understand women being angry enough to destroy them. We were also concerned about complaints we had received from women who said collective members embarrassed them or criticized them for buying our pamphlet. We called the bookstore and asked if we could meet with them. They refused. We waited a few days to see if the book would go back on the shelves. It did not. We made a second request for a meeting and were told that the collective had already made its mind up about S/M and any discussion would be a waste of time. A few days later, one of our members called and asked if they were selling *What Color Is Your Handkerchief?* She was told yes, so she and a friend went to the bookstore to purchase a copy. When they arrived, they could not find it on the shelves. They asked the cashier where the pamphlet was, and she took a copy of it from underneath the counter. The Samois member refused to buy the pamphlet and protested it being sold under the counter as if it were a piece of pornography. She asked once again if the collective would meet with us, and she was told no.

On March 15, a group of 25 Samois members and supporters went into the bookstore to confront the collective directly. We did this only after they had made it clear that they would not meet with us privately, and after they had lied to us about the status of our pamphlet. We were angry that women could not buy the booklet without being harassed or pointed out to other customers in the shop, and we felt that no matter what a woman's position on S/M was, she had a right to get information about the issue from all possible points of view.

The meeting was extremely unpleasant. Samois members offered again and again to meet with the collective, and they refused each time. So we presented our criticisms publicly. We finally received a grudging promise that they might put the booklet out if they could find the time to write disclaimer cards. We produced index cards and pens and offered to put them up ourselves if the collective would write them. They refused. We told them we would monitor their handling of the booklet and return if it was not reshelved, and then we left. We wrote a letter to *Plexus* describing this conflict, and *Plexus* refused to print it. Eventually, the booklet was once again put on the shelves, but A Woman's Place became increasingly unfriendly to anyone even vaguely associated with Samois, S/M, or criticism of the anti-porn movement.

What Color was a 44-page pamphlet and consisted mostly of reprints of articles which had appeared a few years ago in the feminist press. We began to talk about producing another, larger work—a real book, with original material. We wanted a more graphic, erotic book, a book that would be aimed at an audience of S/M lesbians, not an audience of our detractors. We began to publish ads and solicit materials for this book, which you are holding in your hands right now.

Manuscripts poured in from all over the country. Lesbians everywhere had been writing S/M fiction, poetry and essays, and consigning it to their desk drawers. The MOT began to meet regularly to handle this influx of work. We were excited at the thought of getting this suppressed material out into the open, but after all the flap about *What Color,* we wondered if feminist bookstores would carry the book we wanted to publish.

In June, flyers began to appear announcing plans for a book called *Against Sadomasochism.* Some of the women who had spoken at the WAVPM "forum" on S/M were working on it, and so were some of the members of the collective of A Woman's Place. The leaflet stated that the editors had hoped WAVPM would lead the fight against S/M, but WAVPM's failure to take an official position against S/M had forced them to pursue this crusade by publishing a book of "feminist theory" against S/M. I was especially amazed by the leaflet's suggestion that somebody research Krafft-Ebing for damaging information about S/M. Krafft-Ebing was a Victorian sexologist who believed that masturbation caused insanity, that normal women had little or no interest in sexuality, and that sex itself was a disease. This forthcoming book was obviously going to contain some very sophisticated information about sex. Afraid that this book would appear before our own, the MOT worked with increased dedication.

Since most of us retained strong ties to lesbian feminism, the condemnation of our own community was very painful. However, we were even more concerned when the mainstream media began to take an interest in S/M. Sex scandals in the press usually herald stepped-up activity by vice police and more violence in the streets.

Ironically, KQED, the local public television station, ran a documentary on S/M in February that was much more reasonable and sound than anything that had appeared in the feminist press. The reporter, Phil Bronstein, interviewed lots of S/M people (including two Samois members) who gave him a thorough education about S/M culture and sexuality. Bronstein presented good basic information: S/M is consensual, it is mutually pleasurable, it's safe, it's not anti-feminist. The show was followed by a panel discussion. Despite their lack of an "official" position on S/M, a WAVPM member appeared on the panel and spoke against S/M. KQED received about ten times the number of calls they normally got on documentaries, and 70% of those calls (according to them) were favorable.

Incidentally, the Samois members who appeared on KQED were later attacked by black feminist Alice Walker ("A Letter of the Times, or Should This Sado-Masochism be Saved?", *You Can't Keep A Good Woman Down: Stories By Alice Walker,* reprinted in *Ms.* magazine and *Against Sadomasochism).* In an attempt to prove that S/M is racist, Walker describes these women as a white woman top and a black woman bottom. In fact, the top in this couple is a Latina lesbian.

Two other media events had a much greater impact and were much more sinister. The first was the protest over and release of the movie *Cruising.* Very few of the vanilla lesbians and gay men who protested *Cruising* did so because it presented a horrifying and false picture of S/M. They did it because they were freaked out about straights discovering that leathermen existed. There was a lot of rhetoric about *Cruising* reinforcing the stereotype of gay people as victims and encouraging queer-bashing. I saw *Cruising,* and it seemed to me that the movie's message was that "normal" (i.e., vanilla) gay men had a lot of good, hot sex, and that as long as you stayed in the bar and danced and sniffed poppers or went to the baths, you would be fine and have a good time—but if you went home with somebody wearing leather, they would tie you up and stab you to death. The muddled ideology of the *Cruising* protest created more hostility toward S/M in the lesbian and gay community, and the movie itself made sadomasochists more visible to straight America and a greater object of hatred and fear.

Activists were so exhausted by their protests of *Cruising* that when CBS showed "Gay Power, Gay Politics," a program that actually did everything *Cruising* was accused of doing, nobody had much energy to mount a successful campaign against CBS. This infamous pseudo-documentary informed a queasy America that queers had taken over San Francisco, forced its mayor to attend leather bars to beg for votes, and that when faggots weren't running City Hall they were flocking to S/M palaces to fist-fuck each other to death. Erosion in the public parks was attributed to the thousands of gay men who overran them, day and night, to fuck in, behind and on the bushes. A badly focused film clip of men walking around the park was shown to document this vicious exaggeration, and a tearful family testified that the kiddies had been run out of the park by aggressive fags.

In San Francisco, the airing of "Gay Power, Gay Politics" was followed by a panel of gay leaders. Most of them simply disavowed the notion that public sex or S/M had anything to do with serious gay politics. Only gay city supervisor Harry Britt had the guts to say that S/M and public sex were issues that could be discussed in an objective, serious way, but CBS had misrepresented and sensationalized these issues.

The most effective protest of "Gay Power, Gay Politics" was mounted by one man, a gay journalist, Randy Alfred. Alfred filed a complaint with the National News Council against George Crile and Grace Diekhaus, the producers of the CBS documentary. One of the major points of this complaint was the documentary's treatment of S/M. For one thing, the documentary had stated that 10% of all deaths in San Francisco were the result of S/M activity. That statistic was an inaccurate rendering of a statement made by the San Francisco coroner that 10% of all deaths in the city were gay-related (including the murders of gay people by straight homophobes). This spurious statistic has been widely quoted since the special was broadcast, and turned up most recently in *Off Our Backs*. Alfred's complaint was eventually sustained by the news council, and the producers were censured.

Progressive institutions made it clear that their positions on S/M were not much more sophisticated than Criles' and Diekhaus's. In August, the National Lawyers Guild passed an anti-porn resolution that condemned "violent" pornography (which by now most of us in Samois interpreted to mean images of our sexuality as well as genuinely violent imagery). The guild asked its members not to defend people arrested on porn charges. Since the vice police were using obscenity laws to harass S/M people in Canada and the United States, this was frightening. The guild has traditionally defended people who are critics of the established order. What if Samois were to be prosecuted under obscenity laws for any of our publications? Who would defend us?

In October, NOW passed a resolution (ludicrously billed as its "gay rights" resolution) which condemned S/M, pornography, public sex and pederasty and denied that these were issues of sexual or affectional preference. Instead, the resolution defined these activities as "issues of exploitation and violence." NOW stated that it was interested in working with groups which shared its definition of sexual and affectional preference. It seems our choice of the slogan "the leather menace" was prophetic. Subsequent attempts to repeal this resolution have been scuttled by NOW.

Public events by Samois included speaking at the National Gay and Lesbian Healthworkers Conference in June, participation in the San Francisco and the East Bay lesbian/gay parades, and running a booth at the Castro Street Fair in August.

An attempt was made in October to get various S/M groups to form some kind of coalition. Representatives of the Society of Janus, the Chateau (a business offering professional S/M sessions), the Gemini Society (a male dominant/female submissive S/M support group), the SM Church (female dominant/male submissive), Samois, Backdrop (another heterosexual professional S/M service) and some of the more established professionals met to discuss the possibilities. But it was too difficult to get people to work together on common interests. There were too many divisions of gender, class, sexual orientation, etc. Gay male bar owners couldn't envision working with heterosexual female dominants, lesbians didn't want to work with male dominants, and nonprofessionals had judgmental attitudes toward professionals. San Francisco sadomasochists still need a broad coalition to deal with police harassment, attacks in the media, and bad attitudes in City Hall. We are too fragmented, and every group is too small to be effective alone. But until we have a common identity as *sadomasochists* (instead of gay men who are into leather, lesbian feminists who are into S/M, businessmen who are clients of professionals, etc.), such a coalition has little hope for success.

The Michigan Women's Music Festival had yet another S/M workshop, with about 50 women in attendance. After the festival, we heard that women were organizing S/M support groups in Portland, Ann Arbor and possibly even Vancouver.

In 1981, the anti-porn movement's stranglehold on the feminist press and ideology was finally broken. The *Heresies* special issue on sexuality was the most important publication to challenge the anti-porn movement's simplistic merging of sex, violence, porn and S/M. It not only included good material on S/M, it included articles on prostitution, lesbian role-playing, heterosexual promiscuity and fag-hagging that were not derogatory or hackneyed. More good stuff was out in the July-August issue of *Socialist Review*. In "Talking Sex: A Conversation on Sexuality and Feminism," Deirdre English, Amber Hollibaugh and Gayle Rubin dissected the feminist tendency to reproduce Victorian sexual ideology and pointed the way toward a more sophisticated, sex-positive feminism. *Gay Community News* did a special issue on lesbian S/M, which included a positive article by Janet Schrim, and in July and August they published a two-part interview with me and Gayle Rubin.

Of course, our old friend *Off Our Backs* continued to run anti-S/M material, but they were also forced to run some letters which attempted to demystify S/M and claim a feminist identity for S/M lesbians. Publication of my book, *Sapphistry,* also provoked a flurry of anti-S/M articles in the guise of "book reviews." The most vicious reviews appeared in *Off Our Backs* and *Big Mama Rag* (Constance Perenyi, "Sapphistry—Striking Out at Feminism 'Til it Hurts," Feb. 1981).

Early in the year, Samois went through another upheaval that resulted in reorganization. The group had tripled in size in a short time, and once again the leadership was feeling tired and over-burdened. Most of our outreach had been done in the lesbian feminist community, so most of our new members had fairly traditional politics about sex. They had not been through the bitter fight with WAVPM, the struggle over accepting bisexual women as part of our community, working with gay men who shared their social and sexual space with us, and the whole long process of compromise and negotiation that made it possible for bar dykes, activists, separatists, professionals and other sex industry workers, bisexual women, city dykes and country dykes, and witches to be in the same group together. Older members felt suspicious of and alienated from newer women. The new members were frustrated because they did not know the history of Samois, didn't understand why we did things the way we did, felt pressured to take on responsibility without having the experience to know what should be done or how, felt paranoia and resentment from older members, and wanted to belong to Samois without sacrificing treasured political beliefs.

March 15, we gathered to discuss all of these issues and let off some steam. We met again on April 6 and 13, and out of these meetings, made some badly needed changes. We wrote up our structure and policies so that new members could easily find out how Samois worked. We began to elect our officers, instead of having people volunteer at business meetings. We set up some committees to take care of ongoing business. And we set up a yearly evaluation meeting (since these had been happening annually anyway, planning for them might make them less disruptive and decrease friction). We set up a new members' meeting in addition to orientation to help new members form a small support group to help them get integrated into Samois. We defined criteria for denying membership and a fair process for removing someone from the group. The "no sex at meetings" rule was dropped since it had been impossible to define or enforce it. After all, what was sex? Flirting? Bondage? Whipping? Instead, we decided to tell all new members that we were not a sex club or an introduction service. We also reaffirmed the fact that members were not required to define themselves as lesbians as long as they were interested in S/M sex with other women.

This reorganization made it very difficult to keep doing business as usual. Our regular program meetings were suspended. The MOT, hard at work on the book, was wondering if there would *be* a group to publish *Coming to Power*. And we had scheduled a benefit for the book which had to go on despite our internal chaos.

The women who planned and produced this event, "Spring Fever," at Ollie's on April 12, deserve a special vote of thanks. Ollie's was a new lesbian bar in Oakland. Behind the bar was a large room, Radclyffe Hall, which is where most of Samois' recent public events have taken place. The owner of Ollie's had previously worked at The Bacchanal, where she had organized "Sex Month." It was wonderful to work with someone who supported us and was willing to do business with us.

Spring Fever was very different from previous Samois programs. Instead of lectures (which we were all tired of giving), instead of coming from a defensive place, we wanted to entertain and seduce the audience. The women who organized the event put out posters inviting only women with positive or neutral attitudes toward S/M. By restricting the audience this way, they hoped to avoid arguments or hecklers and reach women who really wanted to learn more about sex. Spring Fever included a humorous skit on the conflicts between S/M and vanilla dykes at The Sutro Baths (a basically heterosexual bathhouse which had one day for women only), a pickup and negotiation for an S/M scene conducted in a lesbian bar, a medley of S/M rock from the sixties (remember "Chains" and "Torture"?), a dictionary reading of dirty words and a personal account (read from a journal) of coming out as an S/M lesbian. More than 100 women came to this event, and it was very well-received. The professional production was due in large part to a Samois member who had a background in television, and Samois owes her many thanks for sharing those professional skills with the group.

For the 1981 Lesbian and Gay Freedom Day Parade, we also planned something new—a meeting with out-of-town women who were interested in starting a group like Samois. One of our members had reserved space at the Women's Building for this event long ago. However, when we called to confirm the reservation, we were told that they would have to meet with us before they could let us use the space. Those of us who had already been through fights with WAVPM and A Woman's Place bookstore groaned and said, "Here we go again!"

The Women's Building postponed this meeting until it was too late for us to list the location of our event in the parade program. Instead, we put in a contact phone number and hoped out-of-town women could reach us. Then we attended a series of meetings with the Women's Building staff, most of whom were convinced that Samois contradicted the purposes of the building. Each meeting was set up during the day and at the Women's Building. This was very convenient for them, but it meant that Samois members who worked during the day had a hard time coming to the meetings. They refused to change the time or location. Despite the fact that the meetings were arranged for their convenience, some of the staff who didn't want to honor their agreement to rent us space could not be bothered to come to all of the meetings. This meant that whenever an agreement was made by the staff at one meeting, staff who had not been present could protest the decision and demand a new meeting (which they often would not bother to attend).

We were expected to defend ourselves against accusations that we were racist, we were told that battered women would be upset by our presence in the building, and we were asked to explain how we did not contradict the building's purpose (which includes a statement that the building will not discriminate on the basis of sexual orientation and recognizes the diversity of the women's community). This seemed very weird to us, since the building had been used for high school dances, weddings and meetings of many non-feminist (and even all-male) groups. It was especially difficult to educate the staff since none of them had read our pamphlet or attended any of our public education programs. We got them a copy of *What Color Is Your Handkerchief?* and Samois' statement of purpose, but this material got lost, so many of the staff never read it. They were more impressed by a petition which about 30 prominent local feminists signed, urging the building to honor their agreement to rent us space.

Finally, the staff agreed to let us use the space. But after we signed a rental agreement and paid for the room, we were told

276

that other conditions were being imposed on us. These conditions had never come up at a meeting. We were told that we could not engage in any "offensive" behavior in the halls and bathrooms of the building. When we insisted that the term "offensive" be defined, we were told that we could not lead each other around on leashes, whip each other or have sex in the hallways and bathrooms—and that building security women would monitor our behavior to make sure we complied! The staff did inform us that we could dress however we liked, which they apparently thought was quite generous.

After going through these tedious and inconvenient meetings, we were very angry about having these conditions imposed outside of any kind of democratic process. We decided to hold the meeting without agreeing to refrain from being "offensive" and hope we did not get expelled from the building. I continue to be amazed at the humiliation and degradation which vanilla lesbian feminists force on S/M lesbians against our will.

Despite the embittering process of getting the space, the meeting itself was joyous. Women came from New Mexico, Portland, New York, Canada and other areas and told us what their lives were like and how their efforts to find other S/M lesbians had succeeded or failed. It became clear that every city and large town in America has a nascent S/M lesbian community—a friendship network of women who share this sexuality. If only we could find a reliable way to contact and communicate with one another! Through 1981, these friendship networks in New York, San Jose and Los Angeles turned into public support groups. The isolation was ending.

On June 28, we marched for the third year in the Gay Freedom Day Parade. We had the largest contingent so far—more than 30 women, many of them from out-of-town. And the crowd response was the most positive it had ever been, although we still got hissed and booed occasionally. However, it made me sad that oppression was still so intense that only one-eighth to one-quarter of our members felt they could be public enough to march in the parade with Samois.

In July, the *Lesbian Insider/Insighter/Inciter (LIII)* ran a short pro-S/M article. After much debate, the collective had agreed to print it only if it was accompanied by a much longer, negative article. I mention this because it is pretty typical of the way most feminist papers have dealt with lesbian S/M. *LIII* later refused to run ads for a lesbian S/M support group in Minneapolis (they ran only one ad, no more) and refused to run ads for Samois or any group which advocated S/M (or the use of alcohol or tobacco). *LIII* also has a "policy" that they will print S/M material only in every other issue. In fact, they run negative material about S/M in every single issue, and only the positive material is censored.

This constipated behavior on the part of the lesbian intelligentsia is removed—even alienated—from grassroots dykes who want to know more about all kinds of sex, not just S/M. When women can get together without their self-appointed leaders censoring and controlling them, they discuss this important subject freely. The 1981 Michigan Women's Music Festival was a case in point. There were a total of three workshops on three different days dealing with different aspects of S/M. The first meeting was attended by over 300 women!

In September, Samois sponsored our first annual leather dance and Ms. Leather contest at Ollie's Radclyffe Hall. More than 300 women attended, many of them in outrageous sexy attire. The dance was truly sleazy, nasty and unbelievably fun. And it certainly was a long way from that first crowded meeting at Old Wives Tales! We had all worked so hard for progress, to feel that our place in the women's community was secure, but none of us had ever dared hope for this much success.

In November, *Coming to Power* was finally published. The dedicated and weary women of the MOT had produced something unique in lesbian literature, a book that was destined to have a tremendous and irreversible impact on the way every lesbian viewed her sexual options. The book party was held at Amelia's, one of San Francisco's most popular lesbian dance bars, and about 200 women attended to dance, drink and buy copies of our book.

However, it's important to remember that Samois does not represent or include the entire lesbian S/M community of San Francisco. I saw many, many women in leather or other S/M costumes at the dance that I had never seen at a Samois meeting. Samois retained a lesbian feminist, political tone that made it an irrelevant or boring place for many S/M lesbians. Because of its structure, Samois did not meet the social needs that a bar or a bathhouse could meet. If San Francisco has a lesbian leather bar, that place is Scott's. A small bar with a bad reputation, Scott's is a haven for role-playing dykes, punk dykes, black lesbians, and lesbians in leather. During November, Scott's was bought by some gay men who changed its name to the Detour and tried to kick out the lesbian clientele and turn it into a gay men's cowboy/leather bar. The women who had made Scott's their home-away-from-home vigorously fought this change, and insisted on keeping the bar a lesbian space. Eventually the owners were forced to change the name back to Scott's, quit harassing women customers, and even institute a leather night.

The book sold rapidly. All 2,000 copies were sold out by mid-1982. We were surprised and pleased by its success. However, none of us were prepared for the impact producing and distributing a book would have on Samois. Samois had been organized as a social/educational group, not as a business. Conflicts over the book became a major source of tension and dissatisfaction.

Coming to Power got positive reviews in *Dinah, Gay Community News, The Advocate, Plexus* (well, quasi-positive), *Atalanta, Drummer, The Body Politic,* and many other publications. Of course, a few women's bookstores refused to carry it, and *Off Our Backs, Big Mama Rag, LIII* and *Feminist Connection* refused to carry ads for it.

Samois was continuing to grow, and we became too large to have meetings in members' living rooms. So we asked the Women's Building if we could rent space there without having extraordinary conditions imposed on us. We received a letter from them in February telling us that they could not rent us space since they could not reach consensus to do so. I didn't understand why they couldn't rent us space anyway, since a lack of consensus meant they hadn't agreed unanimously to *deny* our request. Anyway, they also promised to "document their process" and tell us why we couldn't use the building within a month or two. That documentation has never arrived. The building is in financial trouble, and today has a large poster outside it saying, "Rent Me." We would still like to. Instead, we began to rent space at a gay male art gallery/performance space South of Market. Those who accuse Samois of being male-identified should remember that the group has always gone first to feminist institutions, and has been forced to find alternatives when those institutions won't accept our support.

The year's big wave of negative press about S/M was occasioned by the April 24 Scholar and the Feminist conference Towards a Politics of Sexuality. Samois was not invited to speak at the conference and had absolutely nothing to do with planning it. It took place in New York, on the other side of the continent. Nevertheless, Women Against Pornography chose to target the conference for a smear campaign and succeeded in spreading a false impression that it was in fact an "S/M conference." In the grand old anti-porn tradition of suppressing discussion and trashing critics, WAP distributed a scurrilous leaflet at the conference. The controversy over the conference and WAP's attack on it is too complicated for me to cover completely here, but since the WAP leaflet has been circulated widely among women who did not attend the conference, I think it's important to correct a few of its most obvious errors.

Samois was not "represented" by anybody at the conference. A Samois member did give a workshop, but this workshop was not about S/M and had nothing to do with Samois. Samois does not support child abuse. We have signed a petition protesting FBI harassment of the North American Man-Boy Love Association (NAMBLA). NAMBLA is a support group for pedophiles which lobbies for the repeal of age-of-consent laws. Samois has passed a resolution supporting young peoples' right to complete autonomy, including sexual freedom and the right to have sexual partners of any age that they wish. However, this is not the same thing as supporting "the sexual abuse of children," as stated in the WAP leaflet. Samois has no official position on pornography. Samois does not "imitate and mock the historical patriarchal atrocities of the slavery of Blacks, the Nazi's genocide of Jews, the persecution of homosexuals, and the sexual slavery of women." And finally, despite the fact that I am mentioned and attacked in the leaflet, I had nothing to do with planning or presenting the conference. I merely attended it. Nor am I a representative of or a spokeswoman for Samois.

The saddest development after the conference was *Off Our Back's* and WAP's trashing of any lesbian who discussed sexuality as a "secret" sadomasochist. Women who practiced butch/femme roleplaying were singled out for especially cruel attacks. *OOB's* coverage of the conference controversy included a report from an anti-S/M feminist who infiltrated a lesbian S/M sex party and wrote a hostile, nasty account of it. Despite the fact that the anti-porn movement is losing its control over feminist sex ideology, they seem determined to become more vicious and more personal in their attacks on women who don't agree with them. *OOB's* collaboration in this unfair and hysterical behavior is especially sad, but not unexpected.

Happily, S/M lesbians continue to meet, talk, party and sex it up. On June 26, 1982, the day before the gay parade, Samois sponsored another leather dance at Ollie's. About 300 women attended for another outrageous time.

This year, Samois did not march in the parade. However, an unaffiliated group of S/M lesbians formed a contingent and put in an appearance.

Against Sadomasochism appeared in Bay Area bookstores in October. The book consists mostly of reprints and relies heavily on personal attacks, misinformation about Samois, misquoting, confessions of "cured" lesbian sadomasochists, and accounts of lesbian battery as "examples" of S/M sex and relationships. This book is a work of hate and bigotry. It may unfortunately provide some women with a rationale for their prejudice against S/M; however, it contributes nothing to women's understanding or exploration of their own sexuality. Instead, it promotes a climate of suspicion and fear, a false conformity (where all lesbians pretend to be the same for fear of being condemned and excommunicated) and divisiveness in a community that needs all the unity it can get to face the Christian New Right and Reagan's repressive regime.

In re-reading this history, I think I have focused too much on Samois' relationship with the outside world and not enough on the way we felt about each other. It would have been impossible for us to face the amount of shit that we did and survive it without getting tight and close. This meant that when we disagreed with each other, it was volcanic—but I have never been in a group that risked so much, held together so well, or took care of its members as well as Samois did. In Samois, for the first time in my life, I found women who made sex a high priority, women who talked honestly about their sexual experiences, fantasies, fears and limits. I found women who really wanted sex that was satisfying, even if it seemed weird or strange or scary. We helped each other cope with the dangers of being a sexually active woman in this culture. We also had a hell of a lot of fun. In between rows with the uptight bureaucrats of the women's movement, we amused and educated ourselves with programs like Ask the Doctor Night (where we grilled a panel of medical experts about S/M safety and health concerns), an S/M fashion show (the poodle was a special hit), a panel on sexual minorities other than sadomasochists, demonstrations on flagellation and bondage, painful and revealing conversations about feminism and coming out as an S/M person, porn swaps and erotic readings, show-and-tell-your-favorite-toy nights, workshops on how to be a top, discussions of butch/femme roles, potlucks, a liberated slave and mistress auction, a play-room tour, and a program on lesbians working in the sex industry.

Some of the most irreverent, funny, talented, gutsy and intel-ligent women alive today have passed through Samois. That's why we could do what we have done. All of this took a lot of energy, but we spent our energy freely, for each other, out of love. And that's the real kind of love that comes from sticking with each other through bad times, personal disagreements, broken relationships and bad dreams, misunderstandings and power struggles and broken promises. It's a love of strong women who have built a community together.

And S/M lesbians *have* built a community. As I conclude this article in September of 1982, there are lesbian S/M support groups in San Jose, New York, Seattle, Los Angeles, Portland, Phila-delphia, St. Paul, Denver, Amsterdam, London, Helsinki, Copen-hagen, and other cities in this country and abroad. There are now three lesbian S/M groups other than Samois in the San Francisco bay area. The progress we have made since 1974, when feminists assumed lesbians just didn't do S/M, is incredible. I can only see this as a healthy and necessary process. Self-doubt, self-hatred and self-deception; loneliness, isolation and stigma can never be good for anyone. If our lives are to contain any meaning or happiness, we must find each other, find partners and friends and sisters who can understand our poetry, our erotic longing, our fantasies. We need allies and accomplices. We need a place where we belong.

Any work that builds that community is good work. I hope we can continue our fight for freedom no matter what the odds. Until women own their own bodies and have the right to seek erotic pleasure completely, with no restrictions, women will not be free. By coming out and coming together, S/M lesbians have made a valuable contribution to the sexual freedom of all women.

Acknowledgments

No project this huge can be completed without the help of many people. Thanks to Susan la Muffin for going through my files with me and writing literally hundreds of index cards, each listing a separate event in our history; thanks to the Clipping Fetishist for creating a Samois newsletter that was a document of our trials and tribulations in the feminist press; thanks to the MOT who produced this book and encouraged me to write this history; and a special thanks to It, who wears her keys on the right and her blue pencil on the left (sexually submissive, editorially dominant). It has been ruthless, and I will probably enjoy "rewarding" her for that a great deal more than I enjoyed pounding the typewriter to produce this monster of an article. If there are any inaccuracies or omissions in this history, however, I alone am responsible.

For DAVID & JERRY & CYNTHIA
& MARK & now CHRISTOPHER too...

SCARLET WOMAN

I am becoming excessively familiar with
        Death,
    Sick of this hard face
        Shadow over my friends:
I am weary of grieving and thoughts of coming
    Home to Her good earth are
        Not consoling me.

The mystic association of sex and death
Intrigued me once – but
These are not little deaths, and
A conspiracy of half-alive invaders
Seeking out warm
        highways
            between us
Is not what I meant by intrigue.

We have been adventurers down
        these warm highways:

Mappers of forbidden territories of our experience,
Discoverers of names for the unspeakable,
Explorers who made a lifestyle out of
        Jumping off of cliffs.

Easy, we have been called
    by those who find their passions dirty,

285

As if there were some virtue in being difficult.
Dirty, they have called us,
As if passion does not cleanse.

We call ourselves the risk-takers.
You have been titillated by our riskiness,
And sometimes we aroused
                              your fears
As we bridged the gaps between us
        over these warm highways,
Gasping proudly in the heady air
As we plunged,
        hand in whatever,
            to yet new depths to conquer
Yet higher peaks:

And I tell you it was always easy.
Because, you see, the risk of sex
        Was never a risk.
Our fears were of nothing more fearful
        Than each other
            or our Selves:
The voyage was always cleansing.
The highways were always
                        warm.

Now we who celebrated
        Her good earthiness
Are become the at-risk population.
We share these warm highways
        with a hard disease
        that passion will not cleanse.

Now we are pioneers
        over cold highways with no bridges,
Adventurers in another realm
        more difficult than sex,
            the final

unmapped territory of
Her good earth
that we will know.
It seems we are called upon to discover
An ultimate passion for that good earth,
As if by taking risks we should have
lost all fear,
Or by easily accepting each others' bodies
we should have come to accept
Disease and death.

I do not want to fear death.
I would rather look forward to
a transformation in that good earth.

But as I am moved by
My brave friends who seek to make
Their final voyage
Clean and easy,
Still I am not comforted.

At times like this I often
Laugh at my tears and mutter
"Back to Philosophy:"
But in my deepest meditations
Still a voice within me insists:

Fuck it. I think this is
awful.

*A wide variety of books with gay and lesbian
themes are available from Alyson Publications.
For a catalog, or to be placed on our mailing list,
please write to:
Alyson Publications
40 Plympton Street
Boston, Mass. 02118.*